Outrageous Macintosh Filters

Outrageous
Macintosh Filters

By David D. Busch

A Subsidiary of
Henry Holt and Co., Inc.

First Edition—1995

Printed in the United States of America.

Busch, David D.
    Outrageous Macintosh filters / By David Busch.
        p. cm.
    ISBN 1-55828-429-X
    1. Macintosh (Computer) 2. Computer graphics. 3. Electric filters, Digital. I. title.
QA76.8.M3B865 1995
006.6'865--dc20   95-10900
                                                               CIP

10 9 8 7 6 5 4 3 2 1

Editor-in-Chief: Paul Farrell   **Managing Editor:** Cary Sullivan
Development Editor: Laura Lewin   **Copy Editor:** Sara Black
Technical Editor: Rich Santalesa   **Production Editor:** Anthony Washington

Table of Contents

PART I
Getting Started
with Filters

PART II
Using Your Application's Built-In Filters

PART III
Creating Your Own Filters

PART IV
Third-Party Filters

PART V
Putting Filters to Work

Preface

Photoshop-compatible filters and plug-ins for image editors like Photoshop 3.0, Fractal Design Painter, or PixelPaint Pro 3 may be your most valuable tools in your quest to create outrageous graphic effects with your Macintosh. This book is your no-nonsense guide to understanding how all those controls and options, which are built into your favorite program, affect your image. Learn exactly what each mysterious slider control does and which filters produce each dazzling effect. You'll find complete discussions of exciting third-party add-ons, like KPT Convolver, Intellihance, and Adobe Gallery Effects, along with a CD-ROM with free filters, tons of photo images, and try-out software. The gems include the fabulous Plug-In Manager, which lets you turn whole groups of filters on and off as you need them!

What you won't find is a lot of useless background material, sketchy descriptions where you expect solid how-tos and tips, or examples that feature endless clones of the same image over and over. Whether you're looking for an idea sourcebook, a filter reference guide, or just an extra nudge down the road to creativity, you'll find inspiration and imagination in the chapters that follow.

Chapter Outline

This outline can be your quick guide to finding the topic and type of effect you want to explore:

Part I: Getting Started with Filters

1. **Filter Magic.** This chapter explains what filters are and how they work and offers an overview of what sorts of effects can be produced using plug-ins.

2. **What Are Filters?** A brief description of what filters are, how to install them, and how to use them appears in this chapter.

Part II: Using Your Application's Built-In Filters

3. **Sharpening and Blurring, Despeckling.** This chapter explains how to apply the exact amount of sharpening and blurring required, how to remove spots and dust from images, and how blurring can improve an image.

4. **Distortion Filters.** This chapter describes how displacing, twisting, twirling, and spherizing filters can be used effectively if you know how to use the options provided with them.

5. **Painting Filters.** This chapter explains how to recreate Old Masters effects and minimize the defects in less-than-perfect images with crystallizing, pixelating, faceting, fragmenting, pointillize, and other effects.

6. **Rendering Filters and Lighting Effects.** This chapter explains how lighting used in photo studios can be applied to "flat" images using the Lighting Effects filter, which has dozens of options that can generate some amazing effects.

7. **Other Built-in Filters.** This chapter explores using noise, rendering, stylizing, transparency, video, and other filters to modify images.

Part III: Creating Your Own Filters

8. **Custom Filters.** Most image editors have "custom" filter options but offer users little more than a dialog box where numeric values can be typed in. This chapter explains and how to create useful filters.

9. **Introduction to Filter Factory.** Adobe didn't even describe how to use Filter Factory in the printed documentation—supplying, instead, a README file on the disks and CD-ROM shipped with Photoshop 3.0—this chapter can help you decide whether you have enough programmer in you to put this tool to work.

Part IV: Third-Party Filters

10. **Kai's Power Tools.** This chapter explains how to use Kai's Power Tools because this top-selling filter toolkit has a weird interface and a radical number of options.

11. **Using KPT Convolver.** This chapter explore KPT Convolver, which was introduced at COMDEX 94. Convolver is a revolutionary way of exploring effects with plug-in filters, offering ways to explore and preview the capabilities of existing filters, and design "new" ones by tweaking parameters.

12. **Using Aldus Gallery Effects.** This chapter looks at applications for the three sets of filters offered by Aldus, which are among the best on the market.

13. **Other Commercial Filters:** This chapter explores the capabilities of filter packages like those from Andromeda, Second Glance, Paint Alchemy, Terrazzo, Intellihance, Color Bytes, and Specular Collage.

14. **Shareware Filters.** This chapter discusses where to find dozens of great filters that are available in try-out versions and how to use them.

Part V: Putting Filters to Work

15. **Using Filters with Text.** This chapter shows how filters can be applied to text in creative ways, producing 3-D effects, flowing characters, and other transformations.

16. **Working with Textures.** Because Pixar 128 isn't the only source of texture plug-ins; this chapter explains how to use textures.

Glossary. A complete imaging/effects glossary explains terms like *convolution*, and *unsharp masking*.

PART I

Getting Started with Filters

This section introduces you to the world of filters and plug-ins and get you started in exploring these tools. Chapter 1 provides a briefing of what I hope to accomplish in this book and how I'll go about doing it. You'll learn what topics, tools, and techniques are within these covers and on the bundled CD-ROM. Chapter 2 introduces the concept of filters and includes some clever installation tips you might not have thought of.

CHAPTER 1

Filter Magic

If you thought you knew everything there is to know about Adobe Photoshop—or another high-end image editor like Fractal Design Painter or PixelPaint Professional—prepare to be surprised. You're probably seriously underusing your most powerful creative tool—Photoshop-compatible filters and plug-ins. Even familiar filters like Add Noise or Blur can accomplish incredible image sorcery. This book shows you many of the spells and incantations needed to work this magic.

On the other hand, if you just wish you knew everything there is to know about Photoshop or another image editor, you too are in for a surprise. Some amazingly effective special effects are relatively simple to achieve if you know the tricks presented in this book. Even apprentice image magicians can perform startling feats of filter legerdemain without hours of practice and study.

There's no doubt that plug-in image-processing filters are very popular. New tools like Filter Factory, KPT Convolver, and Terrazzo let graphics workers explore millions of different effects or create their own stand-alone filters. There are dozens of other filter products already on the market, from Aldus Gallery Effects to Chromassage to Kai's Power Tools. The latest versions of Photoshop 3.0, Fractal Design Painter 3.0, and PixelPaint Pro 3 include complex new filters, each flexible enough to be mini-applications on their own.

Unfortunately, most Macintosh owners don't know how to use these powerful add-ons. Even though many filters have multiple parameters that users can set, most just apply the default values because few understand the effects of each control. If you're reading this, you're probably a graphics worker who knows you are only scratching the surface of what plug-ins can do but don't know where to turn for help.

Outrageous Macintosh Filters has everything you need to wring every last bit of creativity out of your images through the filter tools you already own. If you're looking for new filter horizons to conquer, you also will find tips and techniques for getting the most out of third-party plug-ins.

Outrageous Macintosh Filters offers step-by-step instructions that will let you:

- Apply photo-studio quality lighting effects to scanned images, using three or more virtual "lights" with reflectors users can vary from a diffuse plastic texture to a glaring metallic sheen.

- Add 3-D surface textures based on any image you have or can scan.

- Create wild psychedelic or solarized effects with new ways of using common plug-ins.

- Understand the difference between confusing or seemingly similar filter options: Blur and Gaussian Blur, Sharpen and Unsharp Mask, Trace Contour and Find Edges.

- Experiment with Photoshop's new Filter Factory (which is undocumented in the printed Adobe manual) to create vibrant, stand-alone filters that readers can share with others—for free or for fee!

- Through complete descriptions and bountiful examples; learn which of the third-party filter products like Pixar 128, Second Glance, Paint Alchemy, Kai's Power Tools, or Intellihance should be added to readers' toolkits.

- Combine filters with other tools to generate entirely new effects. For example, if you apply a Chrome filter to an image and then paste the original image on top using varying degrees of transparency, the effect looks like the image has been encased in plastic!

Outrageous Macintosh Filters attacks plug-in confusion with in-depth coverage of all common plug-in packages for the Macintosh.

What's in This Book?

In this book and the CD-ROM packaged with it, you will find:

- A comprehensive look at each of the filters provided with Photoshop and other image editors, with explanations and examples of the images that benefit most from the plug-ins. All the variables are fully explained so that your image tweaking can be planned rather than executed on a trial-and-error basis.
- An introduction to using Photoshop 3.0's mysterious Filter Factory.
- Dozens of unique filters prepared exclusively for the readers of this book, along with instructions on how to use them.
- More shareware and freeware plug-ins, culled from the best available online, along with demo filters from manufacturers like Adobe, Alaras, and Alien Skin.
- Dozens of textures that can be used with filters you already have.
- All the photographs used in the book's examples so that you can duplicate techniques.
- More photographs: royalty-free TIFF files—outdoor scenes, glamour photos, flowers, kids, portraits, abstracts—that you can experiment with.

Why This Book?

Book sellers offers dozens of generalized Photoshop books aimed at all levels of users. I've bought and read most of them. When a product dominates a market the way Photoshop has, users of the product can expect a continual parade of books that show them how to learn the basics, master the depths of the feature set, and then eventually tweak, supercharge, power-accelerate, or hyperventilate the program to new heights. Most of these books tend to rehash and reexplain the basic features of Photoshop.

If you've been using Photoshop for more than a few months, you don't need a book like that. If you're using PixelPaint, Fractal Design Painter, or some other image editor, you don't need a book like that ever. Yet, at least two of the last few Photoshop books I've read started off along the lines of "Why do you need yet another Photoshop book?"

You don't. You need *this* book. I won't bore you by explaining how to make basic selections (unless I discover a nifty new way you might not have thought of) or to combine images or to shift from one mode to another. Dozens of books already do that—the best of them being, I think, *teach yourself Photoshop 3.0 for the Macintosh* by Karen Winters and David D. Busch (MIS:Press) (if you happen to be using Photoshop).

Outrageous Macintosh Filters is one of the few books that concentrates on one of the most-misunderstood aspects of image editing—Photoshop-compatible filters.

Outrageous Macintosh Filters the ultimate filter and plug-in book for the following reasons:

- Instead of just telling you how a filter works and giving an example or two, it will help you explore every parameter, every setting in depth. You'll learn how angles, rotations, pixel settings, percentages, and other controls can be used to provide the exact effect you want.

- The illustrations in this book and the 8-page color insert will help you visualize what's happening. The CD-ROM includes hundreds of examples of images with every imaginable filter and combination of filters provided with them. Instead of trying to figure out exclusively from the printed page just how a filter looks, you'll be able to load dozens of examples right into your image editor. Even with a Power Mac it can take many seconds for a filter to be applied to an image (trust me, thumbnail previews are not sufficient). Instead, load one of my sample images and see many variations, side by side.

- Unlike last year's books, *Outrageous Macintosh filters* covers KPT Convolver, Filter Factory, and other recently introduced tools. There's even a section on creating your own custom filters.

- If you like, you can follow the exercises using the same files I used. I include the working files on the CD-ROM, along with a good supply of try-out filters and photo clip art.

Who Needs This Book?

Outrageous Macintosh Filters will appeal to five different types of readers:

- Curious graphics workers who want to see what they're missing. They'll use this book to add to their image-editing repertoires. A reader of my last book, *Macintosh F/X* (Mis:Press), contacted me over the Internet (I'm 75725.1156@compuserve.com) to say that he enjoyed reading about graphics effects that he never planned to use himself—just to see how they were done. Although most of you will actually want to try out many of these techniques, this book will help educate you about the possibilities that exist.

- Power users trying to tweak Photoshop with some new techniques, tips, and add-ons. Even the most sophisticated graphic artist doesn't have time to try out every filter on the market or to experiment with every possible technique. If you're a really savvy user of your image editor, you'll find many ideas in this book to make your work even more awesome.

- Corporate graphics department decision makers seeking more information before purchasing new third-party filter plug-ins. This book can help them decide where to spend their bucks. Just because you're in charge doesn't mean you have the time to bone up on every possible add-on for your company's main image-editing application. You can get a good idea of what products you need to consider from this book.

- Trainers who need a guide they can use in advanced courses. If you're teaching Photoshop classes and want a book with ideas to challenge students who've gone beyond the basics, this is it.

- End users who want more detail and explanation about new features in Photoshop or other image editors than can be found in the vendor manuals and generalized third-party books. If this lack of detail frustrates you, I've got a dozen and a half chapters of detail and explanation for you in the following pages.

Why Me?

Books of this type always stand on firmer ground if the writer understands photography, imaging, and graphics. That description pretty well represents me. Although I was a writer before I was a photographer, I was a professional photographer before I was ever a professional writer.

A regional newspaper hired me right out of high school as a news photographer. Then they discovered that they had little use for a reporter on my assignments, when I consistently turned in carefully crafted two- and three-page "captions" with my best shots. I "graduated" from photographer-writer to writer-photographer and writer-about-photography for several public relations agencies,which were hired by a well-known imaging company based in Rochester, N.Y. I've operated a commercial photo studio, took a turn as a wedding photographer, and served as a photoposing instructor in fashion photography for a Barbizon-affiliated modeling agency. My pictures and articles have appeared in publications as diverse as *Petersen's PhotoGraphic*, *The Rangefinder*, and *Professional Photographer*.

I'm more of a newcomer to personal computer technology, not getting my first desktop computer until 1977, eventually migrating to IBM PC and then Macintosh systems when they were invented. For the last 10 years, I've combined my love of photography and computers and written three Mac-oriented scanner books and a clutch of other imaging-oriented works like this one.

Do you really need to know all this stuff about me to use this book? Probably not. The only really important fact about me that you must keep in mind is that my first Computer Press Award was for a book of computer humor. To this day I refuse to take all of this too seriously. I think you'll find *Outrageous Macintosh Filters* fun to read and use.

Special Note for Readers of *Macintosh F/X*

If you've already explored Macintosh special effects with my last book, I'm glad you've come back for more. There's not much overlap between this book and *Macintosh F/X*. Even though some of the same filters described in that book appear here, in all cases, the coverage is deeper here, and the example illustrations are different.

The TIFF files on the CD-ROM are generally different as well. If you liked the snapshots of Spain, the glamour photos, and the shots of pop and blues musicians and other images on the first CD-ROM, you'll appreciate the illustrations in *Outrageous Macintosh Filters*. In any case, I've tried to include a mixture of image types to keep things interesting.

In *Macintosh F/X*, I promised to include only as much of that boring background material as was absolutely necessary. That approach worked so well that I've put even less background in this one. Any background information that remains is well hidden and diluted by outrageous techniques and ideas.

About the Example Photographs

Every photograph and image in this book is my own. The examples represent actual images that I created myself, often expressly to illustrate one type of filter or special effect. Several books available "showcase" the work of many different artsy types, using complex images that incorporate a dozen or more sophisticated techniques. I found the explanations of these effects difficult to understand and impossible to follow.

I think you'll find the images in *Outrageous Macintosh Filters* impressive enough, even though you can easily duplicate the effects yourself. Instead of layering technique on technique, I'll generate a group of pictures that may use only a couple different effects.

The images and working files you'll be using from the CD-ROM aren't all picture-perfect photos. That's the whole point of this book. I'll provide you with some good basic images that can be improved using filters. If you find yourself working with images that may have imperfect color balance or a few dust spots or need some touching up in contrast or brightness, we'll discover ways of using filters to cover blemishes, disguise goofs, and rescue even still-born photographs from the scrap heap.

Finally, because I was disappointed with lack of lack of variety in the example images shown in other works on this topic, I'll mix things up quite a bit in this book. In some cases, I'll apply a dozen or so variations of the same filter to a given image; at other times, I'll work with one image and a dozen different filters. But, as we explore the world of filters, I'll choose images that can benefit most from the type of effect under discussion.

CHAPTER 2

What Are Filters?

Filters can perform some amazing magic on your images. They can transform a dull image into an Old Masters painting with delicate brush strokes, or they can create stunning, garish color variations in a mundane photograph. Blast apart your images into a cascade of sparkling pixels or simply add some subtle sharpness or contrast to dull or blurred areas. Plug-in image-processing accessories have the power to effect a complete makeover on an entire or parts of a scanned photo or bit-mapped painting you created from scratch. You can also use these add-ons to produce undetectable changes that make a good image even better.

So, what are filters? Photoshop-compatible plug-in filters are actually miniature programs in their own right, designed in such a way that they can be accessed from within an image-editing application to manipulate the pixels of a file that is open in the parent application. Some plug-ins can also load files on their own.

They are called *filters* because in the most general sense they function much like filters you're familiar with in the real world. Air filters in air conditioners, and oil filters in cars are designed as a sort of barrier that lets desirable elements—air or lubricating oil—pass through unimpeded, while things we want to keep out—such as dirt particles—are left behind. Filtering is a conversion process, converting dirty air or oil, say, into clean air or oil.

The computer world picked up on the filtering concept long ago. You may have used word processing conversion filters, which take a stream of text data, grab all the formatting control codes inserted by one program, and substitute the equivalent codes for another application. Image-processing filters advance the idea a step further, working on individual pixels in a bit-mapped image.

For example, the Invert filter found in all image editors looks at each pixel in turn and simply "flips" it to the exact opposite value. That is, a pure white or light gray pixel will be changed to pure black or dark gray. The color value of the pixel will be changed to the color opposite it on the Apple Color Picker "color wheel." A dark blue pixel will become light yellow, and so forth. This is the simplest kind of filtering possible because the values being modified are already stored as numbers, from 0 to 255 for each of the three color channels, plus gray. A single mathematical algorithm can be applied to each pixel to produce the filtered image.

Other filters may remove pixels entirely or shift them around in an image in relation to others that remain in place. The programs that make up filters can be very simple or extremely complex and require no user input or bristle with dialog boxes, slider controls, buttons, preview windows, and other features.

NOTE You can thank the wonderful space program, which also brought you Teflon and integrated circuits, for the early impetus to develop image-processing techniques of the sort we use in filters today. When imaging for scientific and military purposes moved from high-flying airplanes to satellites and other space-based platforms, computerized techniques for manipulating the digitized images were developed. The same enhancement techniques used by Jet Propulsion Labs and the CIA are applied to your snapshots today. And don't forget to thank the entertainment industry, which discovered new applications for these capabilities (starting with *Star Wars* in 1977) and paid the bills until they trickled down to us ordinary folk.

Image-processing filters resemble photographic filters in some ways, too. You can buy special effects filters to screw onto the front of a lens to provide wild diffraction, break an image into dozens of "bug's eye-view" elements, and even blur an image across the board—or only selectively at the edges.

Before applications like Adobe Photoshop added support for plug-ins, image editors were limited to the special effects that could be built into the program. There were several drawbacks to that approach. Fixing a bug or making an improvement to an existing effect required issuing an upgrade to the entire program. In addition, a particular application was limited to the filters included in a particular release. There was no way to add filters created by the original designer of the program or by third parties without revising the entire application.

Plug-ins were a brilliant fix, even if the idea was not original to Adobe; it was adapted from a facility in the Digital Darkroom program marketed by Silicon Beach. All Adobe had to do to provide the same capabilities was build certain *hooks* into Photoshop, bits of program code that allowed Photoshop itself to temporarily turn over control to an outside module, which could then work with and manipulate the pixels within currently open images. In effect, the add-on module "plugged in" to Photoshop and became part of it, much as you plug a modem or printer into your Mac.

Some plug-ins use part of Photoshop itself and are considered *native filters* (which is why you can't access some Photoshop filters from other image editors that are nominally compatible), but most are true programs with a life of their own. Upgrading, adding, or removing a filter is as easy as deleting the old filter file and dragging a new one into the Plug-Ins folder of your application. The next time you start Photoshop or another image editor, the application will "build" itself by looking for available modules, such as filters. Any suitable plug-ins are automatically added to the Filters or Acquire menus.

The ease with which plug-ins can be integrated with Photoshop is undoubtedly one of the reasons behind the popularity of Photoshop—and of the Mac itself—within the graphics community. As good as Photoshop is, its modularity makes upgrading the program or adding specialized functions simple. Even though the last revision of Photoshop—Version 2.5.1—had an amazingly long life in computer-world terms, the capabilities of the program changed vastly between the last "official" upgrade and the latest version, 3.0. Support for products like PhotoCD, scanners that weren't even on the drawing board when Photoshop 2.5 was introduced, and incredible new add-ons like Kai's Power Tools were all seamlessly integrated by most users without missing a step.

And, now that Photoshop 3.0 is here, we can expect a new round of add-ons that take advantage of its new layering capability and other features.

What Kinds of Plug-Ins Are Available?

The plug-ins available for Photoshop and compatible image editors fall into several broad categories:

- **Acquire/Import/Export Modules.** These add-ons provide access within your image editor to file formats not normally supported by the program and to special hardware devices, such as slide, flatbed, or drum scanners. Once a plug-in of this sort has been installed, it becomes part of Photoshop. Scanners were originally furnished with clumsy desk accessory scanning modules, or "lite" editions of image editors that could do little except scan images and make modest changes.

  While bundled programs are still included with scanners, it's becoming more common to include an Acquire module that can be plugged into the purchaser's own copy of Photoshop. There are also third-party scanning plug-ins like ScanTastic from Second Glance. You don't have to learn a new program to operate your scanner, and images you capture are available immediately.

  Other Acquire modules allow you to import new or specialized format images, such as PhotoCD, or to do things like work with portions of an image without opening the entire image. Alaras (formerly Alaris) Corporation's Apertura, shown in Figure 2.1, is one of these.

Figure 2.1 Alaras Corporation's Apertura lets you work with portions of an image.

- **Production Modules.** These filters are designed first to streamline color correction and separation steps and then to generate files in Scitex format. Alaras Tropix is one filter in this category; LaserSeps and PhotoSpot from Second Glance Products are others. While I won't ignore color correction and separation entirely in this book, I will skim over most aspects of production. My guess is that many of you prepare images, and then turn them over to others for actual production and that you would rather see creative ideas and techniques here.

- **Image Enhancement Filters.** I use this term for filters that improve the appearance of images without making basic changes in their content. You have to apply the term loosely, since some of these filters can make dramatic modifications. Sharpen, Unsharp Mask, Dust and Scratches, and similar filters are image-enhancement plug-ins. Intellihance filters—which can automatically improve things like tone, brightness, contrast, and other parameters—also fall within the enhancement category. Blur filters are also image-enhancement filters; there are many images that can be improved through a little judicious blurring. This kind of filter can be applied to an entire image or just to a portion that you have selected.

- **Attenuating Filters.** These filters that act like a piece of glass or other substance placed between the image and your eye, superimposing the texture or surface of the object on your picture. Think of a piece of frosted glass, translucent scrap of canvas fabric, or a grainy sheet of photographic film. These filters, or any of dozens of others, including most Noise and texturizing filters, can add a texture or distort your image in predictable ways. Attenuating filters may be applied to a whole image or just to a selection. Figure 2.2 shows a filter of this type at work.

- **Distortion Filters.** These filters actually move pixels from one place in an image to another, providing mild to severe distortion. Filters that map your image to a sphere; immerse it in a whirlpool; or pinch, ripple, twirl, or shear bits here and there can provide distortion to some or all of an image. The Vortex Tiling filter in Kai's Power Tools is a stunning example of a distortion filter. Figure 2.3 shows Vortex Tiling applied to an image of a 2000-year-old Roman aqueduct.

- **Pixelation Filters.** Adobe's own terminology is good enough for me to use in referring to a group of filters that add texture or surface changes, much like attenuating filters. However, pixelation filters take into account the size, color, contrast, or other characteristic of the pixels underneath.

These filters include Photoshop's own Crystallize, Color Halftone, Fragment, and Mezzotint filters; Adobe Gallery Effects' Dry Brush; or Kai's Power Tools' Pixelwind. The Pointillize or Facet filters, for example, don't simply overlay a particular texture; the appearance of each altered pixel incorporates the underlying image.

Figure 2.2 A canvas texture has been applied to this photograph with a typical attenuating filter.

Figure 2.3 The Vortex Tiling filter in Kai's Power Tools provides an amazing effect.

- **Rendering Filters.** Again, Adobe's terminology is a good way to describe filters that create something out of nothing, in the way that a 3-D rendering program "creates" a shaded model of an object from a wireframe skeleton. These filters may or may not use part of the underlying image in working their magic: Photoshop's Clouds filter creates random puffy clouds in the selected area, while Difference Clouds inverts part of the image to produce a similar effect. Lens Flare and Lighting Effects generate lighting out of thin air, while Gallery Effects' Chrome filter produces *Terminator 2*-like surfaces. Alien Skin's Drop Shadow filter belongs in this category, too; it takes the edges of your selection and creates a transparent drop shadow "behind" it.

- **Contrast-Enhancing Filters.** Many filters operate on the differences in contrast that exist at the boundary of two colors in an image. By increasing the brightness of the lighter color and decreasing the brightness of the darker color, the contrast is enhanced. Because these boundaries mark some sort of edge in the image, contrast-enhancing filters tend to make edges sharper. The effect is different from pure sharpening filters, which also use contrast enhancement. Filters in this category include all varieties of filters with names like Find Edges, Glowing Edges, Accented Edges, Poster Edges, and Ink Outlines as well as most Emboss and Bas Relief filters.

- **Other Filters and Plug-Ins.** You'll find many more different add-ons that don't fit exactly into one of these categories or that overlap several of them. Xaos Tools' Paint Alchemy is a kind of pixelation filter, that has so many options for using varieties of brush strokes that it almost deserves a category of its own. Terrazzo, another plug-in from Xaos, creates repeating tile patterns from your selection, making it a distortion filter— but you can apply the patterns so that they attenuate your image. Kai's Power Tools Convolver is a kind of "filter's filter," which is used to modify the behavior of other filters. We'll look at many different odd-ball filters throughout this book. Figure 2.4 shows an image that has been modified with Terrazzo, which can create an infinite number of textures from your own images.

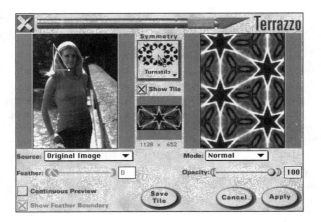

Figure 2.4 Terrazzo seamlessly tiles portions of your image in a kaleidoscopic effect.

What Vendors Don't Tell You about Installing Filters

Most commercial filter packages for the Mac come with an Installer program that asks where you store your plug-ins and then decompresses the files in the correct location. Some filters, particularly shareware offerings, must be manually dragged to your Plug-Ins folder. This seems pretty simple, right? Think again. If you accept the default installation routines, you're missing out on some valuable options, including the ability to organize your burgeoning filter collection in a reasonable manner.

In most cases, you're better off customizing your filter installations. Here are some key points to keep in mind:

- Photoshop 3.0 automatically hunts through any subfolders within the folder you have designated for storage of your plug-in filters, searching for additional filters. Therefore, you don't need to keep all your filters at the same folder level. My "main" filter folder is called Plug-Ins. Within it are additional folders labeled Filters (Photoshop 3.0's own filters), Intellihance; Alaras; KPT 2.1; Gallery Effects Vol 1, 2, 3; Chris' Filters; and so forth. Keeping all the filters separate makes it easy to delete batches you no longer use and to perform updates. Photoshop will find these filters with no trouble if they are all within the folder you've identified as your Plug-In folder. Figure 2.5 shows a typical Plug-In folder.

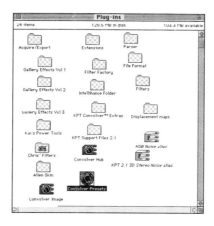

Figure 2.5 Filters can be arranged in subfolders within your Plug-In folder.

- Use **File:Preferences:Plug-Ins** to select your filter folder. It doesn't have to be named Plug-Ins, and it can be located anywhere. That means you can share the same set of filters with several compatible applications. PixelPaint Pro 3, for example, uses a similar command, **File:Preferences:Plugins** (not Plug-Ins) to identify its plug-ins folder.

PixelPaint and Photoshop can actually access new plug-ins immediately when you change the Plugin folder. You don't have to exit the program and reload.

N O T E

- Filters have the built-in capability to "tell" your application in which menu they should appear. Filters can be "installed" within existing Photoshop menus. That is, Kai's Power Tools' Diffuse More automatically shows up in Photoshop's Stylize menu. Others are designed so that they are added to Blur, Sharpen, or other menus. Filters can also be coded so they appear in menus of their own, as in KPT's Fractal and Texture Explorers or grouped together with other KPT filters under a general menu entry as in Gradient Designer. Intellihance, Alien Skin, Pixar 128, Gallery Effects, and other packages also create their own menu entries.

These locations can't easily be changed by the user (without fiddling with the filter code itself), and Photoshop will place all the filters in their intended menu locations even if you've arranged them into subfolders.

- Some applications like PixelPaint 3 don't search subfolders for additional filters. If you've selected a particular folder as your Plug-ins folder for these applications, only filters in that folder will be loaded. If you still want to organize your filters into subfolders, simply create an alias for each plug-in and install the alias in the main Plug-Ins folder for your application. If you find that some filters work with one application but not with another, you can use this trick to create separate plug-in folders for each program—and include only the aliases for the filters that you know will work in each.

- The **About Plug-in** option in the Apple menu will show you what filters have been loaded by Photoshop. You don't have to wend your way through nested menus to view this list.

Using Filters

I'll explain how to use particular filters in the upcoming chapters, but some general tips apply to nearly all the filters that we'll be working with. To apply a filter, follow these steps:

1. Choose the portion of the image that the filter will be applied to.

   - Use any of the selection tools, including the Marquee, Lasso, Magic Wand, or one of Photoshop 3.0's new tools, such as **Select:Color Range**.

   - It's often smart to copy the entire image to a duplicate layer (Select **Duplicate Layer**, from the Layer Palette's fly-out menu) and make your selection on a copy. That way you can play around with different filter effects without modifying your original image.

   - If you don't select a portion of an image, the filter will be applied to the entire image. Because it can take anywhere from a few seconds to several minutes to apply a filter, you may want to work with a representative section of the image before applying the filter to the whole thing.

- Don't forget about Photoshop 3.0's Quick Edit facility in the Acquire menu. It lets you load a small portion of a large image so that you can bring only the portion you'll be filtering into memory.

2. Select your filter from the Filter menus.

- Some filters (**Sharpen:Sharpen, Sharpen:Sharpen More,** etc.) operate immediately. Others cause a dialog box to pop up with controls you'll need to set.

- Most filters will also include a Preview window you can use to get an idea of what your filter will do when it is applied to a selected portion of an image. You'll find this useful to make broad changes in parameters, but I think it's still a good idea to select a somewhat larger area of an image and apply the filter to that on a duplicate layer.

3. Apply the filter by clicking on **OK** or the **Apply** button.

- If you have a slow Mac or a slow filter, find something to do. This might be a good time to set up your PowerBook next to your desktop Mac and get some work done. Even filters that work their magic in a minute or less seem terribly slow when you're sitting there staring at the screen.

- When the filter is finished, be careful not to do anything else (e.g., move the selection) until you've decided whether the effect is the one you want. That way, you can quickly undo the filter and apply another rendition. You save your work often, of course, and you are using a duplicate layer instead of your main image, but using Undo is always quicker than reverting to the last-saved version of a file.

4. When you're really certain that the effect is what you want, save the file under another name (**File:Save As...** or use **File:Save A Copy**). Then, and only then, flatten the layers to merge the effect with your main image. Some day, you may be glad you saved a copy of the file.

Additional General Filter Tips

- If you apply a filter to a duplicate layer, try adjusting the Transparency slider in the Layer's palette while that layer is highlighted (and both the layer and background are visible) to apply different "strengths" of a filtered selection to an image. This is similar in concept to the old Composite Controls command in Photoshop 2.5. We'll play with this option later in the book.

- To experiment with a filter without duplicating the whole image, fill a new layer with a color and apply the filter to that, layer instead. Use the **Fill with Neutral Color** option from the dialog box that pops up when you select **New Layer** from the Layer Palette's fly-out menu.

- Learn the keyboard shortcuts for using filters: **Command-period** to stop a filter in its tracks as it is being applied, and **Command-Z** to undo the filter if the application is already complete. You can reapply the last filter used to a selection (a new selection or the same one) by pressing **Command-F**. If you want to make some changes first, use **Command-Option-F** to bring up the last filter's dialog box.

The Next Step

In this section, you learned about the different categories of filters, a little about how they work, some installation tips that vendors haven't shared with you, and a few guidelines for applying filters in general. Now, let's jump right in and begin working with some specific filters to see what they can do. We'll explore Photoshop's own plug-ins in the following chapter, before going on to look at filters you can develop yourself or obtain from third-party sources.

PART II

Using Your Application's Built-In Filters

You can accomplish a great deal of filter magic using nothing more than the plug-ins that are built right into your image editor. This section explores the basic filter set found in every imaging application, using Photoshop's filters for our examples. However, you'll find that filters like Sharpen, Blur, or Find Edges work virtually identically in every application. The in-depth discussions of filters that follow are refreshing and thought-provoking.

CHAPTER 3

Sharpening, Blurring, and Despeckling

The filters we'll work with in this chapter are all image enhancers. None of them change the basic content of an image—they just make the image more pleasing to look at by sharpening details, smudging distracting parts, adding neutral noise to barren areas, or removing unwanted specks and spots.

Although these filters are fairly simple to use, they have not been discussed in much detail. When do you use Sharpen and when do you use Sharpen More? Why does Unsharp Mask make things sharper instead of unsharper? Why is there a Sharpen Edges filter? Why on Earth would you ever want to blur an image? We've all had these questions from time to time.

Many of the filters we'll be looking at are found under the **Filter:Sharpen** or **Filter:Blur** menus, but others are in other locations. Noise filters, for example, are used to soften and blur an image, but you'll find them in a submenu of their own. I'll explain several different related filters in this chapter, regardless of where you may find them on the menu tree.

Sharpening Techniques Explained

Your application uses some simple techniques to sharpen images. For example, increasing the contrast of adjoining pixels makes details stand out more and edges appear sharper. If the pixels in one part of a picture all fall within a given range of gray, while those in an adjacent part are mostly of a slightly lighter range of grays, the boundary between them will be difficult to discern. However, if you make all the grays in the light section a little lighter and those in the dark section a little darker, the difference between the two will be more pronounced and easier to see. By concentrating the contrast changes at the boundary between the two sections, you'll enhance the edges. Figure 3.1 shows a portion of an image—a door of a Spanish cathedral—in which I used sharpening to make the edges more easily visible.

Figure 3.1 Only the edges have been sharpened in this photograph.

You can see what's going on a little better if you use your own image editor to work with some files that need sharpening. Throughout this discussion, I'll use one of three examples I've included on the CD-ROM packaged with this book. You'll find them in the Chapter 3 folder, under the names DAVISOR1.TIF, DAVI-SOR2.TIF, and DAVISOR3.TIF.

NOTE If you frequently exchange files between Mac and PC platforms, you'll find it useful to store your TIFF files using file names that conform to the DOS eight-character root name, three-character extension convention. That way, your Mac and a PC running DOS, Windows 3.1 or even OS/2 or Windows 95 (which do allow Maclike long file names) will preserve the file name. If you use PC Exchange or AccessPC on your Mac and specify the .TIF extension as belonging to TIFF files created by your image editor, image files can be smoothly imported back when they return from the PC environment.

I'll use DAVISOR2.TIF (Davis Original 2—the original scanned version of the image), but you can play with any of the three. These are all photographs I made of legendary blues/folk artist Reverend Gary Davis some years ago. I lost the negatives and all I had left were proof sheets made from the original negative strips.

These contact sheets were made with the emulsion (image) side of the 35mm negative placed in direct contact with a sheet of photosensitive enlarging paper, held in place by a clean sheet of glass and exposed under an enlarger light. Properly made contact sheets are surprisingly sharp because the image is made directly from the negative, with no intervening enlarging lens to diffuse the detail. Contact sheets are also largely unaffected by any vibration of the enlarger during exposure. Inch for inch, they are sharper than enlargements made by projection.

Unfortunately, they're a little small. Each of my images of Reverend Davis measures 24 x 36 mm, or about 1 x 1.5 inches. I scanned them in at 800 dpi, which gave me individual 800 x 1200-pixel images that had a lot of detail, but still were not as sharp as I would have liked.

That's where Photoshop's sharpening tools came in. I deployed several of them on DAVISOR2.TIF and achieved the results shown in Figure 3.2 shows the original image without any enhancement. I left the edges of the film frame so you can see that this picture was scanned from a contact sheet.

Figure 3.2 Unenhanced image of Reverend Gary Davis scanned from a contact sheet.

Sharpen vs. Sharpen Edges

Your first decision when working with any image that could be crisper will be whether to use Sharpen, Sharpen More, or Sharpen Edges. The difference between the basic Sharpen tools and Sharpen Edges is easy to see. Sharpen and Sharpen More increase the contrast between all the pixels in an image. It's as if a huge number of tiny edges were everywhere in the picture. Sharpen/and Sharpen More find these myriad edges and darken or lighten the pixels at them. Sharpen Edges, on the other hand, looks only for grosser, or larger edge boundaries and enhances the contrast only between them. The broad range of tones between these edges is not modified.

So, when you use Sharpen/and Sharpen More, the sharpening effect is applied everywhere. When you use Sharpen Edges, only the most significant edges of the image are modified. Figure 3.3 shows a section of the original image at left, the same section with Sharpen More applied in the center, and the section with Sharpen Edges used at far right. Because the differences may be minimized by halftoning during the printing process, you may want to examine the original figure, located in the Chapter 3 folder on the CD-ROM. The sharpening produced by Sharpen Edges is easiest to see if you compare the edge of the earlobe in the example at far right with the original at far left.

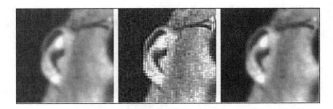

Figure 3.3 Original image (left), Sharpen More (center), and Sharpen Edges (right).

You may have heard or read elsewhere that Sharpen More is the equivalent of using the Sharpen filter three times in a row. That's simply not true. In my extensive tests, I found that multiple passes with the Sharpen filter gave different results than the Sharpen More filter, probably because sharpening an image that has already been sharpened is different from performing a greater degree of sharpening on the same image one time. You'll find that Sharpen applied twice provides a little less of the effect than Sharpen More, while three applications of sharpen gives you a much coarser texture. Figure 3.4 shows a portion of an image with no sharpening, Sharpen More applied once, Sharpen applied twice, and Sharpen More applied twice. If you want to examine the images more closely a copy of the uncropped image is included on the CD-ROM as a Photoshop 3.0 file, with each version in a separate layer. You can make each layer visible in turn to see the changes. The file is called SHARPEN.PSD.

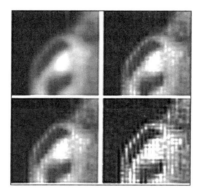

Figure 3.4 Unsharpened image (upper left), Sharpen More applied once (upper right), Sharpen applied twice (lower left), and Sharpen More applied twice (lower right).

Using Sharpen and Sharpen More

The Sharpen and Sharpen More filters can bring blurry images into focus. When applied directly to an image, you have no control over how much sharpening is applied. Sharpen adds a little bit of crispness, while Sharpen More provides a lot of crispness. Here are some tips for using each of these filters:

- You can always reapply either of these two filters to keep sharpening an image, although after two applications Sharpen More begins to look more like a special effect than an image enhancer.

- These sharpen filters increase contrast. If your image is low in contrast, experiment with applying sharpening first and then adjust brightness/contrast of your sharpened image. If you reverse the order of the steps, you may end up with an image that is too contrasty for your taste.

- Because you can't vary the strength of Sharpen or Sharpen More, duplicate the layer or selection and then sharpen the copy in its own layer. Adjust the transparency of the sharpened layer using the Opacity slider controls for that layer (see Figure 3.5) to give you more or less sharpening.

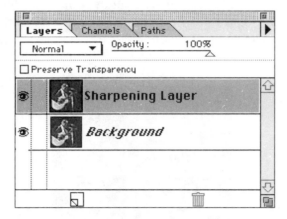

Figure 3.5 Sharpen an image in a separate layer and then combine it with the original image using the layer Opacity slider control.

Figure 3.6 shows the image from Figure 3.2 with Sharpen and Sharpen More filters applied. Because the differences are subtle, you can view the original file on the CD-ROM or look at two other samples I've provided, DAVIS1SH.TIF/DAVIS3SH.TIF (Sharpen) or DAVIS1SM.TIF/DAVIS3SM.TIF (Sharpen More).

Figure 3.6 Reverend Gary Davis with Sharpen (top) and Sharpen More (bottom) filters applied.

Using Sharpen Edges

Think of Sharpen Edges as a "quickie" version of the Unsharp Masking filter, which is described in the next section. Like the Sharpen and Sharpen More filters, you have no control over the amount of sharpening that is produced. For that reason, you may want to use Sharpen Edges only on images that don't require a lot of fine-tuning, reserving the more sophisticated Unsharp Masking technique for pictures that demand the extra control.

As mentioned earlier, Sharpen Edges differs from the Sharpen and Sharpen More filters by sharpening only the significant edges—it doesn't produce the grainy effect that results when the image or selection is made crisper in its entirety. Most of your image will remain as smooth, or blurry, as it was, but by sharpening the edges it may look quite a bit sharper.

As you gain experience using these filters, you'll learn which images can benefit from Sharpen Edges and which need Sharpen or Unsharpen. The following guidelines may also help.

- Buildings and other heavily textured objects that contain many fine details can benefit from overall sharpening. Use Sharpen or Sharpen More.
- People and faces often look better with only the edges enhanced. With most portraits, the outlines of eyes and other features should look sharp, but you don't want every flaw in the skin to be accentuated. Use Sharpen Edges.

Unsharp Masking

Unsharp Masking, like many features of Photoshop, is derived from a photographic technique. Despite the conclusion you might draw from the name, Unsharp Masking is used to make images sharper.

The technique was first applied to images made on sheet film, in sizes from around 4 x 5 to 8 x 10 inches or larger. To produce the effect conventionally, a film positive is made from the original film negative (a negative of the negative, so to speak). The positive is slightly blurred, which spreads the image slightly. When the positive and negative are sandwiched together and used to expose a new image, light areas of the positive correspond very closely to the dark areas of the negative, and vice versa, canceling each other out to a certain extent. However, at the edges of the image, the blurring in the positive produces areas that don't cancel out, resulting in lighter and darker lines on either side of the edges. This extra emphasis on the edges of the image adds the appearance of sharpness.

It's fairly easy for a computer to simulate the blurry positive mask and then mate it with a negative image of the original picture—with an added advantage. We can have greater control over the amount of blur in the mask, the radius around the edges that are masked, and a threshold level (relative brightness) at which the effect begins to be applied. The Unsharp Mask filter is similar in many ways to the Sharpen Edges filter, but with this enhanced control. We'll look at how you can use each of the parameters in this section.

Figure 3.7 shows Photoshop's Unsharp Mask dialog box (select **Filter:Unsharp Mask...**). The elements you'll be using include:

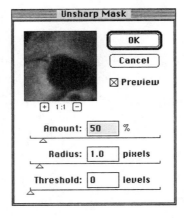

Figure 3.7 Photoshop's Unsharp Mask dialog box.

- **Preview Window** Like all Photoshop filter Preview windows, this window can be turned on or off by clicking on the checkbox next to it. Switching off previews will eliminate the delay that constantly updating the window can produce in slower Macs. On my Quadra 650, only a slight delay— usually less than 1 second—results when parameters are changed. You can change the area of your image shown by the Preview window by placing the cursor inside the window and dragging with the hand that appears.

Zoom in and out from one viewing ratio to another by clicking on the plus and minus buttons below the window. A 1:1 ratio is the default.

- **Amount Slider.** This slider controls the amount of edge enhancement used. You can vary the sharpening effect from 1 to 500%. Figure 3.8 shows a section of our Gary Davis photo with 0, 100, 200, and 500% sharpening applied.

- **The Radius Slider.** This slider determines the width of the edge that will be operated on, measured in pixels, with valid values from 0.1 (very narrow) to 250 pixels (very wide). You should adjust the range to take into account the resolution of your image. Low-resolution images (under 100 dpi) can't benefit from much more than 1- to 3-pixels worth of edge sharpening, while higher-resolution images (300 dpi and up) can accommodate values of 10 or more. You'll know if your values are set too high—you'll get thick, poster like edges that aren't realistic, accompanied by a high degree of contrast. You may, in fact, like the weird appearance, but you've left the realm of sharpening and ventured into special effects at this point. Figure 3.9 is a close-up of our test photo with no sharpening (upper left), a radius of 1 pixel (upper right), 8 pixels (lower left), and 16 pixels (lower right.)

Figure 3.8 The Amount slider controls the degree of edge sharpening applied.

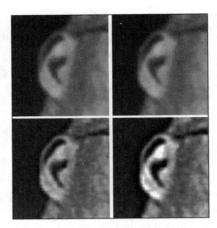

Figure 3.9 *Various radius settings produce different sharpening effects.*

- **Threshold Slider.** This slider is used to set the amount of contrast that must exist between adjacent pixels before the edge is sharpened. Values from 0 to 255 can be used; a very low value means that edges with relatively small contrast differences will be accentuated. High values mean that the difference must be very great before any additional sharpening is applied. Normally, you'll need this control only when the default value produces an image with excessive noise or some other undesirable effect. To be honest, in my tests, changing the Threshold slider produced effects that were hard to predict because they varied widely depending on how the other two controls were adjusted and the nature of the image itself. Your best bet is to set the Amount and Radius sliders first and then to experiment with Threshold to see if you like the results any better.

Blur Filters

To repeat a question posed earlier in the chapter, why on Earth would you want to blur a picture? In practice, you'll find many instances in which an image contains excessive noise or the transitions from one portion of an image are too abrupt. You may have a scanned image with dirt, an unwanted texture, or just a grainy appearance that detracts from the effect you want. If the details in that image area are unimportant, you can benefit from some blurring.

For example, a simple way to create a shadow is by duplicating or cloning the object casting the shadow and then flipping the image around and placing it where the shadow would naturally fall. Darkening the duplicate can obscure most detail, but not all of it. Your Blur filter can quickly soften the image to generate the shadowlike effect you want.

Blur and Blur More

For my examples, I selected a heavily textured photographic print of La Giralda, an ancient Moorish bell-tower that now stands next to Seville's mammoth cathedral. Although I was able to eliminate some of the texture by selecting the sky area and substituting fluffy new clouds, the texture in the tower itself still shows through strongly in the scanned image (Figure 3.10).

Figure 3.10 Original textured image of La Giralda tower in Seville.

Blur and Blur More are like Sharpen and Sharpen More in that a fixed amount of blurring is applied, which you can't control without resorting to the layer trick described earlier. Even so, their blurring effect can be useful when administered "straight." Figures 3.11 and 3.12 show the same image of La Giralda with Blur and Blur More applied.

Figure 3.11 La Giralda with Blur applied.

Figure 3.12 La Giralda with Blur More applied.

Some tips for using these blur filters include:

- As with the Sharpen and Sharpen More filters, you'll get different results when you apply Blur several times in succession as compared with fewer applications of Blur More.

- Try using one of these blur filters to blend smoothly a selection you've pasted down into an image. The effect is different from the **Select:Feather** option and may provide a smoother transition if the area being pasted has more noise, grain, or sharpness than the background it is pasted into.

Radial Blur

Strictly speaking, Radial Blur can be considered a kind of special effects filter because its effects are so drastic when applied to an entire image that the whole picture is changed significantly. However, you can also apply Radial Blur to selected portions of an image to produce a more subtle effect. I'll use the Giralda tower picture for my examples so that you can easily see what's going on.

Radial Blur is another effect derived from photography. When zoom lenses first became popular, some experimental souls discovered that by zooming in or out while a picture was taken (long exposures of half a second or more are sometimes required), an image that contains blurry intermediate versions of the original subject is produced.

A related effect can be generated by spinning the image around a selected access, producing blur in the direction of the spin. Either type of radial blur adds a feeling of motion to an otherwise static image. You can choose between the two types of blur by clicking on the **Spin** or **Zoom** radio buttons in the Radial Blur dialog box (Figure 13.13).

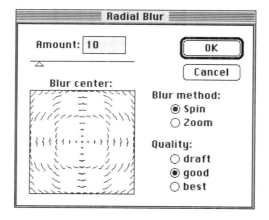

Figure 3.13 Radial Blur dialog box.

Move the axis on which the blur will be applied by sliding the centerpoint in the "Preview" window (which doesn't show a preview at all) and adjust the amount of blurring from 1 to 100, using the slider control. Since both types of Radial Blur take a long time to calculate, Photoshop gives you a "quality" mode. Use Draft mode to get a quick idea of what the effect will look like. Good mode may be good enough for some applications. If you check off Best mode, you'll get the smoothest blur, but sit back and be ready to wait awhile for your finished image. On my Quadra 650, a 20% Spin blur of Reverend Gary Davis at Best quality took 4 minutes to generate. Figures 3.14 and 3.15 show examples of Spin and Zoom radial blurs.

Figure 3.14 Radial Blur. Spin

Figure 3.15 Radial Blur. Zoom

Gaussian Blur

You'll see Gaussian Blur applied more often than the other stock blurring options because it provides you with a healthy degree of control. The blurring is not applied linearly over the entire image or selection as you might expect, but according to a bell-shaped curve Photoshop calculates using a weighted average of the pixels in the selection. Gaussian Blur reduces the contrast of an image.

In addition, whereas Blur and Blur More simply diffuse the area they are applied to, Gaussian Blur has the added effect of putting a hazelike noise in the blurred area, which can be desirable when generating shadows. Figure 3.16 shows a selection blurred using this filter. I selected an oval against a black background, filled it with white, and then copied the selection to the Clipboard. Then I reversed the selection (so that everything except the oval was selected) and applied a 16-pixel Gaussian blur. Finally, I pasted the selection back, positioned slightly to the side to allow easy comparison.

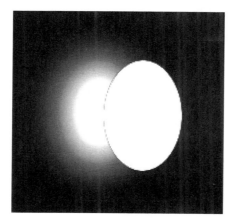

Figure 3.16 Gaussian Blur.

The only control you need to worry about with the Gaussian Blur filter is the radius setting, from 0.01 to 250 pixels. The higher the radius setting, the more pronounced the blurring effect. You can get an advance idea of the effect in the Preview window (Figure 3.17).

You'll want to play with Gaussian Blur quite a bit because it can be your best friend when you have noisy, scratchy images that badly need cleaning up.

Figure 3.17 Gaussian Blur dialog box.

Dust and Scratches

Your other friend in such situations may be the **Noise:Dust & Scratches** filter, which selectively blurs areas of your image that contain dots spots, scratches, and other defects. When the filter is applied, Photoshop examines each pixel in the image, moving outward radially to look for abrupt transitions in tone that might indicate a dust spot on the image. If it finds a spot, it blurs the area to minimize the appearance of the defect. This filter has two controls (Figure 3.18).

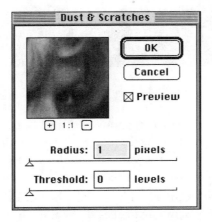

Figure 3.18 Dust & Scratches dialog box.

The Radius slider adjusts the size of the area searched for the abrupt transition, measured in pixels. You can select from 1 to 16 pixels. If your image is inhabited by really humongous dust spots, you might find a value of about 4 pixels useful, but for most pictures either a 1- or 2-pixel radius should be sufficient. The larger the radius you select, the greater the blurring effect on your image. Always use the smallest radius you can get away with.

Figure 3.19 shows another photo scanned from a contact sheet, but this one wasn't nearly as "clean" as the Gary Davis example. It had plenty of dust spots, and I added a few more with a 1-pixel brush to give the Dust & Scratches filter a workout.

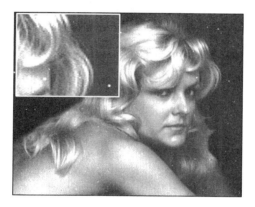

Figure 3.19 Original photo scanned from a contact sheet.

Figure 3.20 shows the same photo, cleaned up with a radius of 1 pixel. In Figure 3.21, I used a radius of 2 pixels to remove the dust. As you can see from Figure 3.20 and 3.21—or even more clearly from the original files on the CD-ROM—the 2-pixel setting does a good job of mopping up the dust spots and scratches, while blurring the picture somewhat. The added diffusion doesn't harm this picture much, but you should keep the inevitable loss of sharpness in mind when selecting your own images for processing through the Dust & Scratches filter.

Some defects are still visible, but these can be cleaned up by using the Rubber Stamp tool, which clones parts of the image over the dust or scratches that remain. The filter did most of the job, saving hours of hand-retouching with the Rubber Stamp.

Figure 3.20 Dust removed with radius set to 1 pixel.

Figure 3.21 Dust removed with radius set to 2 pixels.

The Threshold slider tells the filter just how drastic a transition must be before it should be considered a defect. Your image may be infested with nasty white spots (or black spots if made from a transparency), or you may have some gray spots that crept in. Once you've set the Radius slider to the lowest setting that eliminates the spots in the Preview window, adjust the Threshold slider up from 0 until defects begin to reappear.

Your goal in balancing these two controls is to eliminate as many defects as possible, without blurring your image too drastically.

Despeckle

The Despeckle filter is in some ways similar to the Sharpen Edges filter. Instead of increasing the contrast in the edges and leaving the rest of the image or selection alone, the Despeckle Filter decreases the contrast in all the selection except for the edges. In both cases, the edges end up with relatively more detail than the rest of the image. Don't confuse this filter with the Dust & Scratches filter, which can remedy dust spots in an image through its blurring effect, but that's a bonus—Despeckle is a much "dumber" filter that doesn't specifically search for spots.

You can tell which filter to use by following these guidelines:

- If your image has dust spots in random locations and you don't need edge enhancement, use Dust & Scratches.
- If your image is already relatively sharp, to the point where there is objectionable detail or noise in the image areas, use Despeckle to provide a blurring effect that doesn't mask edge detail.
- If your image doesn't contain excessive noise, use Sharpen Edges to sharpen it up a bit without introducing an undesirable texture.

Despeckle has no controls you need to adjust. An image that has been modified with this filter is shown in Figure 3.22. Note that the sky area in the original image at left has a lot of noise; in the despeckled version at right, the noise has been removed.

Figure 3.22 The Despeckle filter applied to remove noise from the sky.

Motion Blur

Like the Radial Blur filter, the Motion Blur filter verges on being a special effect. It duplicates the blurring you get when a fast-moving subject races across the field of view when a photograph is taken with a shutter speed that is too slow to freeze the action. Motion blur can also occur when an object is moving toward or away from the camera, but the effect is much less pronounced at a given subject speed. In fact, photo gurus recommend shooting pictures of things like oncoming trains as a way to stop action at relatively slow shutter speeds.

The Motion Blur dialog box is shown in Figure 3.23. You have two controls to work with: an angle for the blurring effect, which represents the direction of motion of the subject, from –90° to +90° (type in a figure, or drag the dial of the "clock"), and a blur amount, continuously variable from 1 to 999 pixels through the slider at the bottom of the dialog box.

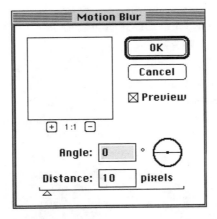

Figure 3.23 Motion Blur dialog box.

Motion Blur can really shake things up when applied to an entire image, but you can achieve some cool effects by selecting an individual object and blurring only that object. A guitar player's hands, a dancers head and feet, a racing car, a moving athlete, or some other subject can be given a dynamic feeling. Figure 3.24 shows an image with Motion Blur applied.

This picture was easy to do: I just selected the taxi at the right in the background of this photo, enlarged and pasted it into the foreground, and applied about a 50-pixel motion blur. I then pasted a copy of the taxi image into a separate layer and adjusted the transparency so that a faint sharp image would show through the blur. When I was done, I flattened the image.

Figure 3.24 Motion Blur adds a feeling of action to an otherwise static photograph.

Noise Filters

Noise filters blur images in their own way, by adding random pixels to an image or selection, thereby replacing details that are there with the noise. Adding noise blurs an image without reducing the contrast.

Standard blur filters obscure details in an image by smoothing everything out and reducing contrast. You may not want that effect if you end up with a smooth surface that looks fake because it should contain some texture.

Noise filters add texture to areas that have been made too smooth by other effects or filters or that have been painted in from scratch using a nontextured brush. Adding noise can actually help these smooth areas blend into other parts of the image that already do have texture. In other cases, a bit of noise can mask very fine scratches or dust spots in an image.

Because of the random nature of the noise, the added texture often won't be too apparent, especially when applied to monochrome/grayscale images. Noise added to color images often has specks of random colors that don't look right, but there is a way around this.

Photoshop has several noise filters, which include Add Noise and Median. The Add Noise dialog box is shown in Figure 3.25.

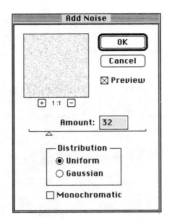

Figure 3.25 Add Noise dialog box.

Working with Noise

You'll need to work with the following controls in the Add Noise dialog box:

- Select an Amount from 1 to 999. The default is 32. This value is used to determine how much the random colors added to the selection will vary from the color that is already present (or from the gray tones if you're working with a monochrome image).

- Choose either **Uniform** or **Gaussian** distribution of the noise. Uniform distribution uses random numbers in the range from 0 to the number you specified with the Amount slider. The random number is then added to the color value of the pixel to arrive at the noise amount for that pixel. Gaussian distribution uses a bell-shaped curve calculated from the values of the pixels in the selected area, producing a more pronounced speckling effect.

- Check off the Monochromatic box to apply the noise only to the brightness/darkness elements of the image without modifying the colors themselves. This choice can reduce the "color specks" effect that often results from applying noise to an image. Figure 3.26 shows a section of an image with noise added.

Figure 3.26 Noise added to an image.

The original, noise-free image is at upper left. At upper right, I've added Gaussian noise to the sky using a value of 25. At lower left, the same amount of noise was added using Uniform distribution. At lower right, the Monochrome box was checked. If you review the original color image of this figure on the CD-ROM, you'll see that only the monochrome version is free from a confettilike appearance.

Regressing Toward the Median

The Median filter reduces noise by minimizing the difference between brightness values of adjacent pixels, blending them together when possible. The filter works by replacing the center pixel of a group with one having the median brightness value of those pixels. You can specify the radius of the search using the only control offered with this filter (Figure 3.27).

Other filters could be dumped into the Noise, Blurring, and Sharpening categories, but they are useful almost exclusively as special effects, so I'll leave them for other chapters. These filters include Find Edges and Trace Contours, which produce effects so dramatic that they can hardly be lumped together with the image enhancers we have looked at so far. We'll also investigate at some useful noisemakers available in Kai's Power Tools and other third-party products.

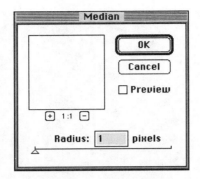

Figure 3.27 Median dialog box.

Working with Blur and Sharpen Filters

We'll use blur and sharpening filters extensively in this book, and I'll provide examples throughout the book of ways you can apply these handy plug-ins. To end this chapter, lets see how you can use these filters in your own work.

Figure 3.28 is a view of the famous Alcazar (castle) in Segovia, Spain. You've probably seen dozens of photos of this prototypical castle in Spain taken with the plain in the background. Its turrets and parapets and towers, perched on a hill overlooking the countryside, are what we all imagine when we picture castle. This one, located in the mountains outside Madrid, happens to be the one in which Queen Isabella was crowned. I took this picture from an even higher tower on the street side of the castle.

I performed the following steps on the castle, which you can duplicate on the original file, CASTLE02.TIF:

1. I traced the outline of the castle using the Pen tool. Because the castle had so many straight lines and angles, creating a path that closely followed its outlines was easy.

2. I selected **Make Selection** from the Path Palette's fly-out menu and converted the path to a selection.

3. I selected some tiny details, such as the weathervane/lightning rods, by painting them in Quick Mask mode and then used **Select:Save Selection** to store the selection in an alpha channel.

4. I applied the Unsharp Mask filter to the castle, using a Radius of 2 pixels and an Amount of 200%.

Figure 3.28 Photograph Segovia's Alcazar, prior to manipulation.

5. Reversing the selection (**Select:Inverse**), I applied Gaussian Blur with a Radius of 5 pixels to blur the background.

As you can see in Figure 3.29, using sharpen and blur tools together can improve a picture by diffusing elements that you want to de-emphasize (the background), while sharpening elements to which you want to draw attention (the castle). Photographers use a similar technique, called selective focus, to highlight a subject by blurring everything else in the picture.

Figure 3.29 The background has been blurred and the foreground sharpened.

You can take the technique even further by using extremely heavy Gaussian Blur (Figure 3.30) to turn the background into a foggy haze. In this case, the background actually is transformed into an interesting gradient blend, with a smooth transition from the blue sky to the green-brown plains surrounding the castle.

Figure 3.30 Further blurring turns the background into a gradient blend.

Finally, I added some noise (I used Gaussian noise, with a value of about 50) to create a realistic, foggy texture to the background. The original background of the image was scenic enough, but contained some distracting buildings. The final image, shown in Figure 3.31, presents an eerie, Medieval image of Isabella's castle. You can view the original files on the CD-ROM, or check out Color1 in the 8-page color insert.

Figure 3.31 A little noise gives a foggy texture to the atmosphere around the castle.

The Next Step

In the next chapter, you learned how images can be improved by selectively blurring, sharpening, or adding noise. Our tour of Photoshop's basic filters continues in the next chapter with a discussion of filters that can be used to distort, twist, and reshape images in creative ways.

CHAPTER 4

Distortion Filters

Imagine that your image is printed on a piece of rubber. Now, pretend that you can wrap and stretch the rubber sheet around a basketball, rolled-oats cereal container, or other object. Yank on opposite corners to stretch the image or poke the center of the sheet with your finger. Just for good measure, fold the sheet a few times or twist it around. By now you have a pretty good idea of the distortions that you can create with your image and an editor like Photoshop.

In this chapter, we'll look at ways to twist your image in a variety of directions. Most of the filters we'll be working with aren't difficult to use or understand, and many of them have only a few parameters that you need to learn. Despite their simplicity, you'll find dozens of uses for them in your own work.

These filters are all "pixel movers." They operate by shifting pixels from one location to another, enlarging or reducing them as required to simulate images applied to spheres, cylinders, or stretched rubber sheets. The changes they make are never subtle.

Because distortion filters cause such dramatic changes, you'll want to select the images you use them with carefully. I'll use a portrait for most of the examples in this chapter to give you a basis for comparing one type of change to the other. Most of these special effects don't lend themselves to human subjects, however. I already apologized to the model, who says some of the pictures make her look fat (models always complain about this!).

All the filters in this chapter can be found in the Photoshop **Filter:Distort** submenu. Similar filters are provided by other image editors in corresponding menus. The only Distort menu filter I didn't address in this chapter is Displace, which has some special tools and gets a longer discussion in Chapter 7 (Other Filters).

Pinch

The Pinch filter squeezes an image toward its center or pushes it out toward its outer edges. You can pinch the entire image or just a selection. The only control you have available is an Amount slider, which can be varied from 0 to 100% (to pinch inward) or from 0 to –100% (to push outward). The Pinch dialog box is shown in Figure 4.1.

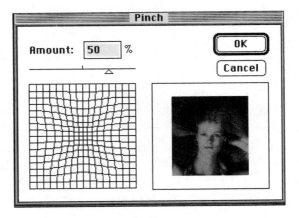

Figure 4.1 Pinch dialog box.

The grid shown in the window next to the Preview window gives you an idea of the amount and direction of distortion you're going to get. The only way that you can change the center point is by reselecting a different portion of your image. The pinching effect is always applied around the centerpoint of the selection.

Figure 4.2 shows an unpinched portrait at upper left. The entire image has been pinched by 50% at upper right and by 100% at lower left. At lower right, the same image is pinched outward (using –100 percent). Note that this version is similar to the Spherize effect described later in this chapter. In truth, pinching with negative values is more or less the same as spherizing with positive values, and vice versa. The spherize filter allows you to apply the effect only in one direction (either vertically or horizontally), whereas Pinch does not.

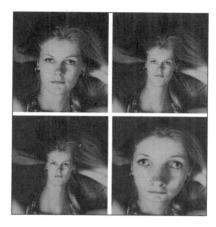

Figure 4.2 Applying the Pinch filter by 50% inward (upper right), 100% (lower left), and outward (lower right).

If you're pinching a rectangularly shaped selection, the filter automatically blends the affected area into the surrounding image. There's a simple reason for this. When you administer Pinch to a rectangular image or selection, Photoshop applies the filter to an elliptical section of the selection—the largest ellipse that will fit inside the square or rectangle. The effect is feathered into the rest of the selection, providing a smooth transition.

If your selection is round, elliptical, or irregularly shaped or if it consists of discontinuous multiple selections, the Pinch effect will be applied to the largest ellipse that can fit inside the selected area, but there will be an abrupt boundary at the selection border. To avoid this, make your selection, choose **Select:Feather**, and specify 5 pixels or more as your feather radius. The Pinching effect will be applied to the entire selection, gradually tapering off in the feathered portion.

Most illustrations of the Pinch filter feature images that look like those in Figure 4.2, but let's get real for a moment. Would you really want to do something like that to a human being? Is Pinch just for weird effects? Take a look at Figure 4.3 for two examples of how this filter can be effectively applied without making your subject look like something from another planet.

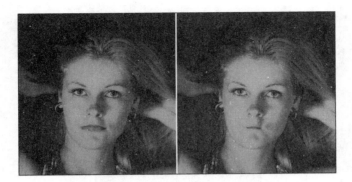

Figure 4.3 The Pinch filter can provide more subtle effects.

In both cases, I selected a small section around the mouth, and then pinched outward (at left) and inward (at right). Both effects aren't all that strange unless you compare them to the original. Remember that you saw an actual useful treatment of Pinch here first. This filter can provide a limited type of "warping" that you might otherwise have to use a morphing program to achieve.

Polar Coordinates

The Polar Coordinates filter takes quite a while to get used to, because its function may be difficult to understand—unless you work with maps a lot. Those who create world maps have a real problem: the Earth is a sphere, more or less, but maps are most convenient when expressed in a flat, two-dimensional format that can be printed in a chart book.

Some maps cut the Earth into sections, like the peel of an orange, with the cuts concentrated in ocean areas that contain few land masses. Ocean navigators hate maps with the seas cut up like that. They'd rather have a version in which the oceans are intact and the land masses dissected. However, in either mode, with many sections, the distortions are minimized.

Other maps, like the infamous Mercator Projection, exaggerate the distance between the horizontal lines of latitude as you move from the equator, giving us a Greenland, Alaska, and Antarctica that are enormously out of proportion. Still other maps view the world from a polar perspective, giving a reasonably accurate view of what the Earth would look like from space, if viewed from above the north or south poles.

The Polar Coordinates filter can take a rectangular image (it doesn't have to be a map) and distort it as if it were that view from space. You end up with a circle with the bottom portion of the original image wrapped along the outside of the circle, while the top portion of the original image is squeezed into the center of the circle.

The same filter can take a circular image (or even one of another shape) and change it back to rectangular format—cutting the peel off, so to speak, and filling in the missing sections. The Polar Coordinates Filter can perform some useful effects if you take the time to experiment with it. The dialog box for this filter has just two buttons: Rectangular to Polar and Polar to Rectangular and an inadequate Preview window, so I won't waste an illustration with it.

Instead, I'll help you visualize how this filter works with two examples. Instead of a map, I'll use the landscape shown in Figure 4.4. I added some text at the top and bottom to make it easy to see what the Rectangular to Polar conversion does to the image.

Figure 4.4 Rectangular image before conversion to polar coordinates.

Figure 4.5 shows the same image after conversion. See how the text that was originally at the bottom is now arrayed along the outer edge of the circle that is produced? If you have good eyes or examine the original file for this filter (it's on the CD-ROM), you can make out the text that was on the top line in a tiny little circle in the middle.

Figure 4.5 Image converted to polar coordinates.

The top image in Figure 4.6 shows a "globe" viewed from the top, with a shish-kabob skewer stuck through the middle at the "equator." At the bottom is the same image after the Polar to Rectangular conversion has unwrapped it.

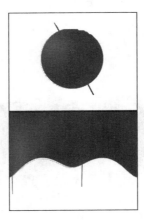

Figure 4.6 Polar to Rectangular transformation.

Unless you work with maps a lot, your chief uses for the Polar Coordinates filter will be to produce some interesting textures and shapes from images that you have on hand. The effects can be quite extraordinary and a lot of fun to play with. The Adobe manual mentions something called *cylinder anamorphosis,* which was a way of producing an image so that it looked distorted except when viewed as a reflection on a mirrored tube. Apparently this was an 18th century method for disguising racy pictures so that they could be distributed freely and viewed in privacy using chromed plumbing fixtures or something. Keep this in mind just in case the technique comes back into popularity.

Ripple

The Ripple filter gives you a wavy effect, supposedly something like the ripples on a pond, except when we think of those we usually expect them to be concentric. If that's what you want, investigate the Zigzag filter instead. Personally, I think Adobe has the names of these two filters reversed.

The Ripple dialog box, shown in Figure 4.7, allows you to specify an Amount from 0 (little ripples) to 999 (big ripples) or 0 to –999 (the ripples go the other direction). You can also click on **Small**, **Medium**, and **Large** radio buttons, which control not the size of the ripples (as you might expect) but rather how closely spaced together they are. This ripple frequency is calculated in proportion to the selection: choosing **Small** will produce differently sized ripples in small selections than in large selections.

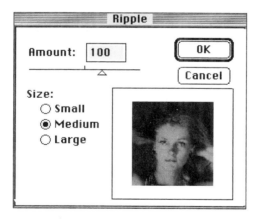

Figure 4.7 Ripple filter dialog box.

The ripple filter produces a stark transition with the rest of your image unless you feather the selection before you apply the effect. You can also produce some wonderful textures by applying the Ripple filter to the same selection multiple times, alternating negative and positive values, or mixing small, medium, or large frequencies.

Indeed, Ripple lends itself to experimentation. Don't limit yourself to using it to create a liquid effect. Figure 4.8 shows what you can get when you use small, medium, and large frequencies and apply Ripple to clouds to generate different artistic effects.

Figure 4.8 Clouds with no ripples, and with a value of 100 applied using small, medium, and large frequencies.

Shear

The Shear filter distorts the pixels in an image or selection based on a curve you specify in the dialog box (Figure 4.9). When you first activate the filter, the "curve" shown on the grid is a straight line with draggable endpoints at the top and bottom ends. Each time you click on the line, a new control handle appears. You can create a total of 16 handles on the curve (plus the two endpoints), and any of them can be dragged to produce complex curves. If you goof or just want to start over, click the **Reset** button to return to the basic straight line you first saw.

Click on either the **Wrap Around** or **Repeat edge pixels** radio buttons to specify how areas that are empty when the image has been dragged to fit your curve should be filled in. The **Wrap Around** option uses pixels from the opposite edge of the image to fill in the blanks, while the **Repeat edge pixels** option just adds pixels of the same tone and color as those just outside the empty area boundary. Figure 4.10 shows an image that has been manipulated by the curve in Figure 4.9. I used the **Repeat edge pixels** option.

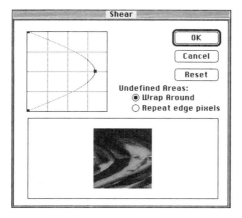

Figure 4.9 Shear dialog box.

Figure 4.10 Sheared image.

Spherize

The Spherize filter maps your image or selection onto a sphere, represented by the wireframe shown on the grid in the dialog box (Figure 4.11). You can specify an "outward" bulge from 0 to 100%, or an "inward" indentation of 0 to –100%. As mentioned earlier, the effect is quite similar to that of the Pinch filter.

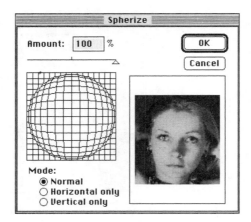

Figure 4.11 Spherize dialog box.

However, the Sphere filter also lets you distort your image around a vertical or horizontal cylinder, by clicking on the **Horizontal only** or **Vertical only** radio buttons. Figure 4.12 shows four variations on images that you can produce with the Spherize filter.

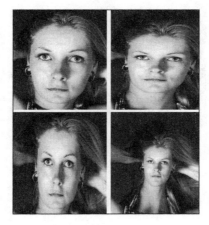

Figure 4.12 A 100% Spherize effect (upper left), vertical cylinder (upper right), horizontal cylinder (lower left), and inward-oriented bowl effect (lower right).

The image in the upper left was produced using the Normal mode, with a 100% setting. The image at upper right was generated with a 100% setting and the **Horizontal only** option. At lower left is the same image wrapped around a cylinder standing on end, using the **Vertical only** option. The final version shows a pinching effect achieved by using the −100% setting.

If your selection area is not round, this filter will carve out a circular area in the middle of the selection and warp that instead. You can use feathering to blend the selection into the rest of your image.

You'll probably use the Spherize filter a lot, and not just for mapping images onto globes. You can also use it to create spheres from scratch. I once needed to create a "moon" for a science-fiction-type painting. I drew a circle, added craters (which I raised above the surface using the Emboss filter), added shading to give the moon a sphere like appearance, and then applied the Spherize filter, which realistically manipulated the surface details of the satellite, such as the craters. It really looked three-dimensional.

If you want a plain sphere, try this trick: select a circle and fill it with a radial gradient. Position the center of the gradient up and to one side of the circle. Use **Filter:Render:Lens Flare** to make the surface even more realistic. Then apply the Spherize filter. Presto! One ball-shaped object, ready to roll.

Twirl

The Twirl filter acts like one of those rotating paint swirlers that creates art by spinning a turntable full of wet paint. The pixels in the center of your image or selection move more drastically than those on the periphery, which lag behind. The effect is quite striking. The Twirl dialog box is shown in Figure 4.13.

Your only control is the slider that specifies degrees of twisting; you can use from −999° to +999°. That range is not a misprint. A setting of 180° would cause the center to spin a half revolution more than the edges; at 361°, the center actually "laps" the edges. The maximum 999° is nearly three full spins, producing a whirlpool like effect. I used only a couple hundred degrees of spin for Figure 4.14.

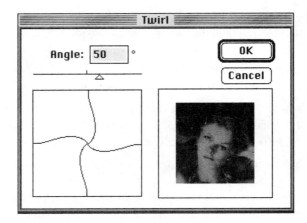

Figure 4.13 Twirl dialog box.

Figure 4.14 A twirled image can produce a whirlpool effect.

Positive numbers give a clockwise spin effect; negative numbers reverse the spin to counterclockwise. Use the Twirl filter to create whirlpools, paint swirls, or special textures.

Wave

The Wave filter's flexibility comes from the no less than 13 different controls you can use to specify how your image is stirred up. You get three kinds of waves; can specify the number, size, and frequency of the ripples; and can even randomize things if you want a natural appearance. You can spend a lot of time figuring out how the Wave filter works but, on the plus side, you can achieve effects that are unlikely to be duplicated. Think unique. Figure 4.15 shows the Wave dialog box.

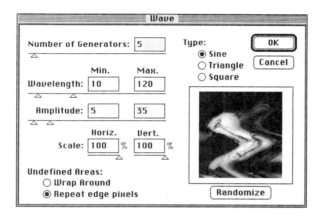

Figure 4.15 Wave dialog box.

The key controls that you can work with are:

- **Number of Generators.** The number of points where waves are created. Up to 999 different little wave generators can be entered, but that's far too many for most images—the effect is so muddled that each wave may be only a pixel or two wide. In my tests, high numbers ended up producing areas with plain tone, and no waves at all! You'll want to use from 5 to 20, tops.

- **Wavelength Minimum/Maximum.** This parameter sets the distance from one wave crest to the next. In this case, wavelength minimum and maximum (from 1 to 999) refer to the number of individual waves produced by each generator.

- **Amplitude Minimum/Maximum.** The height of the waves can also be set from 1 to 999.

- **Horizontal/Vertical Scale.** How much distortion you get per wave can be set here, with values from 1 to 100%

- **How Undefined Areas Are Filled In.** You can have pixels wrap around from one side to another or just stretched from the edge to fill the empty spaces.

- **Type of Wave.** Choose from smooth sine waves, pointy triangle waves, or chunky square waves (which are more blocks than waves to my eye). I have an example of each in Figure 4.16.

- **Randomize:** If you just want waves, and don't care what they look like, click on this button to supply random values. Keep clicking until you find an effect you care for.

Figure 4.16 shows our sample picture with sine, triangle, and square waves applied. I left the other parameters the same so that you could see how the shapes differ.

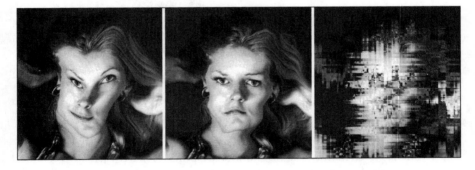

Figure 4.16 Sine, triangle, and square waves produce different effects.

Zigzag

The Zigzag filter is my choice for producing ripples in an image, because you don't really get zigzags at all (unless you count the **Around center** option, which does alternate the direction the ripples rotate). You can specify an amount of distortion from –100 to +100, which is reflected in the grid shown in Figure 4.17. The number of ridges (1 to 20) can also be specified.

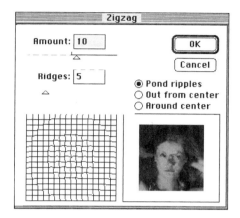

Figure 4.17 Zigzag produces three kinds of ripple effects.

You may select from:

- **Pond ripples,** which Adobe defines as ripples that progress from the upper left or lower right (depending on whether you've entered a positive or negative number).

- **Out from center,** which produces ripples that are generated from the center of your image or selection.

- **Around center,** Whirlpool-like ripples that revolve around the center of the image or selection, first in one direction, and then in the other.

In Figure 4.18, I've partially submerged our model in a pool of water, created by flipping a copy of the image, adding some noise, and then using the Pond Ripples filter. The Zigzag filter is a good choice for creating any type of water effect, assorted liquids, and special textures.

Figure 4.18 The Zigzag filter's Pond Ripples effect can produce realistic-looking water.

The Next Step

The filters in this chapter all distort images in ways that range from subtle to drastic. You can use them to produce interesting backgrounds or to warp your image. In the next chapter, we'll investigate Photoshop's "painting" filters. You'll find that poor images can be salvaged by adding an arty texture to them that resembles brush strokes, frescoes, or mosaics. Good images may become outstanding with the creative application of some painting effects.

CHAPTER 5
Painting Filters

Digital effects applied with filters can produce in seconds results that can't easily be achieved by an artist equipped with paints, brushes, and other traditional tools. It's also fairly easy to generate effects that are strongly reminiscent of the styles of "real" artists, using a group of filters found in the Pixelate and Stylize menus of Photoshop, or their equivalents in other image-editing programs.

PixelPaint Pro, for example, has Oil, Emboss, and Mosaic filters in its **Filter:Other** menu, which can create interesting painterly effects. Fractal Design Painter is another case entirely, since you don't even need plug-ins to add brush strokes to your image—it's whole raison d'être is to mimic natural media painting.

These kinds of filters all have one thing in common: they reduce the amount of information in an image by combining or moving pixels. Some overlay an image with a texture or pattern, while other plug-ins group similar colors together or transform groups of hues into new tones. The result is an image that has been softened, broken up, selectively increased in contrast, or otherwise *pixelated*.

At first glance, these filters seem to have turned a photograph into a painting. Instead of the harsh reality of the original image, we have a softer, more organic picture that appears to have been created rather than captured. The process resembles the way in which video and film cameras convert moving images.

Just as the crystal clarity of video productions adds realism to documentaries and intimacy to videotaped stage plays or situation comedies, original photographs look real to us. For romantic stories and fantasy images, motion picture film provides a softer look with a feeling of distance, much like digital processing of still images. Would *Star Wars* or *Forrest Gump* have been as effective if originated on video? Do hyper realistic original photos qualify as portraits?

Of course, both kinds of images have their place. Painting-oriented filters are excellent for portraits, figure studies, or landscapes in which fine detail is not as important as general form, colors, or groups of shapes. Indeed, brush strokes or other textures can mask defects, disguise or diminish distracting portions of an image, and create artful images from so-so photographs. That's especially true when the original image was too sharp or, paradoxically, not sharp enough. Filters can tone down excessive detail while masking the lack of it.

You'll want to select your subjects for painting filters carefully. Pictures of older men and women may not look right when you blur all those hard-won wrinkles and character lines. Teenagers of both sexes, on the other hand, may prize the improvement to their complexions. Judicious application of a painting filter can add some softness to a glamour portrait, too.

Keep in mind that painting filters mimic but do not duplicate the efforts of an artist. In real paintings, each brush stroke is carefully applied with exactly the right size, shape, and direction needed to provide a particular bit of detail. Years of experience and a good dose of artistic vision tell the artist where and how to put down those strokes.

A filter, in contrast, can base its operation only on algorithms built into it by the programmer. A skilled software designer can take advantage of variables such as lightness, darkness, contrast, and so forth to produce the illusion that an organic human, and not a silicon simulacrum, is behind the effect. You can further enhance the image by using your own judgment to apply parameters and choose which sections of the picture are to be processed by a filter. However, you won't exactly duplicate the efforts of an artist with one of these plug-ins. But you knew that. (I'm reminded of the Superman Halloween costume with the notice on the box: "Warning: Cape does not enable wearer to fly!")

In later chapters we'll look at third-party filters that also provide painterly effects, such as Xaos Tools' Paint Alchemy and Adobe Gallery Effects. For now, let's explore the filters built right into your image editor. I spent days working with each of them, trying to uncover features, bugs, and nuances I couldn't find in the documentation or other image-processing books. Some of the things I discovered were surprising.

Pixelate Filters

This group of seven filters ranges from the mildly interesting to the wildly useful, and all of them provide distinct effects. You may have no parameters to enter or just a few simple controls to manipulate. Here's a quick rundown on all of them.

Color Halftone Filters

Most color halftone filters should be considered as a special effect rather than as a way to actually generate color separations with the halftone dots required to print color on a printing press. These plug-ins don't have the accuracy required to produce color separations: all they do is take each color layer of your image and change it into a pattern of dots. The size of the dots varies depending on the darkness or density of that portion of your image. Highlight areas are represented by small dots; shadows and solids are represented by larger dots.

The relationships among these dots in the individual color layers can be complex and quite beyond the scope of a run-of-the-mill color halftone filter. So you should use these plug-ins simply as a way of adding a halftone texture to your images.

WARNING

Tech Alert! This section has a bit of technical background that you don't need to understand in order to use the Color Halftone filter but that you might find interesting. Proceed with caution.

Photoshop's Color Halftone filter differs from real color halftoning in several ways. In traditional color printing, only solid dots of cyan, magenta, yellow, and black color ink can be printed, so the goal is to produce hard-edged dots of many different sizes (expressed as percentages) in the separations. A midtone would be represented by a 50% dot that would occupy exactly half the area of allocated for it—say, 0.01 x 0.01 inch with a 100-line (dots-per-inch) screen.

The Color Halftone filter, in contrast, produces gray dots without the hard edge, as shown in Figure 5.1. Such dots look better on-screen and won't be used by your printer to reproduce the colors. Your printer's own halftoning routines will break down the dots into its own screen equivalents.

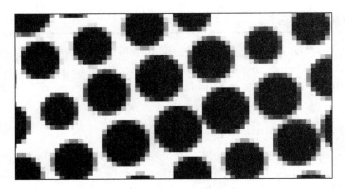

Figure 5.1 Gray dots produced by Photoshop's Color Halftone filter.

WARNING

The second area in which the Color Halftone filter is different is in the angles used for each color layer's dot patterns. Obviously, if you printed or displayed the dots on top of one another, you'd end up with black. To avoid this, each color halftone layer is angled slightly with respect to the others. With true halftones, the angles—usually 105° for cyan, 75° for magenta, 90° for yellow, and 45° for black—produce a neat rosette pattern that avoids troublesome moiré patterns.

The most visible color—black—is placed at the least obtrusive angle (45°) with two of the other colors set 30° apart. The least visible color—yellow—is angled 90°, which is not an ideal position being only 15° from cyan and magenta, but it is not likely to be a problem either.

Photoshop uses 45° for black and 90° for yellow but places cyan and magenta at 108° and 162° respectively. The filter's dialog box, shown in Figure 5.2, doesn't call the cyan, magenta, yellow, and black channels by their names but, rather, Channel 1, Channel 2, Channel 3, and Channel 4, which corresponds to the Channels palette's labels.

If, as is likely, you're working in RGB mode instead of CMYK mode, Photoshop uses only the first three channels and angles, so the ideal 45° setting doesn't get used at all, unless you manually change it.

```
┌─────────────────────────────────────────────────┐
│ ▓▓▓▓▓▓▓▓▓▓▓▓▓▓    Color Halftone   ▓▓▓▓▓▓▓▓▓▓▓▓▓ │
│                                                   │
│   Max. radius:  │  8  │  (pixels)   ┌───────────┐ │
│                                     │    OK     │ │
│   Screen angles (degrees):          └───────────┘ │
│      Channel 1: │ 108 │             ┌───────────┐ │
│                                     │  Cancel   │ │
│      Channel 2: │ 162 │             └───────────┘ │
│                                                   │
│      Channel 3: │ 90  │             ┌───────────┐ │
│                                     │ Defaults  │ │
│      Channel 4: │ 45  │             └───────────┘ │
│                                                   │
└─────────────────────────────────────────────────┘
```

Figure 5.2 Color Halftone dialog box

Using the Color Halftone Filter

One thing you may not have seen emphasized elsewhere is that the Color
Halftone filter provides distinctly different effects when applied in RGB or
CMYK modes. In RGB mode, three sets of dots are created: one each for the red,
green, and blue color channels. In CMYK mode, four sets of dots are generated
for the cyan, yellow, and magenta colors plus black. You'll get very different
effects in each mode, and you can create the halftone in one mode and then
switch back to the other to continue working on your image.

N O T E   Because some colors are lost when you switch from RGB to CMYK
and back (and vice versa), you may want to apply the filter on a
copy of a selection and then paste that selection back in the
main image, so that only the selection is affected by the color loss.

The Color Halftone dialog box has only five settings for you to control. You
already know about the angles of the dot patterns for each color layer. (The
Channel 4—black—angle is used only when you're in four-color CMYK mode.)
The fifth parameter is the maximum width of the dots that will be created, and is
measured in pixels.

Another point often overlooked is that the effects of this filter—or any of the pixelation filters that let you specify a cell size—vary depending on the resolution of an image. That is, with a 100-dpi image, an 8-pixel cell size will generate relatively large dots, with a maximum of about 12 cells per inch of your image. At 300 dpi, you get 36 cells per inch—still coarse, but your image would be recognizable.

Why would you want to use a larger cell size in the first place? Bigger cells can represent a wider array of tones. At the default setting of 8, the largest 8 x 8-pixel dot could theoretically represent 64 different tones. The actual number is different because round rather than square dots are created. (You'll never get a full 8 x 8-pixel dot; some are always left off the corners.) In addition, Photoshop uses intermediate shades of gray pixels rather than just white and black pixels to create its dots, effectively providing more tones per given cell size.

However, while larger values can represent more tones, they also provide a coarser image. Figure 5.3 shows an original 400-dpi RGB image at left and the same image processed by the Color Halftone filter at its default settings at right. As you can see, the dot pattern is very coarse. The upper inset is a blow-up of the RGB dots, while the lower inset is an enlargement of the same dots produced in CMYK mode.

Figure 5.3 Original image (left) and same image with Color Halftone effect using default settings (right). Insets show the dot patterns for RGB and CMYK modes.

If you use smaller dots, you'll get a tighter dot pattern that robs your image of detail. Figure 5.4 shows two examples using a value of 4, the smallest pixel diameter cell size allowed. The image at left uses Photoshop's default screen angles, while the image at right shows the traditional angles used in color separating. The insets show the dot patterns enlarged. You can experiment with angles to get different effects.

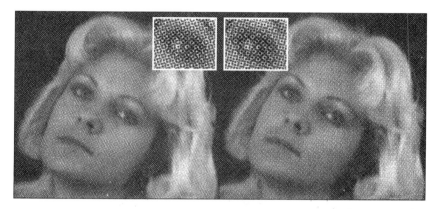

Figure 5.4 Reducing the dot size to four or smaller using Photoshop's default screen angles (left) and the traditional screen angles (right) each produce a different effect.

In Figure 5.5, I played with setting all channels to 45° (left) and 90° (right). These settings give you two more effects, however, because the dots are superimposed on one another.

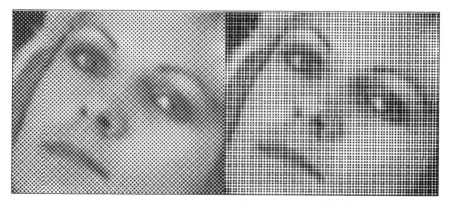

Figure 5.5 Setting all channels' screen angles to 45° (left) and 90° (right) produce these effects.

You can apply the Color Halftone filter to a grayscale image, producing the variation shown in Figure 5.6. Only the screen angle specified for Channel 1 will be used; the others are ignored.

Figure 5.6 Color Halftone applied to a grayscale version of the image.

Crystallize Filter

The Crystallize filter converts your image or selection to random polygons, each with a maximum cell size that you specify, from 3 to 300 pixels. The value can be typed in or entered using the slider shown in Figure 5.7. That's the only parameter you can control; the color of each cell is determined by the average underlying tone of the image beneath the cell.

As with the Color Halftone filter, the smaller the cell size, the more detail is retained from your original image. Larger cells simplify your picture and mask defects. Figure 5.8 shows our sample picture crystallized using a 3-pixel cell at left and an 8-pixel cell at right.

Just because this filter doesn't offer several different parameters to play with doesn't mean you must settle for a few limited effects. As with any of the filters discussed in this book, you can get numerous variations by combining one or more filters or by adding the filtered image back with the original in different "concentrations." That is, you can merge the modified image with the original using one of Photoshop's merging modes (Normal, Lighten, Darken, etc.) or by adjusting the transparency of one or more layers when the image is flattened.

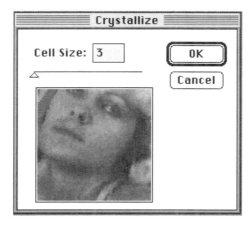

Figure 5.7 Crystallize dialog box.

Figure 5.8 Crystallize, using a 3-pixel (left) and 8-pixel (right) cell size.

With Photoshop 2.5, you used the Composite Controls dialog box. In Photoshop 3.0, you use layers instead. Follow these steps to produce the images shown in Figure 5.9.

1. Use the Layer Palette's fly-out menu to select **Duplicate** and create a new layer identical to the original background image.

2. Apply the Crystallize filter to the new layer, using a cell size of 8.

3. Adjust the Opacity slider in the crystallized layer to 50%, so that the image is half the original and half the filtered image. This version is shown at left in Figure 5.9.

Figure 5.9 Image half crystallized, half unfiltered (left) and same image merged using Dissolve control (right).

4. Use **Image:Duplicate** to create two more copies of this image so that you can produce a couple of variations. I left the Opacity setting for the pixelated layer at 50% in both copies.

5. Flatten the layers in the original version shown at left in Figure 5.9, using the Normal composite setting (see the dialog box in Figure 5.10), and save that file.

6. Using the first copy, flatten the layers using the Dissolve composite setting, which randomly mixes in foreground-colored pixels, producing a beautiful feathery effect, as shown at right in Figure 5.9.

7. Using the second copy, flatten the layers using the Difference composite setting, which reverses pixels in the background layer if the equivalent pixel in the foreground layer is brighter. If the resulting image is low in contrast, add some snap with the **Image:Adjust:Brightness/Contrast** sliders. The final image is shown at bottom in Figure 5.11.

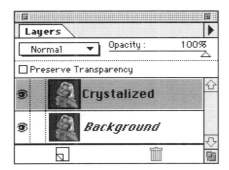

Figure 5.10 Layers palette and its merging controls.

Figure 5.11 Half-crystallized image merged with unfiltered image using Difference composite setting.

Facet Filter

The Facet Filter changes blocks of pixels that are similar in color to one tone, producing a faceted effect like the face of a diamond (or maybe like the face of Bizarro Superman, if you remember him). This is a kind of posterization, but with the reduction in number of colors taking place in a seemingly randomized way over the entire image. Details are masked, so this is an excellent filter to use with grainy, dust-laden, or otherwise imperfect photographs. Figure 5.12 shows a baby picture that was pixelated using the Facet filter (right). The unaltered image is shown at left.

Figure 5.12 Normal image (left) and same image
softened using the Facet filter (right).

The Facet filter has no dialog box or options; you apply it directly to any selection or an entire image. The effect becomes more pronounced with repeated applications. Just use **Command-F** to apply the filter several times until you get the look you desire. Figure 5.13 is a close-up of the baby picture from Figure 5.12, showing before and after images. In the version at right, the Facet filter has been applied six times.

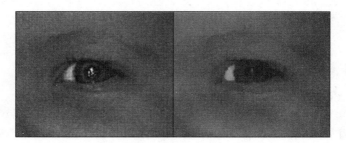

Figure 5.13 Unaltered image (left) and same image
with six applications of the Facet filter (right).

Fragment Filter

If you want to duplicate the Fragment filter without using your Mac, peel an onion, and then look at the world around you through tear-filled eyes. If you live in California, you can also get the same effect by taking a few snapshots during the next earthquake. This filter produces a shaky image that doesn't have a lot of application when applied to entire images (although I provide you with an example in Figure 5.14). It can be used to add some random texture to backgrounds or to apply a little motion blur to edges of an object.

Figure 5.14 Using the Fragment filter to shake things up.

Like the Facet filter, the Fragment filter has no options or parameters. Just apply it until you're happy with the results, or else give up and access the **File:Revert** command. If you want to amaze your friends or would just like to see how the Fragment command works, follow these steps.

1. Open an image and use the Layers palette to duplicate the image four times onto new layers.
2. Switch to each layer in turn, use **Select:All** to select everything in the layer.
3. Jog the image on the first duplicate layer 4 or 5 pixels to the left by pressing the **Left Arrow** key four or five times.
4. Jog the image on the second duplicate layer 4 or 5 pixels to the right by pressing the **Right Arrow** key four or five times.

5. Nudge the images in the third and four duplicate layers to the left and right (respectively) by pressing the **Left Arrow** and **Right Arrow** keys twice, as appropriate.

6. Set the Opacity for each of the four layers to 40% using the slider.

7. With the four duplicate layers (but *not* the original background layer visible), flatten the image.

The result looks a lot like what you get with the Fragment filter, which operates in a similar way.

Mezzotint Filter

The Mezzotint filter, another technique borrowed from traditional printing, is a special overlay that is placed on top of a photograph to add a pattern during duplication. Digital filters offer much the same effect with a little less flexibility, since the range of mezzotints you can achieve with Photoshop is fairly limited. Only dots (fine, medium, grainy, or coarse) and lines or strokes (in short, medium, and long varieties) can be applied, as shown in the dialog box in Figure 5.15. You can rotate your image, apply this filter, and then rotate it back to the original orientation if you want to change the direction of the lines or strokes.

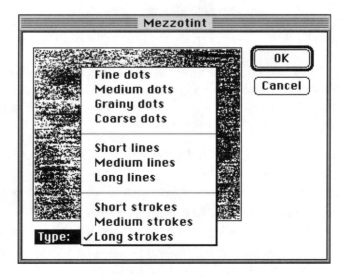

Figure 5.15 Mezzotint dialog box.

Figure 5.16 shows an original image at left and the same image with Grainy dots applied at right. Different effects can be achieved using the lines and strokes option (Figure 5.17).

Figure 5.16 Original image (left) and same image with Grainy dots.

Figure 5.17 Long lines (left) and Long strokes (right) applied to the image.

Mosaic Filter

At last! Now you can apply the very same effect used in cop reality television shows to mask the identities of alleged offenders or those who refused to sign a release. Better yet, simplify images with too much troubling detail, creating a blocky computerish effect at the same time.

The Mosaic filter divides your image into an array of blocks, using a cell size you specify. Then, it averages the color and brightness of all the pixels in each cell and creates a new mega-pixel from the value that results. Figure 5.18 shows the dialog box for this filter.

The Mosaic filter can actually be a pretty cool filter to use when you want to create an abstract image of a subject that screams "Computer generated!" at the viewer but still can be recognized if you squint or move back a little. Mosaic is a popular effect among graphic designers preparing illustrations for magazines. You can choose a cell size from 2 to 64 pixels; Figure 5.19 shows the baby picture pixelized using both 4- and 8-cell settings.

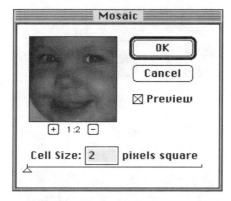

Figure 5.18 Mosaic dialog box.

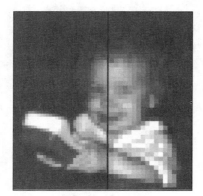

Figure 5.19 Using 4- and 8-cell settings with the Mosaic filter provides different effects.

Pointillize Filter

The Pointillize filter will enrage artists and please everyone else. It purports to create a pointillistic image, but don't expect to generate anything that reminds you of Georges Seurat. What you end up with is more of a randomized image with lots of little dots on it (many in colors that you may not remember seeing in the original). Generally the pixelation represents the detail in the original photograph. You can select a cell size from 3 to 300 pixels, using the dialog box shown in Figure 5.20.

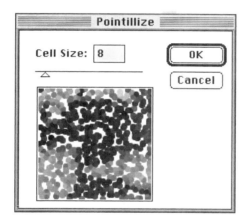

Figure 5.20 The Pointillize dialog box.

The most difficult thing about using this filter is selecting a compatible background color. All the spaces between dots are filled in with your current background color. If you're using the defaults, that's white. Softer pastels that match the predominate tones of your image make a better choice, unless you want the image to look as if it were overlaid with a snowstorm, as in Figure 5.21.

As you can see from the unfiltered portion of the image at left, this scene originally featured a house in snow, perhaps suitable for the owner's holiday greeting card. At center, the same image has been pointillized with a fine, 3-pixel cell size, and a white background, achieving a blizzardy look. At right, a larger 8-pixel cell size was used, and the white background isn't nearly as appropriate. You'll always want to work with a copy of your original (or better yet, duplicate the original onto another layer) and experiment.

Figure 5.21 Snow scene left pointillized using 3-pixel cell (center) and 8-pixel cell (right).

Stylize Filters

Filters found under Photoshop's Stylize menu sometimes add pixelating effects (Diffuse and Extrude are good examples of this type), but they go beyond mere pixel jumbling to add new types of image processing. This section will get you started using each of the eight filters listed under Photoshop 3.0's revamped Stylize menu.

Diffuse Filter

The Diffuse filter divides your image or selection up into 4-pixel elements (you can't control the size of the cell); then it moves pixels toward the edges or higher-contrast areas of your image. As a result, the image is smudged in a pleasing way, producing a very nice artistic effect.

WARNING

If you know a bit about photography, don't confuse *digital diffusion* with the kind of diffusion that can be produced by a conventional filter with a texture. Something as simple as women's hosiery stretched over a frame is sometimes used in the darkroom to provide a diffusing effect when a print is exposed. A glass filter placed in front of the camera lens with petroleum jelly applied also can be used to create diffusion.

In photography, diffusing a positive image "spreads" lighter areas into darker areas, so an on-camera filter smudges highlights into the shadows. Diffusing a negative image during printing also spreads lighter areas into the darker areas, but in that case they are the more transparent shadows of an image, smudged into the denser highlights. The final image diffused under the enlarger has a much different look than one diffused in the camera.

Photoshop's diffusion does not work in this way, so don't bother inversing a picture or selection before applying the diffusion filter and then converting it back. Even with multiple applications, the effect is virtually identical whether you diffuse a positive or negative image.

Your only controls, shown in the dialog box in Figure 5.22, are options to perform this diffusion on all pixels, only darker pixels, or only lighter pixels. It takes experience with hundreds of images to acquire an idea of which mode is best for which image.

To experiment with diffusion, zoom in on the area being previewed by clicking on the plus box under the preview window. Then click on the **Normal, Darken Only**, and **Lighten Only** radio buttons to get a close look at how the diffusion will appear. Your original image or selection will also be diffused in the main window. Wait a few seconds until Photoshop has a chance to apply the filter while the dialog box is still on-screen and check out the full effect while looking at the zoomed-in preview.

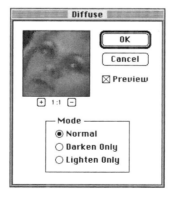

Figure 5.22 Diffuse dialog box.

Figure 5.23 shows the same image with Diffuse applied in Normal mode (left), Darken Only (center), and Lighten Only (right). You can see that the Normal mode provides the strongest diffusing effect but that the differences between it and the other too modes are subtle, at best. You'll want to apply the filter several times to get the maximum effect.

Figure 2.23 Diffuse applied in Normal mode (left),
Darken Only (center), and Lighten Only (right).

Emboss Filter

The Emboss filter raises the edges of your image above its imaginary "surface" much like an address embosser presses a 3-D version of your name, address, or monogram into stationery or an envelope. This digital filter more or less discards most of the colors in your image, providing a stamped-metal effect. The controls are shown in the dialog box in Figure 5.24.

You can modify:

- The angle for the imaginary light source that casts the shadow of the raised surface. Type in a value in degrees or drag the pointer on the clock face at right. Because we're most accustomed to overhead lighting, values from 0° (right side of the image) to 90° (directly overhead) and on to 180° (left side of the image) produce a raised effect. From –1° (right) to –90°

(directly underneath) to -179° (left) make the image seem to be pressed into the surface.

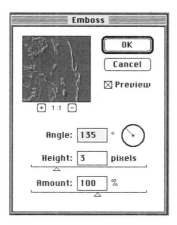

Figure 5.24 Emboss dialog box.

- The Height of the embossing, from 1 to 10 pixels. The larger the number, the greater the 3-D effect. Use this control with the Amount slider, which is described later. You can get some lovely, grainy effects even with only a 1-pixel-high emboss if you ramp up the contrast by specifying 500% with the Amount slider.
- The amount of embossing, from 1 to 500%. This control adjusts the contrast between the embossed edges and the rest of the image so that you can fine-tune the effect to a surprising degree. I've gotten some great results from using a very small height with a large Amount setting—and vice versa.

On its own, the Emboss filter often isn't particularly useful with some images, since the 3-D effect, while interesting, has bland coloration and featureless backgrounds. You'll want to combine this filter with other effects—pixelation, distortion, or even sharpening—to create a really outrageous image. Figure 5.25 shows an image that has been embossed using the maximum 10-pixel Height and a 500% Amount settings.

Figure 5.25 Embossing creates a 3-D stamped image.

Extrude Filter

Combine the Mosaic filter with the Emboss filter and you get something like the Extrude filter, which squeezes your image through an imaginary mesh, something like a Play-Doh Fun Factory for photographs.

The controls for this filter, are shown in the Extrude dialog box in Figure 5.26. Note that this filter does not have a preview box; it's a processor-intensive effect that takes so long to produce that you couldn't realistically be presented with a preview in anything approaching real-time. The parameters you can work with are

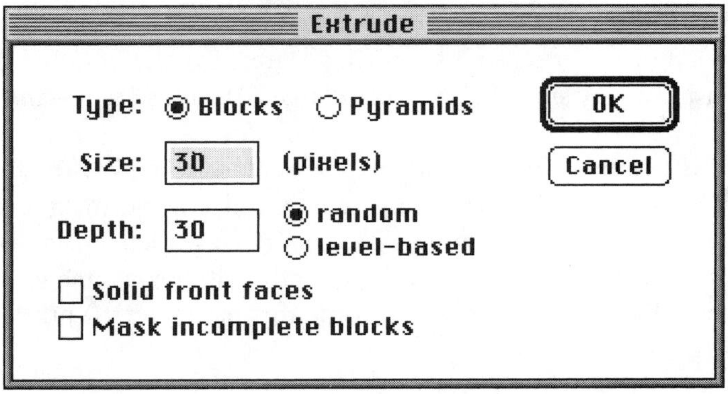

Figure 5.26 Extrude dialog box.

- **Type.** You can choose rectangular blocks or pointy pyramids.
- **Size.** The dimensions of each cell in the square grid are used to extrude your image, from 2 to 255 pixels.
- **Depth.** You can choose the maximum height of each block squeezed from your image, from 1 to 255 pixels. You can further select random depth (adjacent blocks may be any size up to the maximum you specified) or level-based (the lighter blocks are higher; the darker blocks are shorter).
- **Solid front faces.** Check this box and the faces of the blocks are the predominant color of the block. Unchecked, the faces retain the original image detail of the block.
- **Mask incomplete blocks.** Hidden areas of blocks are not shown.

Figure 5.27 shows an original image at upper left, and the same image at upper right was extruded with a large block size of 60, low height (5 pixels), and front faces that retain the original image. At lower left and lower right, the block size was reduced to 5 pixels, the height was raised to 30, and with the Solid front faces and Mask incomplete blocks boxes were checked. The two images were produced using blocks (left) and pyramids (right).

Figure 5.27 Effects produced with the Extrude filter.

Find Edges Filter

You'll love the Find Edges filter because it's so easy to use and produces such dramatic effects, much like drawings created with colored pencils. There are no controls or dialog boxes to worry about: you simply select a portion of your image, or the whole thing, and drag your mouse to the **Filter:Stylize:Find Edges** choice.

The filter works so quickly that you can experiment on many different images, discovering those that are most suitable. After playing with it awhile, you'll discover that the Find Edges filter emphasizes the transitions between one color and another and changes solid colors to softer pastel versions of the complement (opposite color) of the tones in those areas. That is, blues are changed to yellow, cyans to reds, and so forth, much as if you were producing a negative of the original. In fact, you can get some great effects by inverting your image after applying the Find Edges filter, as you'll see in Figure 5.28.

The Find edges filter is a great springboard for combining several filters or using other controls to generate outrageous variations. Use the **Image:Adjust:Hue/Saturation** dialog box's sliders to warp the colors in your edge-enhanced image, juice up the saturation, or lighten/darken the effect. Pixelate your image or merge it with a copy of the original image, adjusting the Opacity slider in the Layers palette to combine varying percentages of the unaltered and edge-enhanced versions.

Figure 5.28 Find Edges applied to an image (left), and then inverted (right).

Solarize Filter

Photoshop's Solarize filter is not the best I've seen, since it has no controls. You can't specify the amount of solarization, although different effects can be produced by applying the filter to selections of an image, or by inverting the effect, as shown in Figure 5.29.

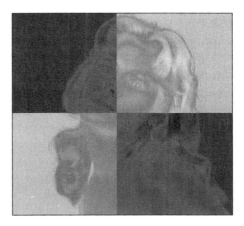

Figure 5.29 Image solarized (upper left, lower right) and inverted (upper right, lower left).

Solarization was originally a photographic effect produced (by accident or on purpose) when a negative or transparency being developed is exposed to light part way through the development process. The denser sections of the image that have already been developed are affected differently than the parts of the image that have not been fully developed. What you get is a partial reversal of the image. (When I first saw this effect in color on the cover of Frank Zappa's first album in the mid-1960s, I was awestruck. I bought the record without first listening to it; in those days album cover creativity was often directly related to the creativity of the music.)

Tiles Filter

Like the Mosaic filter, the Tiles filter divides your image into individual squares, but it retains all the detail in each section. You can specify the number of tiles, from 1 to 99, and the amount of space each will be offset, in percentages from 1 to 90. The "grout" between tiles can be filled with either the current foreground or background color, a negative version of the image that would normally appear in the grout space or an unaltered version of the image. Figure 5.30 shows the Tiles dialog box.

```
┌─────────────────────────────────────────────┐
│══════════════════ Tiles ═══════════════════│
│                                             │
│    Number of Tiles: [10]     ┌──────────┐   │
│                              │    OK    │   │
│    Maximum Offset:  [10] %   └──────────┘   │
│                              ┌──────────┐   │
│  Fill Empty Area With:       │  Cancel  │   │
│    ● Background Color  ○ Inverse Image  └──┘ │
│    ○ Foreground Color  ○ Unaltered Image    │
│                                             │
└─────────────────────────────────────────────┘
```

Figure 5.30 Tiles dialog box.

This filter doesn't have a preview window. You can tile a smaller selection to see how it looks if you don't want to wait for the entire image area to be tiled. Figure 5.31 shows an original image (upper left) and the same image tiled with a 10-pixel block, white grout, and a 10% offset in upper right and larger 30-pixel blocks with unaltered image (lower left) and inverted image (lower right) used as grout.

Figure 5.31 Various Tile effects create interesting patterns.

Trace Contour Filter

The Trace Contour filter is often lumped in with the Find Edges plug-in, but they are very different in practice. For one thing, you can adjust the brightness level that the Trace Contour filter uses as the threshold to outline edges in your image. That is, you can change which edges of an image are lined, with the Level slider. Higher values set the threshold so that lighter edges are outlined; lower values apply the effect to darker edges. Clicking the **Lower** or **Upper** radio buttons tells Photoshop to outline values either above the level set on the slider, or below.

The Trace Contours filter creates different outlines for each color channel, so you can sometimes get interesting effects by separating the color channels and working with them individually before recombining. (Use Photoshop's Channel's palette; separating and combining each color is virtually automatic and not difficult to do with the **Split Channels** and **Merge Channels** choices from the palette's fly-out menu.)

Don't get confused by this concept: what you're really interested in is how your image will look with Trace Contour applied, and you really can't tell by estimating numbers. You're better off using the Preview window and playing with the slider to see what effect works best for a given image. The numbers that appear in the Levels box are really useful only when you want to repeat an effect, using a previously used value. Figure 5.32 shows the dialog box.

Figure 5.32 Trace Contour dialog box.

The Trace Contour filter is another filter that can be used as a jumping off point. Try different level settings, merge a contoured image with the original, or invert your contour to create new effects. Figure 5.33 shows the same image contoured using different levels, but this is one effect that is best visualized in color. You'll want to load this figure from the CD-ROM to take a look or experiment directly with an image of your own.

Figure 5.33 Image contoured using different levels.

Wind

You'll love this filter! If you've tried it a few times and didn't like the jarring effects it produced, prepare to be converted. Wind is much more versatile than you might think if nobody has explained it to you.

Wind can create a variety of wind-blown and streaky effects, in virtually any direction you please. It can simulate dripping paint or create an image reminiscent of superhero The Flash streaking by on his way to a crime scene. There are several secrets to using Wind effectively.

- Choose your images carefully. When you have a picture with an empty or dark area that the wind effect can smear your image into, the results are much more impressive. It also helps if your subject can be enhanced by the streaky effect. A house may look pretty blah when streaked, but adding a wind effect baseball player sliding into second base raises the action level several notches.

- You're not limited to left and right wind directions, regardless of what you may think from the dialog box in Figure 5.34. I've gotten some fabulous effects by rotating an image, applying Wind, and then rotating it back to its original orientation. Instead of a gust of wind from the left or right, you end up with a dripping effect. You can even rotate the image in other than 90° increments to create interesting smearing.

Figure 5.34 Select strength (Wind, Blast, Stagger)
and direction from the Wind dialog box.

- Try different wind effects on each image. Figure 5.35 shows the same image with the mild Wind setting (left), a stronger Blast (center), and the chilling Stagger (right). Remember that you can always apply the filter to a duplicate copy of the image on another layer and then combine it with the original using various percentages of opacity.

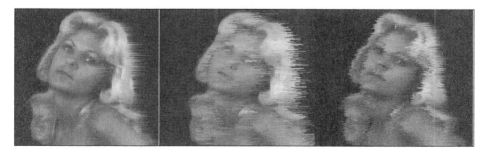

Figure 5.35 Various amounts of wind effect applied to an image.

Here's the best tip of all! Streak your image from two different directions to create a wild, wet-paint, splotchy effect that looks a lot more like something created by a real artist than most of the filters discussed in this chapter. For the image in Figure 5.36, I applied wind from right to left, rotated the picture, and then applied the filter again. After I restored the original orientation, I ended up with the picture you see here.

Wind looks especially good on silhouetted images, like the one shown in Figure 5.37. The interesting, streaky texture makes the model look as if she had stripes painted on her. In this case, the effect was applied from right to left, so the streaks push highlight areas into the shadows. Wind from the other direction wouldn't be nearly as effective.

Figure 5.36 Wind applied from two different directions, 90° apart.

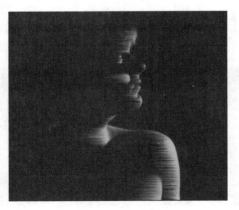

Figure 5.37 Wind creates special effects.

The Next Step

This lengthy chapter looked at some of your image editor's key filters in a great deal of detail. I devoted this much space to these filters because they are workhorses that most of us apply in some combination to many different images. Despite the fact that most filters are so widely available, they are often misunderstood, misapplied, and not used to their full potential. I wanted to give you some examples and techniques you haven't seen elsewhere as an incentive to explore these basic tools more completely.

In the next two chapters, we'll look at other built-in filters that you may have used before, but never fully understood. The fun is just beginning.

CHAPTER 6

Rendering Filters and Lighting Effects

The filters we'll work with in this chapter literally give you something for nothing. The plug-ins described in Chapters 3–5, work their magic by moving or changing the pixels in an existing image. Rendering filters, on the other hand, create new artifacts in your pictures or add things that weren't there in the first place.

You'll discover two kinds of Clouds filters, which conjure fluffy puffs of cumulus from thin air, and a lens flare filter capable of generating a mighty sun from nothing at all. Even if your original image was illuminated by a single, on-camera flash, you can add three or more studio lights to spotlight portraits or let still lifes bask in a wonderful glow. You can even fill selections with textures.

Rendering Filters

Although we'll look at just five filters in this chapter, you'll find the effects described here among the most useful in the book. I find myself turning to Photoshop's rendering filters over and over when I work with images that need a little extra excitement.

Clouds Filter

The Clouds filter is an incredibly useful plug-in that can be used to add realistic cloud textures to any picture that has a flat, uninteresting sky. You can also use this filter to create cloudlike mist or smog behind any object. There are no controls or dialog boxes to fool with nor is there a need to have any texture in the area to be filled. Just select the sky or other area you want to fill with clouds and apply the filter. Opaque clouds are created using fractal algorithms, producing a highly realistic effect.

Figure 6.1 shows the famous castle of Segovia, Spain perched on its hillside. At left, the original image has a plain, featureless sky. At right, the Clouds filter has filled the heavens with a rich, puffy texture.

Figure 6.1 Castle with featureless sky (left) and same castle where clouds have been added (right).

Although this filter doesn't use a dialog box, you still have some control over its effects. Here are a few tips you'll find useful.

- Clouds uses the current foreground and background colors to generate its cloud effects. You can select a blue and white tone to produce realistic clouds.

- If you forget to choose these colors or just want to fine-tune your clouds, go ahead and use the default black-and-white foreground and background tones. Then select **Image:Adjust:Hue/Saturation**. When the dialog box shown in Figure 6.2 pops up, click on the **Colorize** button and then move the Hue slider to a sky color you like. Don't just settle for blue. I've gotten some great science-fiction effects with yellow, orange, and magenta skies!

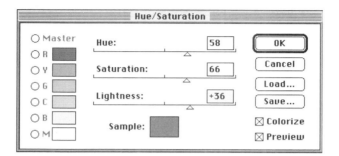

Figure 6.2 Use the Hue/Saturation dialog box to adjust the sky color.

- You can also fine-tune your clouds with the Saturation and Brightness controls, in the Hue/Saturation dialog box changing from dark, ominous clouds to lighter, more subtle sky effects. Don't be afraid to use other filters to enhance the effects of your clouds. Figure 6.3 shows the Segovia castle with darker, foreboding clouds at left. At right, I applied the Wind filter discussed in Chapter 5—but only to the sky selection. So, the clouds have a streaky texture, while the castle remains sharp.

Figure 6.3 Darker clouds (left) and clouds streaked with the Wind filter (right).

- While the Clouds filter produces opaque clouds in any selected area (that's good, since you don't need any texture or color there already for the filter to work with), you can create them in a layer and combine with existing portions of the image in the same area by adjusting the Layer palette's Opacity control for your cloud layer.

- If you don't like the clouds you get on first try, just reapply the filter (**Command-F**) to create a whole new set of random clouds.

WARNING

Tech alert! The reason why so many of your pictures have bland skies is that film is sensitive to ultraviolet light, which you can't see but, which is present in the sky. Those fluffy clouds you saw in the original scene may not show up as vividly in your finished picture: the clouds are transparent to the ultraviolet (UV) light in the sky, and that's what your camera records. If you want to avoid using the Clouds filter, your best bets may be to

- Keep the sun more at your back or to one side, which will reduce the amount of UV light reaching your film.
- Use a polarizing filter with color film. These filters skim off some of the UV light, favoring directionally polarized photons to produce richer, contrastier colors.
- Darken the skies in black-and-white photos by using a filter that removes some of the blue light, including ultraviolet. A light yellow filter has a mild effect; red filters have the strongest.

Difference Clouds Filter

The Difference Clouds filter works much like the plain Clouds filter, but it uses the current image information in the scene to calculate the difference in pixel values between the clouds and the underlying image. The end product is an image that is a combination of clouds and a weird, negative image.

Figure 6.4 shows two versions of Seville's Giralda tower with clouds added. At left, I selected the tower, used the Find Edges filter to emphasize its fine details, and then made a mirror-image copy of the selection. Inverting the selection, I added clouds. Finally, at right, I applied the Difference Clouds filter to the entire image, giving two very different pictures with little extra work.

Figure 6.4 Tower filtered through Find Edges and with Clouds added to the sky (left) and some tower with Difference Clouds applied to the whole image (right).

Here are some tips for using Difference Clouds.

- If you apply the Difference Clouds filter to an image without existing texture, with few contrasting colors, or with a subtle gradient, you'll get a relatively mild cloud effect. This filter really needs some image information to produce dramatic results.

- Try applying the Difference Clouds filter several times in succession to get increasingly interesting results. Each time you use the filter, colors are inverted, and new combinations result. Figure 6.5 shows an image that was processed with Difference Clouds several times. I ended up with almost a solarized look in the final image. (If you check out the original file from the CD-ROM, you'll see that the model's hair is magenta!)

Figure 6.5 The Difference Clouds filter applied several times in succession.

Lens Flare Filter

Lens Flare is a prime example of turning a bug into a feature—in this case, an optical bug found in every camera lens to one extent or another. The (usually) unwanted reflections of light inside the barrel of a photographic lens can produce flaring effects. Although there are various remedies for this "problem," many photographers—and now digital image workers—have learned to incorporate this effect into their pictures. The Lens Flare filter can create this sort of distortion, making your image manipulation seem that much more "real" (photographic) while generating suns, stars, and light sources where there were none.

You don't need to know anything about photography or optics to use Lens Flare. The filter's dialog box, shown in Figure 6.6, gives you enough feedback through the Preview window to let you play with various combinations of parameters until you get the amount and type of flare that you like.

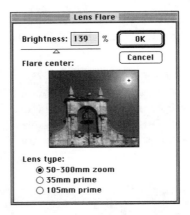

Figure 6.6 Lens Flare dialog box.

The flare is generated inside your image or selection using a center point that you can specify by dragging the cross hair in the Preview window. The amount of flare can be adjusted using the Brightness slider, from 10 to 300% The lens type radio buttons let you choose the particular type of photographic lens that will be simulated. Different optics generate different flare patterns, as I'll explain shortly.

Figure 6.7 shows two views of the bell tower of the City Hall in Ciudad Rodrigo, Spain. That's a stork nesting atop the tower. At left is the original image, while the inset at right shows the same picture with a "sun" created by using the Lens Flare filter's default settings: 100% brightness and a 50–300mm zoom lens.

Figure 6.7 Original image (left) and same image with "sun" added with with Lens Flare filter.

Zoom lenses are notorious flare-producers because they have so many pieces of glass (lens elements) for light to bounce around in. So, the 50–300mm setting generates the largest amount of flare, with lots of the little circle artifacts (actually images of the lens' diaphragm). Different flare effects are produced with the 35mm and 105mm prime (nonzoom) lens settings. An example of each of these is shown in Figure 6.8.

Figure 6.8 Lens Flare filter with 35mm prime (left) and 105mm prime (right) lens settings.

Increasing the Brightness value makes the flaring more pronounced, as if the source light were brighter. The flare spreads into the other areas of the image. The maximum of 300% will usually wash out your picture; use much lower settings in most cases. Figure 6.9 shows the flare that results from a 139% setting.

Figure 6.9 Flare set at 139% Brightness.

When using the Lens Flare filter, keep these tips in mind.

- The flaring effect is limited to your current selection. You can keep the light from spilling over into other areas of your image by creating a selection and applying the Lens Flare filter within it. For example, you can select the sky and add flare only to the sky area. I sometimes select circular areas with the sky and add the flare only to that area, say, when I want to create a sun, star, or point source light effect.

- You can place a flare behind an object by selecting the object, inverting your selection, and then moving the flare center behind the object in the Preview window. The flare effect will be applied only to the area outside the object. I use this technique to create a light source peaking out from behind a building or to backlight a person.

Figure 6.10 shows two young rock stars in concert. At left, the original picture had a modest amount of lens flare already from the light sources in the background. I applied Lens Flare twice, centered inside each light source, to increase the effect dramatcially. The final image, at right, has lots of extra lens flare.

Figure 6.10 Adding more lens flare to the picture at left increases the excitement in the final image at right.

Tech alert! Ideally, a photographic lens should take each ray of light emitted or reflected by your subject and focus it on an equivalent position on the film. In the real world, these light beams sometimes go astray in the following ways.

- Rays of light just outside your actual subject area can reach the inside of the lens at an angle and, despite dead black internal coatings on the lens barrel, bounce around to produce flare or degraded image contrast. A proper lens hood can shield your optics from these stray light beams.

- Strong light from the subject area can bounce off elements inside the lens instead of proceeding directly to the film plane. Lens manufacturers counter this by coating the front and internal lens elements with nonreflective surfaces, but there is no way to eliminate the effect entirely. The more complex the lens, the more surfaces and more potential lens flare. Zoom lenses, which must change the configuration of many different elements to provide different magnifications, are the worst offenders. Very fast lenses (with wide maximum apertures) or very wide lenses (which need extra elements to simulate very short focal lengths) also produce a lot of flare. Wide angle lenses also tend to scope in broad ranges of the landscape, increasing the opportunity to incorporate a flare-producing light source.

The Lens Flare filter takes all these optical factors into account to reproduce photographic flaring effects in a very clever and realistic way.

Lighting Effects

The Lighting Effects filter allows you to define up to 16 different light sources to "illuminate" your image from any angle you choose in the picture's original two-dimensional plane. That is, you can't move the light sources "behind" any portion of the image, in 3-D fashion. Even so, the effects you can create with this filter are very photographic in nature. If you know anything about photo lighting, you'll love this filter! And if you don't, you'll have a ball playing with it and learning about the various moods you can create through lighting alone.

Not only can you specify the direction and type of light source with the Lighting Effects filter, but you can also add textures and perform other magic. This filter is probably the most complex and versatile filter built into Photoshop, rivaling some Kai's Power Tools add-ons or specialized plug-in tools like Paint Alchemy for flexibility. The number crunching involved may not exceed those of some of the distortion filters, like Vortex Tiling, but this plug-in is unsurpassed among Adobe filter offerings in terms of the number of controls and parameters you can specify when you put it to work. Figure 6.11 shows the Lighting Effects dialog box and its controls, which divided into five different sections. We'll look at each of them shortly.

For photographic neophytes, the best way to learn about this filter is to simply play with it, using the guidelines in the section that follows the next one. You don't really need to understand photography to use it. However, for those of you who want to know more about how lighting works, I'll dig into the subject a little more deeply in the next section.

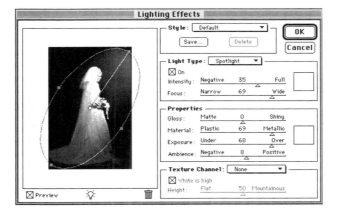

Figure 6.11 Lighting Effects dialog box.

Lighting Primer

Several factors govern how lighting affects an image. Photoshop simplifies most of these, so I'll describe each of them in terms of how they are used within the Lighting Effects filter.

Light Type

Photographers can choose from many different types of light: Photoshop gives you three: spotlight, directional light and omni light. Each has distinct characteristics.

- **Spotlight.** This is a focused source that casts light within an area shown by an ellipse in the Preview window. Figure 6.12 shows an example at far left. The center of the coverage area (but not necessarily the focal point of the light itself) is shown by a circle in the middle of the ellipse. The direction of the light is illustrated by a line radiating from the center out to a control handle at the edge of the ellipse. That control handle represents the position of the light source itself. There are three other control handles along the edges of the ellipse; any of them can be dragged to change the shape of the ellipse.

Spotlighting is tight, dramatic lighting that can be used to draw attention to a portion of an image or to isolate it from the rest of the picture. In a photo studio, a light of this type would typically be encased in a small reflector.

Figure 6.12 Light source preview windows for Spotlight (left), Omni Light (center), and Directional Light (right).

- **Directional Light.** Less focused than spotlighting, a directional light has a broader area of coverage. The Lighting Effects filter reflects this by not providing a bounding ellipse to represent the limits of coverage. Instead, directional light fades off gradually from the center to the edges of your image or selection. The center, direction of light, and position of the light source are represented with a circle, straight line, and control handle, just as with spotlighting. A typical Preview window is shown at far right in Figure 6.12.

  Directional lighting can be used when you want illumination that is less harsh than spotlighting but a definite sense of direction. In a studio, such lights would have larger, more diffuse reflectors. The familiar photographer's umbrellas are a type of directional lighting.

- **Omni Light.** Omnidirectional lighting seemingly comes from everywhere, although within Photoshop, omni light is applied only from the front. The preview includes a center circle and an outer bounding circle that can be resized by dragging the control handles. A typical Preview window for this type of light source is shown in the center of Figure 6.12.

Light Intensity

Lights used in photo studios may have only a limited range of intensities: full power, half power, quarter power, etc. Each of the sources used with the Lighting Effects filter can be controlled continuously from 0 to Full (with percentages used for everything in between). Moreover, your digital lights can be set to a negative intensity; that is, they *darken* the image rather than light it up. This can be useful when you want, say, a spotlight to neutralize the effects of another light in a particular area. Figure 6.13 shows the slider used to control intensity.

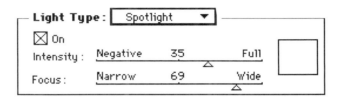

Figure 6.13 Light Type controls.

Light Focus

The Spotlight, only, can be adjusted in focus from Narrow to Wide. If you play with this slider, you'll see that the coverage ellipse doesn't change, only the size of the spot produced. The Focus control is shown in Figure 6.13.

Light Color

Notice the box at right in Figure 6.13. It represents the color of the light source. You can double-click in this box to access the Color Picker and select any color you wish. The default is white.

Light Properties

In addition to focus and direction, light can have several different properties in the Photoshop world, which are limited to four key factors. These factors control how your lighting effects appear in a finished image. Figure 6.14 shows the Properties sliders provided with the Lighting Effects filter.

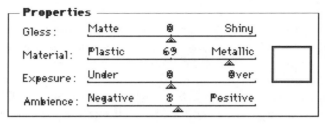

Figure 6.14 Lighting properties sliders.

Gloss: Matte/Shiny

Imagine for a moment the reflectors used to concentrate light onto your image. If the reflector has a rough, matte surface, the light it casts will be soft and diffuse. If the reflector is polished and shiny, the light will be harsher and create harder highlights. The Gloss slider lets you simulate these effects by controlling the amount of the reflector's "hot spot" added to the image. Figure 6.15 shows two spheres that have been illuminated by a matte reflector (left) and a shiny reflector (right).

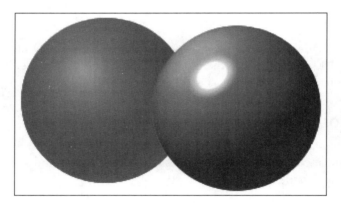

Figure 6.15 Matte (left) and shiny (right) reflectors.

Material: Plastic/Metallic

The Material slider controls how a shiny highlight appears in your image. The concept is subtle. Apparently, even with equally shiny surfaces, plastic looks distinctly different from metal. As you move the control toward Plastic, the highlight takes on the color of the illumination source. Reverse directions toward Metallic, and the highlight becomes more reflective (like chrome) and therefore mirrors the colors of the surrounding image instead.

Exposure: Under/Over

The Exposure slider controls the intensity of the light as it reaches the surface. You can use this control to fine-tune the amount of light illuminating your image.

Ambience: Negative/Positive

Ambient light is the existing light level in a room, before you add extra lights, plus the light the bounces off the new lights from other surfaces. Ambient light is omnidirectional; it seems to come from everywhere. Increasing the amount of ambient light adds light to both the highlights and shadows. You can use this control to increase and decrease the contrast between the portions of the image illuminated by your light sources and the rest of the image. The box at the right of the Properties sliders shows the color of the ambient light only.

Texture Channel

The Texture Channel controls can be used to apply a texture to the area illuminated by your light sources. You can choose from Red, Green, Blue channels in RGB mode: Cyan, Magenta, Yellow, and Black in CMYK mode, or None if you prefer not to add a texture. Texture can also be applied to selections you have saved; they appear as additional numbered channels in the drop-down list, shown in Figure 6.16. You can load grayscale textures from disk and use them as a "bump" map to apply a texture. We'll learn how to do that in the next section.

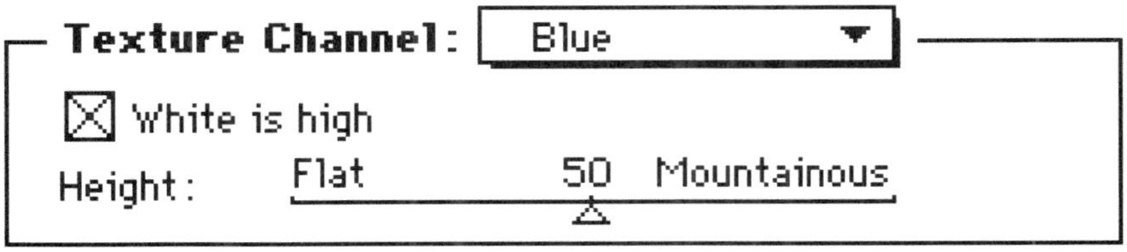

Figure 6.16 Texture Channel controls.

You may move the slider to choose from relatively flat texture to "mountainous" effects. With the default White is high box checked, the lighter areas of the image will seem to come toward you. Uncheck this to have darker areas protrude.

Number of Lights

You can create up to 16 different lights, but you will rarely need that many. To add a light to an image, drag the light bulb icon shown at the bottom center of Figure 6.17 into your picture area. To remove a light, drag the center circle representing the light to the trash can at lower right.

Figure 6.17 Add or subtract lights using the Preview window.

When several lights are present in an image, only one can be active at a time. The active light will display its control handles and bounding circle or ellipse (if any). When a light is active, you can set its properties with the sliders or change its coverage area or position by dragging the handles or center circle in the preview window. A given light can be left in place, but turned off by unchecking the On box under Light Type.

To work with a different light source, click on its center circle. You can also move from one light to another by pressing the **Tab** key. Once you have a suitable arrangement, you can save the lighting effect using the Style controls shown in Figure 6.18. Any saved lighting styles can be loaded by selecting them from the drop-down list.

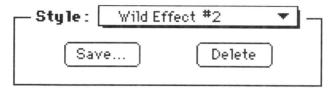

Figure 6.18 User-defined lighting styles can be saved and reused.

Light Style

Photoshop provides you with 16 other lighting setups from the Lighting Type drop-down list, shown in Figure 6.19. These include traditional photographic or theatrical lighting setups, such as crosslighting and downlighting, and several other styles you can experiment with. As you click on each choice, the Preview window shows how the lighting will look with your image or selection. Browsing through all the choices takes only a minute or two.

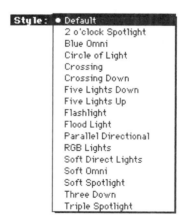

Figure 6.19 Built-in lighting styles can be accessed from this drop-down list.

Using the Lighting Effects Filter

Because this is such a complex filter, it's worthwhile to provide a few examples so that you can see how it works. I'll use several different original images, choosing pictures that lend themselves to particular lighting effects, and even combine a few filters we've used already.

Let's take the bridal portrait shown in Figure 6.20 in the left-hand example. It's not a bad picture, especially when you consider how difficult it is to capture all the detail in a bright white bridal gown. However, we can add a little drama with a judicious application of the Lighting Effects filter. At center is the same picture with a spotlight filter used to provide a vignetting effect. A quite different rendition is at right in Figure 6.20, with two spotlights on opposite sides.

Figure 6.20 Bridal portrait (left), and same portrait highlighted with a single spotlight (center) and with two spots (right).

The next example is a study that was originally taken with a single light to the side and slightly behind the model, with very little ambient light, producing a silhouette effect, shown at left in Figure 6.21. I applied Lighting Effects using a spotlight located at the approximate position of the real light source to create the version shown at the right in Figure 6.21.

After that, I applied a broader, Omni light effect to the same image, and then positioned a Lens Flare effect where the glare was already the strongest (using the 105mm Prime lens setting) to produce the image shown at left in Figure 6.22. At right, I added texture to give the image a rough appearance.

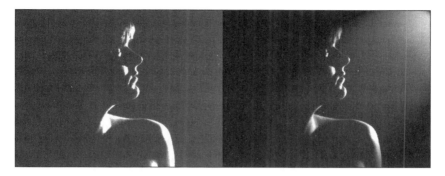

Figure 6.21 Original image (left) and version with a
Lighting Effects spot applied at upper right (right).

Figure 6.22 Adding Lens Flare and Texture further manipulates the image.

For a stronger texture effect, I set Light Properties to Shiny, Metallic, and raised
the texture setting to Mountainous. The finished image shown in Figure 6.23
looks like an engraved copper penny. You can use this effect to add textures to
virtually any image, but you will find that generally pictures with a strong
contrast work better.

Figure 6.23 Shiny, metallic textures can transform an image into a copper engraving.

Texture Fill Filter

Although you can use the Texture Fill filter on its own, you won't want to. This filter is really intended for use with the Lighting Effects plug-in, as a way to provide a separate channel of grayscale that can be used as a texture map. As such, it's nothing more than a fancy File Open dialog box.

Like the standard File Open dialog box, you can use Texture Fill's dialog box to navigate your desktop and hard disks in search of a file to open. It works only with Photoshop 2.5 or 3.0-format grayscale files. You can't open TIFF, PICT, or other format files nor can you access full-color Photoshop files. If you want to use a particular colored texture with Texture Fill, you'll need to load the file into Photoshop, use **Mode:Grayscale** to change it to 256 gray tones, and then save the file in Photoshop format. Figure 6.24 shows the Texture Fill dialog box.

The Texture Fill filter automatically loads this grayscale information into an alpha channel that you've created in the current file. If the active image happens to be larger than the grayscale file (in area, not bytes), the texture fill will be tiled to fill the entire alpha channel. (For best results, then, you'll want to use textures that can be seamlessly tiled—that is, they have been designed so the patterns at the edges on all four sides align when tiled in this way.) If the image the texture is being loaded into is smaller than the grayscale file, the texture file will be cropped.

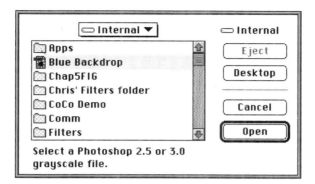

Figure 6.24 Texture Fill dialog box.

If you happened to have a need to load a grayscale image into an alpha channel, this would be a quick way to do it. However, Texture Fill is most useful to load texture information that Lighting Effects can use. Follow these steps to try out this filter.

1. Load an image file. I used CATHYP02.TIF, located on the CD-ROM in the Chapter 6:Working Files folder.

2. Create a selection to be textured. You can apply the texture to your entire image (use **Select:All**) or choose only part of your image. I selected the entire image.

3. Save the selection to create a new alpha channel, using **Select:Save Selection**. I gave the selection the name Texture.

4. Making sure the new Texture channel is selected (use the Channels palette, shown in Figure 6.25), choose **Filter:Render:Texture Fill**, and select Gray Sandstone, which is also found on the CD-ROM. At this point, you'll have an RGB image with a fourth channel containing the grayscale texture.

If you don't save your selection, Texture Fill will flood the selection within your main image with texture.

WARNING

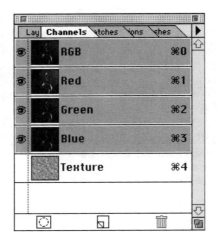

Figure 6.25 Channels palette with new Texture channel.

- Click on the RGB channel in the Channels palette to make it the active channel once again.
- Select **Filter:Render:Lighting Effects,** and select this channel as the Texture channel, as shown in Figure 6.26. I set the Height slider to Mountainous to make the texture show up clearly.

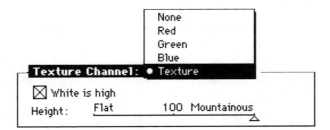

Figure 6.26 The Texture channel can be selected as a "bump map" for the Lighting Effects filter.

- Click on **OK** to apply the lighting effect and texture. Photoshop will use the grayscale information in the alpha channel to create a texture for the image, with lighter tones "higher" than the darker tones, unless you uncheck the White is high box. Your finished image will look like the one in Figure 6.27.

Figure 6.27 Texture applied to the entire image using the Lighting Effects filter.

Try out the Texture Fill feature of the Lighting Effects filter, using your own textures, commercial textures such as those available with Pixar 128 (you'll need to load and save them in grayscale format first), or those provided on the CD-ROM bundled with this book.

The Next Step

We have done six whole chapters and haven't even polished off all the filters built into your image editor! We can take care of most of them in the next chapter, when we'll discover uses for those mysterious Video and Other filters that you may never have understood before. Then, we'll look at some ways you can create filters of your own or add third-party filters from commercial and shareware vendors to your repertoire.

CHAPTER 7

Other Built-In Filters

You may be overlooking some potentially useful filters that have been relegated to the backwaters of Photoshop's Filter menu structure. Many users don't even know what these filters do or why they might want them. It's a safe bet that this is the only book you'll ever see with a chapter devoted exclusively to these "none of the above" plug-ins. Even so, you'll be surprised when you learn more about the mongrels of the basic filter set.

Under the **Filter:Video** entry you'll find De-Interlace and NTSC Colors, while the **Filter:Other** menu lists Custom, High Pass, Maximum, Minimum, and Offset filters. I'll explain all these filters except Custom in this chapter, leaving that versatile filter for Chapter 8, which details ways to create your own filters. We'll also look at the Displace filter in that chapter, because using displacement maps is another way of generating custom filters. With those two exceptions, this chapter will wrap up our exploration of all the filters built into Photoshop 3.0.

Video Filters

Video filters are especially useful for those who must import or export images used for video productions. If you create your own QuickTime movies from images captured from a video frame grabber or want to export color images that will be used on television, you'll want to know about these two filters.

De-Interlace Filter

The De-Interlace filter reconstructs missing information in images captured from video. Each video frame consists of two alternating lines of pixels, each made up of half the entire image and painted in interlaced fashion on your television screen to provide one complete picture. Video frame grabs commonly consist of only one of these two fields, so your digital image is, in effect, missing every other line.

The De-Interlace filter recreates the missing lines either by duplicating the ones already present or by guessing, or interpolating, the value of the pixels using the lines on either side of the missing one. Figure 7.1 shows the De-Interlace dialog box, which allows you to choose which set of lines to use and your preferred method of synthesizing the new information.

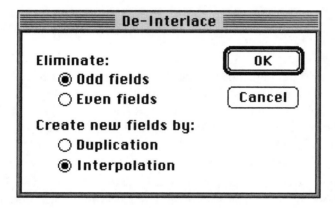

Figure 7.1 De-Interlace dialog box.

Tech alert! If you want to know a little more about interlaced video, read this next section. Of course, working with video images in your Macintosh has some inherent limitations, the most important of which is the reduced resolution of the images. You may scan an 8 x 10-inch photograph at a relatively low resolution of 100 dpi, but that still gives you 800 x 1000 pixels to work with.

Video images, on the other hand, contain no more than 525 lines vertically, with a horizontal resolution of 330 (the minimum that must be met by broadcasters) to more than 500 pixels. As you might guess, a 525 x 500 pixel image is no great shakes, resolution wise—and that's the *maximum* quality you can expect. In practice, the real resolution is much lower because television sets aren't capable of the same quality image as computer monitors. A standard TV picture requires a monitor with a bandwidth of at least 15.75 kHz, while a computer picture with 1280 x 1024 pixels requires a 64-kHz monitor. You don't notice the difference because the television image is always moving, and defects tend to blend into one another.

Worse yet, television sets display only half of each frame at a time; the CRT paints all the odd-numbered lines on the screen first, and then goes back and draws the even-numbered lines before the first set have a chance to fade from the screen. This interlaced picture looks good to the eye, until you capture one of these frames and discover that you have only half the picture information.

Since video frame grabbers capture only one of the two fields that make up each frame, some way is needed to reconstruct the missing lines. If you're preparing your own QuickTime movies from video images, for example, the final product will look much better if you take this extra step. But even if you just want to use video frame grabs in desktop publishing, the extra resolution can come in handy. Since video images are inherently lower in resolution, every little bit helps.

Figure 7.2 shows one field of an actual interlaced image at top. I zoomed in to show that only every other line of pixels is present. While the image looks okay if you step back, viewing the subject (in this case London's Big Ben clock tower) through Venetian blinds is not the best route to clarity.

Figure 7.2 Interlaced image (left) and the same image with missing information supplied by duplication (center) and interpolation (right).

In the version in the center of Figue 7.2, I used the De-Interlace filter to fill in the missing lines by duplicating the one above. For some types of images this can produce results that look sharper. On closer examination, jaggies or staircasing is clearly visible in diagonal lines, such as the minute hand on Big Ben's face.

The version at the bottom of Figure 7.2 was created using interpolation. Instead of just duplicating the line above, the software compared the brightness, contrast, and tonal values of the pixels in the lines above and below and calculated an intermediate value for the line between them. This approach results in a softer and smoother image that doesn't look quite as sharp.

You may want to try both methods on a particular picture to see which provides the best results for your image. How do you choose whether to eliminate the odd or even fields? That's simple—you'll want to get rid of the field opposite the one used to compose your image. (Some video frame grabbers give you a choice of which field to use.) Don't worry if you don't know which field a given image contains—if you eliminate the wrong one, all your image information will vanish!

NTSC Colors

The NTSC Colors filter changes the colors of an image to match the gamut defined by the National Television Systems Committee (NTSC) for reproduction on television.

The NTSC (known within the industry as Never Twice Same Color) is a standards-setting organization that provides specifications for many of the technical standards that must be met by broadcasters in the United States. The television system used in the Western Hemisphere and Japan is called NTSC after this body. Great Britain and Germany use the PAL—phase alternation line—color system, while SECAM—after the French words for system electronic color with memory—is used in France and many countries of the former Soviet Union.

However, it's enough to know that colors that can be reproduced by NTSC systems are fewer than can be handled by your Macintosh, just as the color gamut of CMYK printing systems is different from what you see on-screen in RGB mode.

If you're creating an image that will be displayed on television, such as a digital presentation copied to tape or a title slide used for advertising or other purposes, and color fidelity is important to you, use the NTSC Colors filter. It will modify the colors in your image to match the NTSC gamut. You can preview the final image to make sure it's what you want and then print to a film recorder (to generate a slide) or save to disk for display.

There are no dialog boxes or controls for this filter; just apply it to your image. The changes are rather subtle and wouldn't show up in a black-and-white picture so the effects of the NTSC Colors plug-in's are not illustrated here.

Other Filters

The filters found in the Other menu perform some interesting functions, including a couple that generate abstract effects that complement those we experimented with in Chapter 5. There's even an often overlooked filter that you can use to create seamless textures to use with the Lighting Effects filter and other tools.

High Pass Filter

The High Pass filter is sometimes neglected because it's so hard to imagine what it does. Let's try to picture what it does on your screen and then look at the illustration in this book. A simple way to think about the High Pass filter is as a color-blurring filter that works on those elements in your image that are effected by the Gaussian Blur filter. The latter smoothes out high-frequency information—edges and sharp color transitions, for example. The High Pass filter, on the other hand, keeps those areas sharp and blurs the rest of your image area.

Adobe recommends using this filter to smooth out extraneous detail in a continuous tone image before converting to a one-bit (black-and-white) image. The edges, which will be converted to black lines, are retained while other detail (which will be converted to white) is smoothed out and eliminated. The filter can also make one-bit images look better by removing dirt or other artifacts.

The High Pass dialog box, shown in Figure 7.3, has just one control: the radius of the pixels around the image pixels that you want retained. You can specify from 0.1 to 250 pixels. A low number produces the strongest effects; few pixels next to the edges are left alone. The higher the number, the more pixels are ignored by the filter, and the less dramatic are the changes. You can use this filter to create line art from continuous tone scans. The effects are almost always better than going directly from grayscale to bitmap using the Mode menu.

As you can see in Figure 7.4, low settings give the most interesting results. At left is the original picture of Big Ben, with a white, featureless sky. The center image was processed using a pixel radius of 4. Some of the detail in Big Ben has been suppressed, and the sky is filled in with a bland gray tone. At right, the pixel radius of 8 brought some of the snap back into Big Ben's face and reduced the gray of the sky. In this case, even higher numbers (a pixel radius of 10 to 25) left the image looking a lot like the one we started with.

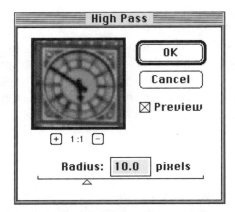

Figure 7.3 High Pass filter dialog box.

Figure 7.4 Clock tower (left) and the same image with High Pass filter applied with settings of 4 (center) and 8 (right) pixels.

Maximum and Minimum Filters

The Maximum and Minimum filters generate interesting abstract effects by adding spreads and chokes to your images. You can even use them to create real spreads and chokes, if you like, but you don't need to understand what either technique is to enjoy using this pair of filters. I'll explain the concept shortly, but let's look at the visual effects of the two filters before we see exactly how they work.

The Maximum dialog box is shown in Figure 7.5. Your only control is a slider to specify the number of pixels evaluated for brightness values. Maximum spreads out white areas and contracts white areas. You can easily see this in Figure 7.6. The original image of Big Ben without any filters appears, at the left, and in the center with a Maximum value of 5. At right, I applied a value of 10 to the same original.

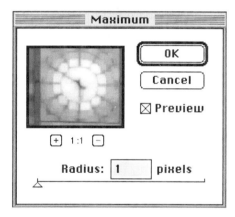

Figure 7.5 Maximum dialog box.

Look closely at the shadows at the left of the tower or the windows at the top. Those dark areas have been shrunk. The hands of the clock have been made thinner. At the same time, the white areas have spread. The clock face has actually become larger. There's actually a technical reason for needing this effect, but you can use it to create some interesting abstracts from your images. Another use is described in the following Tech Alert section.

Figure 7.6 Image with no filtration (left) and with a Maximum value of 5 (center) and of 10 (right.)

Tech Alert! Spreads and chokes are needed because printing presses are not as precise as we might like. If you're printing a red circle inside a black square, for example, two different printing plates are used—one laying down the red circle and the other the black square. You can't print the lighter red color on top of the darker black, of course. All you would see is black. So printers knock out a circle from the black square that's almost the same size as the red circle. When the black square prints, it leaves a white "hole" on the paper that can be printed with the red circle.

Of course, the knockout can't be exactly the same size as the red circle. If it were, any shifting of the paper or change in size of the printing plate would produce an out-of-register condition. The red circle might print a little to one side or another, leaving an unsightly white space.

To prevent this unsightly condition, the knockout in the black square can be choked slightly, making it a little smaller, so that some of the black ink always overprints the red circle, even if either one is a little out of register. Or, you can spread the circle so that its outer edges print over the black ink. We never see this overlapping ink unless we look very closely.

If you are creating masks or other layers that have complementary information you want to overlap without gaps, you can use the Maximum or Minimum filters to spread or choke one or the other (or both of them, by just a little bit). Use the Maximum filter to make the white areas larger and the dark areas smaller and use the Minimum filter to perform the reverse.

What these filters do is look at each pixel in an image, look at the adjacent pixels surrounding that element, and then replace its value with that of either the maximum or minimum value of its neighbors.

Figure 7.7 shows the Minimum dialog box, which looks amazingly like the Maximum dialog box. In Figure 7.8 you'll find two examples of Big Ben with the filter applied in 5-pixel and 10-pixel increments. Notice that the shadows and dark lines have spread and that the white areas have shrunk. If you're not doing spreads and chokes for production purposes, these filters still generate some interesting effects while masking defects in your original image.

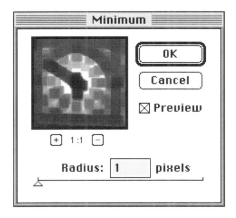

Figure 7.7 Minimum dialog box.

Figure 7.8 Big Ben with Minimum filter applied using 5-pixel (left) and 10-pixel (right) settings.

Offset Filter

Did you read the description of the Offset filter in your manual and then decide that it was terminally dumb? After all, who needs a filter that does nothing but shift your image in one direction or another? Well, you do, for one. It's true that Offset can be used to move a selection in precise increments, say, 5 pixels to the right and 10 pixels down. But, of course, you can do the same thing by pressing the **Right Arrow** key five times and the **Down Arrow** key ten times, right? You can, but Offset can do it faster. The real use for this filter is in what it does with the rest of your image that is left behind. Figure 7.9 shows the Offset dialog box.

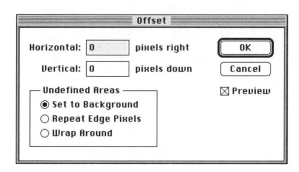

Figure 7.9 Offset dialog box.

Use the Undefined Areas section of the Offset dialog box to indicate what to do with the white space created when you move part of an image.

- You can specify that the hole left by your selection's move can be filled with the current background color. That's the default and is what would happen if you moved the selection using the cursor keys. There's nothing amazing here.

- You can ask that edge pixels be repeated in the undefined area left behind. That options stretches the pixels around the hole to fill in the empty area and eliminates the gaping hole. The results may or may not be pleasing, depending on how much detail was in the image area you moved. If you're moving a section that has an even texture, the transition may be smooth. Otherwise, it might not be much better than just filling in with background color.

- The image can be made to wrap around. That is, image area from the opposite side is used to fill in the empty areas. Believe it or not, this is a profoundly useful feature. It lets you create seamless textures that can be used to tile any size area with Texture Fill or other tools.

A seamless tile is nothing more than one that, when you match it up with another copy of itself, blends in smoothly at any edge you happen to choose. See Figure 7.10 to visualize this technique. It shows Big Ben (at upper left) and then as a seamless tile (at lower right).

Figure 7.10 Seamless tile produced with Offset filter.

You can see that if another copy of the tile at lower right were placed adjacent to the original, it would "fit" together like a jigsaw puzzle to form another piece of the image. I used a photograph because it's easy to see how the pieces were rearranged to produce the tile. In practice, though, you'll create tiles from abstract textures and other images. Figure 7.11 shows how they fit together. Read on to see exactly how to create your own seamless textures with the Offset filter.

The secret to creating tiled images is to offset the selection by half the pixel width and height in each case. This is easier if you have a regularly shaped selection (say 128 x 128 pixels, rather than 257 x 292). Follow these steps to create seamless tiles of your own.

1. Use **File:New** to create a new, empty square image. I specified 200 x 200 pixels, which roughly fit the area of Big Ben that I wanted to include.

2. Copy an area larger than the one you want to tile, with the subject area you're interested in roughly centered in the middle.

Figure 7.11 Tiled images created with Offset filter.

3. Paste this section into the new file, moving it around until it is centered exactly as you want. The rest of the selection will be cropped out.

4. Apply the Offset filter, specifying 100 pixels right and 100 pixels down (half the dimensions of the file), and make sure the Wrap Around radio button is selected.

You'll end up with a perfectly tiled image, ready to be saved and used.

The Next Step

Except for the Custom, Displace, and optional Filter Factory plug-ins, we've covered all the built-in filters that Photoshop offers. In the next section, we'll explore creating your own filters—add-ons you can save and reuse anytime you like, or even share with your friends and colleagues.

PART III

Creating Your Own Filters

With all the hundreds of filters on the market, you might think that all possible plug-in image enhancers have already been invented. Nothing could be farther from the truth. A thriving shareware market, which is discussed in Chapter 14, demonstrates that, when it comes to filters, if you build it, users will come. Indeed, you may find that even the most esoteric and flexible of commercial filters won't provide the exact effect you want.

In this next part of the book, I'll introduce you to three tools for building your own filters and plug-ins. Chapter 8 examines Photoshop's Custom filter routine, which allows you to build your own convolution kernels (don't worry about what those are!). You'll also learn how you can create a displacement map, which can be used to create fairly predictable, repeatable effects. Neither of the techniques discussed require any programming knowledge—a willingness to experiment is all you really need. Chapter 9 unmasks the mysterious Photoshop 3.0 Filter Factory, which is not, as many of us had hoped, a filter construction kit as much as it is a streamlined compiler for use by programmers.

If the two chapters in this part of the book don't satisfy your filter fabrication frenzy, check out Chapters 10 and 11, which discuss Kai's Power Tools and KPT Convolver. Neither one creates stand-alone filters, but both allow you to assemble customized effects that you can save as presets for reuse.

CHAPTER 8

Custom Filters

Photoshop has several facilities that you can use to create customized filter effects in a limited sort of way. In this chapter, we'll look at two of the easiest custom filters to use—Photoshop's Custom and Displace filters. If you're inclined to play with either of these just to see what happens when you tweak here or there and willing to tell your colleagues, "I meant to do that!" when a happy accident occurs, both filters are a great deal of fun. Each can be a little unpredictable when applied to varying images, but you'll soon learn how to create the sort of look you're searching for with only a little trial and a few errors.

Convo-what?

You might as well learn about the term *convolution*, because as you work with filters you're going to hear it a lot. You don't have to pay close attention here, because we'll discuss it again in Chapter 11, when we tackle KPT Convolver.

Tech Alert. In short, a convolution is a series of mathematical operations performed on all the pixels in an image or selection. The math is a bit twisted, or convoluted, because the formulae are applied to one pixel based on the values of the pixels around it, which are themselves processed in turn. So, while the pixel at coordinates 1,1 (upper left and corner) may be brightened or darkened depending on the values of its neighbors (1,2 to the right, 2,1 below it, and 2,2 diagonally), its new value may be used to determine the modifications to the pixel at 1,2 when it's that pixel's turn to be convoluted. Is this confusing or what?

The operations needed to perform a particular effect are arranged in a matrix called a *kernel*, with the pixel being abused represented as a box in the center of the matrix and the pixels surrounding it represented by boxes of their own. Numbers placed in the boxes determine what happens to the poor center pixel. Figure 8.1 shows an example convolution kernel, which just happens to represent the Photoshop Custom filter's dialog box.

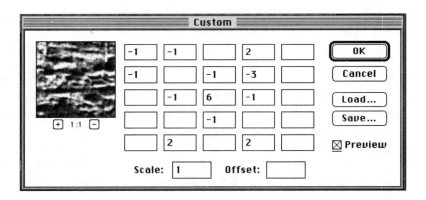

Figure 8.1 The Custom filter's dialog box shows a typical convolution kernel.

If you look closely at the boxes in Figure 8.1, you'll see that there are various positive and negative numbers, which are used at processing time to change the value of the pixel in the center.

There are several kinds of kernels, each relating to a particular property of your image. KPT Convolver, exhaustively described in Chapter 11, works with the Spatial and Color kernels of an image and so is able to modify the image hue, saturation, and brightness as well as the apparent contrast between pixels, along with their positions.

The Custom filter happens to work with the brightness values of the pixels in relation to each other, so most of the effects you can generate with it represent things affected by brightness: contrast, sharpness (which is related to the contrast between adjacent pixels), and 3-D effects, such as embossing (created by lightening or darkening certain pixels to create shadows and ridges).

Using the Custom Filter

To use the Custom filter, you'll need to find it in the **Filters:Other** menu. The dialog box shown in Figure 8.1 pops up and contains some elements you are familiar with, such as the preview window at left, with its plus and minus zoom buttons. At right, you'll find the checkbox to turn previews on and off and several buttons that let you save Custom filter presets that you want to reuse or load previously saved settings.

You may be confused by those other parts of the dialog box. Here are a few hints:

- The center box represents the pixel being evaluated. You can type a number from 999 to –999 to multiply (lighten) or demultiply (darken) the pixel.

- Each of the adjacent boxes represent pixels in adjacent positions. You may type in numbers that will be used to multiply the brightness of the pixel in that position.

In the example shown in Figure 8.1, the center pixel of each convolution will be multiplied by 6 to brighten it. The pixels to the left, right, above, and below the victim pixel will be darkened by a factor of –1. This has the effect of making the center pixel brighter than those which surround it.

When the algorithm moves on to the next pixel, everything cancels out because the new pixel will already have been darkened by the convolution of its neighbor. In practice, you'll get some interesting effects, which you can already see in the preview window.

There are two other boxes in the dialog box, labeled Scale and Offset. The value in Scale is used to divide the sum of the brightness values of the pixels included in the convolution. The value in the Offset box is added to the results of the scale calculation. You may probably get an uneasy feeling about now. If you studied math and maybe calculus in school, everything so far should make perfect sense to you. But what does it mean?

Here's the good news: you don't have to know that. Because one thing you certainly will not be doing is sitting down and trying to figure out how to multiply or divide pixel brightness values in order to achieve special effects. To use the Custom filter, all you really need to do is type values into the available boxes and see what they do.

You'll see a small-scale glimpse of what's going on in the Preview window and a full view of the effect in your main image window. If you position the Custom dialog box off to one side, you can view your entire image and the dialog box at the same time.

All you need to do to have fun is just play around. If you get an effect you like, click on the **Save** button and choose a name that will help you remember what the effect did. I provide about two dozen Custom filters on the CD-ROM packaged with this book to give you a starting point for your own experimentation. Figure 8.2 shows a typical snapshot modified with one of the filters on the disc. At left is the original, unaltered picture. At right, it's been processed using the Ultra Sharp custom filter. This is a quick, one-step sharpen filter that heightens the grain in an image.

Figure 8.2 Original image (left) and version souped up with custom Ultra Sharp filter (right).

WARNING

Custom filters that you create will vary in their effect quite sharply depending on the image that you apply them to. While a filter that decreases contrast or enhances edges will perform essentially a similar function on all the images you try, the effects may be drastically different, because the new image already had lower contrast or fewer sharp edges than the picture you used to create the filter. This is true for all filters, of course, but you can avoid some disappointment if you realize this up front.

Because Custom filters look different with different images, you may find that you use this plug-in most often to create a customized, one-off filter effect for a particular image. That will be the case after you've developed a bit of familiarity with what happens when you type figures into the kernel's matrix. You may find yourself pulling down the Custom filter, typing in a few numbers, tweaking a bit more, and then clicking **OK** when you're satisfied, with no thought of saving the filter for reuse.

Figure 8.3 shows two more examples of the original image shown in Figure 8.2, this time modified with my Ultra Poster and Embosser filters. Try them out on your own images.

Figure 8.3 Image modified with Ultra Poster (left)
and Embosser (right) Custom filters.

None of the other Photoshop books I looked at explained these characteristics of the Custom filter, and it's a shame. This is a virtual special effects playground that more users should be experimenting with.

For Figure 8.4 I switched to a new original image, a telephoto shot of the Spanish Castle at Alarcon, one of a chain of small palaces built for the prince Alaric to wander among as he pursued a career of contemplation and writing, or something along those lines. This castle is out in the middle of nowhere, as you can see from the image on the left. At right, I processed the image using the Faerieland filter, which converted it into a series of light, multicolored lines.

In Figure 8.5 I applied two more filters to the same image. At left I used the Ultra Contrast filter to make the castle stand out from its surroundings even more, while at right I used the Zerox filter, which creates a photocopy like effect. (The particular spelling was chosen to head off any lawsuits from a certain Rochester, N.Y.-based company.) You'll find that Zerox, in particular, looks quite different when applied to images that already have either flatter or harder levels of contrast.

Figure 8.4 Castle in normal view (left) and processed with Faerieland filter (right).

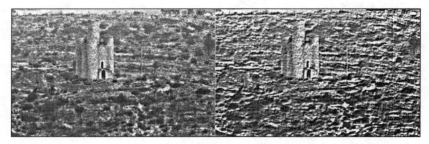

Figure 8.5 Image with Ultra Contrast (left) and Zerox (right) filters applied.

Good News for PixelPaint Pro 3 Users

On at least one front PixelPaint Pro 3 has it all over even the latest version of Photoshop 3.0—how custom filters are treated. With Photoshop, it really doesn't matter where you store your custom filter kernels. Photoshop makes you hunt for them, no matter what. However, if you place these filters in the same directory as your other plug-ins, PixelPaint Pro automatically adds them to your Filter menu under a Custom submenu, which is shown in Figure 8.6.

I must assure Photoshop users that no smoke and mirrors were used in the production of Figure 8.6. PixelPaint Pro 3, without any further instructions, adds the custom filters to its menus. If you aren't a PixelPaint user and want this feature, tear out this page, mail it to Adobe, then buy a copy of this book that hasn't been defaced.

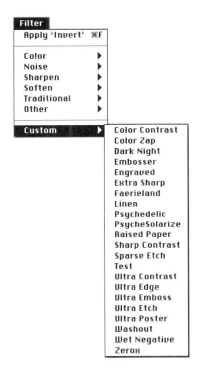

Figure 8.6 PixelPaint Pro 3 adds custom filters to your Filter menu.

If you come up with some particularly cool custom filters, send them to me over America OnLine (screen name Dave Busch) or CompuServe (75725,1156), and I'll either mention you in the next version of this book or speak well of you at authors' bull sessions at Comdex.

Using Displacement Maps

We'll discuss the Displace filter here because this plug-in deserves to be singled out as one of your easiest and most flexible filter-customizing tools. It's related in some ways to the texturizing filters we'll look at in Chapter 12 because it can use additional files to govern how the filter works. However, instead of using the second image to texturize the original photo, Displace uses the color values in the additional file to determine how to move pixels around along a diagonal line.

But how are the pixels moved? The rules are summarized here.

- If the displacement map has just one gray channel, the value of the pixel in the map at a particular position is used to move the image pixel in the same relative position. If the brightness of the pixel is 0 to 127, the pixel is moved southwesterly, with 0 representing the maximum amount of movement, and 127 the least amount of movement. A value of 128 leaves the pixel in place. For values of 129–255, the pixel is moved in a northwesterly direction, with 255 representing the maximum amount of movement.

- If a displacement map has two or more channels (say, a grayscale image with a second, mask channel, or an RGB image), the first channel is used to determine the amount of horizontal movement, while the second channel is used to vary vertical movement. Additional channels are ignored.

- Since gray values are used, black-and-white bitmapped images can't be displacement maps.

Displacement maps are fun to play with because you can generate maps with fairly predictable results, as well as those that do things you never expected. For example, a map that consists of a smooth black-to-white grayscale gradient performs as you might expect. The portions of the map that are very dark will produce the most displacement in one direction, with the movement tapering off until the middle gray tones and then reversing to the other direction for the lighter and lighter tones in the map. You can do all manner of twisting and warping in this mode.

On the other hand, a map that consists of a texture or random lines that you create will do some rather weird things to an image. You'll want to experiment with displacement maps. Some displacement maps are included with Photoshop. Many more are available on-line.

Working with Displacement

To use the Displace filter, just follow these steps:

1. Select **Filter:Distort:Displace**. The dialog box shown in Figure 8.7 will pop up.

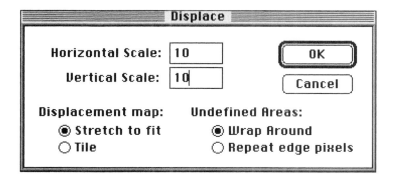

Figure 8.7 Displace filter dialog box.

2. Choose the amount of displacement you want in both horizontal and vertical directions by typing values into the Horizontal scale and Vertical Scale boxes. For example, if you specify 100 for both, a grayscale values of 0 and 255 produces movement of 128 pixels, and a value of 128 generates the least amount of movement. Lower scales create proportionately less movement.

3. If the displacement map is not the same size as the selection, as will probably be the case unless you created the displacement map expressly for this image, you must decide whether Photoshop should stretch the map to fit the selection or tile the map enough times to fill the selection.

4. You should choose whether the filter should fill in undefined areas by wrapping around to take pixels from the opposite edge or simply repeating the pixels at the edge.

5. Click on **OK** and then select the displacement map, using the dialog box like the one shown in Figure 8.8.

I used some of the maps included with the CD-ROM to produce the effects in Figure 8.9, which shows an old Spanish door (left) and the same door displaced with the Streaky map (right).

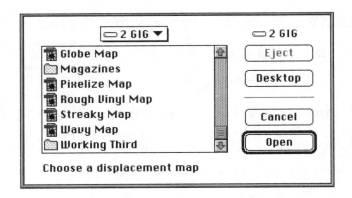

Figure 8.8 Select displacement map dialog box.

Figure 8.9 Normal image (left) and image displaced
with Streaky displacement map (right).

For Figure 8.10, I used a filter called Globe to create a painterly effect at left, while another map called Wavy generated the unique look at right.

Figure 8.10 Image distorted with Globe displacement map (left) and Wavy map (right).

Achieving Predictable Results

While almost any texture or random jottings you may insert in a map will generate some sort of displacement effect, you may want to create some predictable effects from time to time. The following exercise will help you visualize how the Displace filter works.

For my displaceable object, I used the 3-D brick shown in Figure 8.11. You can probably figure out how I created it, using a texture filter and then lightening and darkening various edges to give the 3-D look. You won't have to go through all that, as I've included the image among the working files in the Chapter 8 folder on the CD-ROM that accompanies this book.

Next, I created a pair of gray scale displacement maps. One starts out black in the middle and has a gradient that progresses to white at top and bottom. The other map is simply the first map inverted, using **Image:Map:Invert**. The two displacement maps are shown in Figures 8.12 and 8.13.

Figure 8.11 3-D brick, ready for application of displacement map.

Figure 8.12 DuoGradient displacement map.

Figure 8.13 DuoGradient 2 displacement map.

First, I applied the DuoGradient map to the brick, using horizontal and vertical scales of 10 for each. The results are shown in Figure 8.14. You can easily see that the dark, center portion of the gradient caused displacement quite different from the movement produced by the lighter top and bottom edges of the map. Using the reversed gradient on a new version of the brick, I got the exact opposite type of displacement, as shown in Figure 8.15.

Figure 8.14 DuoGradient map applied to brick
with horizontal and vertical scales of 10.

Figure 8.15 DuoGradient 2 map applied to the brick.

What happens when you alter the scales? For Figure 8.16 I used settings of 15 for both horizontal and vertical scale. And, as the image stretches past the limits of the window at right, it wraps around to the left side, because I checked the Wrap Around radio button.

Figure 8.16 DuoGradient applied with
horizontal scale 15 and vertical scale 15.

Look at Figure 8.17, where I reduced the horizontal scale to 1 and bumped up
the vertical scale to 15. The upper part of the image is stretched more than the
lower part, which is actually squeezed together.

Figure 8.17 DuoGradient map applied with
horizontal scale 1 and vertical scale 15.

Finally, for Figure 8.18, I used a horizontal setting of 0 and a vertical setting of
100, to really stretch things.

It's often a good idea to experiment like this under tightly controlled conditions so that you can see the effects of a filter and achieve more predictable
results in your own work.

Figure 8.18 DuoGradient map applied with
horizontal 0 and vertical 100 scales.

The Next Step

Use the custom filters and displacement maps on the CD-ROM to experiment on
your own. As you learned in this chapter, you don't need to know any programming to get some interesting results. However, if coding is up your alley, the next
chapter will tell you enough about Adobe's new Filter Factory capability to
decide if you want to brew up some stand-alone filters on your own.

CHAPTER 9

Introduction to Filter Factory

If you expected a Filter Factory with Photoshop 3.0, you probably were disappointed when Adobe actually delivered a Filter Research Laboratory instead. Filter Factory isn't a filter-generating plant for every user. Unfortunately, it requires a fair degree of programming skills. That's why this tool is largely undocumented in the printed manual and is not installed by default when you upgrade to Photoshop 3.0. Only a few of you are likely to need Filter Factory, and this chapter is intended to help you determine if this filter maker is for you.

Filter Factory?

Like most Photoshop users, when I heard that Adobe was going to include something called Filter Factory in the latest release, I was excited. At last the everyday user would have a tool for creating stand-alone filters. I envisioned a burgeoning shareware industry with dozens of filters generated by hard-working Photoshop fanatics. After all, creating Photoshop filters in the past has required use of a special developer's kit and at least some experience in programming. Wouldn't it be nice to have tools—a la KPT Convolver—for selecting parameters from a menu and building up your own filters? There are already programming toolkits that let you drag-and-drop dialog box elements, controls, and other components onto "forms" to build applications. If you've used HyperCard to create simple stacks, you know how easy "real" programming can be given the right toolkit.

Alas, Filter Factory is not much more than a developer's toolkit packaged with every copy of Photoshop. You still need to know how to program to use it. However, as a recovering ex-programmer, I know that tinkering around with code can be fun, once you accept the inevitable frustration of trying to get things to work the way you intended. If you have some experience in programming in C or another language, you'll find that Filter Factory can be an important part of your Photoshop repertoire.

What Can You Do with Filter Factory?

Filter Factory is not installed with the rest of Photoshop. You can drag its folder icon to your Plug-Ins folder. You'll then find it under a new **Filters:Synthetic** menu listing.

Filter Factory lets you create filters using arithmetic expressions that operate on each channel of an RGB image, including an alpha channel (Filter Factory filters work only with RGB files). You can include a settings dialog box with up to eight slider controls.

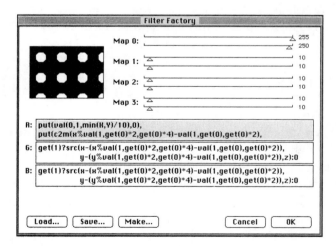

Figure 9.1 Filter Factory's entry screen.

The expressions are typed in boxes allocated for each channel, as shown in Figure 9.1. Filter Factory watches your syntax and highlights the expression with a yellow caution sign until you've typed in a legal equation, with matching left and right parentheses. There's no guarantee that your expression will do what you want, but at least you don't have to deal with the basic syntax checking.

Four pairs of sliders offer previews of the results provided by any controls you define in your expressions. For example, the Map 0 sliders preview your sliders 1 and 2. If you're creating a simple filter to apply just this one time, you can click on **OK** when you're satisfied, and the filter will be applied to your current selection. More often, you'll click on the **Save** button to save the filter program in text form (so that you can edit it later) or click the **Make** button to actually create a new stand-alone filter.

Using Expressions

I won't try to teach you programming for filters in this chapter. Instead, I'll give you a brief overview of what's involved so that you can decide whether Filter Factory is something you want to explore further.

The expressions you create for Filter Factory involve some simple mathematical concepts. You'll be working with some of the following elements:

- *Position of a particular pixel.* The coordinates of each pixel, from 0,0 (upper left-hand corner) to 640,480 or higher (depending on the resolution of your image—this example assumes a 640 x 480 pixel file), are used. You won't explicitly name each position, of course; the program uses variables that, when replaced with values as the filter processes an image, refer to individual pixels.

- *Channel values.* The amount of a particular channel's color in the current pixel can range from 0 (no color) to 255 (the maximum amount of color).

- *Variables.* These represent things like channels (r, g, b, or a—alpha), or coordinates in your image (x or y).

- *Functions.* Filter Factory, like all programming languages, has built-in functions that can operate on the variables you supply. These functions do things like retrieve channel values for a particular pixel.

- *Operators.* The most common operators are used in the mathematical functions like adding, subtracting, multiplying and so forth. There are also conditional operators, which cause the program to do something if a certain condition is present, and logical operators, which compare two values and provide a third value based on the relationship between them.

If you already have done some programming, these elements are all familiar. If not, you'll find that it's not too hard to put together an expression that does something useful. The individual portions of each expression are fairly simple. For example,

```
R:r+50
G:g
B:b
A:0
```

causes Filter Factory to evaluate every pixel in an image, and add 50 to the red channel but leave the others unchanged. You can let the user control how much to add to each channel by using this expression:

```
R:r+ctl(0)
G:g+ctl(1)
B:b+ctl(2)
A:0
```

Other functions manipulate your images in other ways. For example, the rnd (random) function can add noise. Others let you move pixels from one place to another, using a displacement factor and/or angle that you specify or derive from your equation. You can compare one channel to another and add or reduce color to one of them based on the result.

In truth, the hardest part about programming a filter is deciding what to do and why you want to do it. You need to consider what happens when you move all the red pixels diagonally by one pixel to the upper left or what happens when you add random noise pixels just to the red channel. Once you've licked those questions, actually writing the filter is not very difficult.

Adobe includes several examples and tutorial documents (which you can view with Adobe Acrobat reader, also included on the CD-ROM) that can help you. Anyone who has done even a small amount of programming (HyperTalk counts) can get the hang of Filter Factory fairly quickly.

Creating a Stand-Alone Filter

When you choose to make a filter, a dialog box like that shown in Figure 9.2 pops up. You can choose a category, which determines where in the Filters menu your filter appears (select **Synthetic**, or any of the other existing categories such as **Blur** and **Sharpen** or create a new one. You can also add a title for your filter, which will also appear in the menu, and any copyright information to embed in your filter permanently.

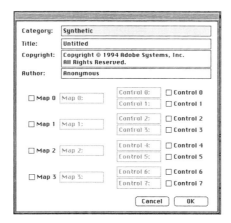

Figure 9.2 Saving a new filter.

At this time you can also choose which of the sliders you want in your dialog box by checking the Map and Control boxes. Each of the four Map boxes allows you to give a category name to each pair of controls and a specific name to individual controls. You don't need to use all the controls for a given Map; you could specify Control 0, Control 3, and Controls 4–5 if you like. Then, click on OK to save your new filter.

The Next Step

Filter Factory may not be for everyone, but it can allow those who have a modicum of programming skills the capability to create their own custom filters. If you'd rather not build your own filters from scratch, you can draw upon a wealth of commercial filters available from third parties like Second Glance,

Intellihance, and HSC (the Kai's Power Tools folks). The next section contains five chapters that describe the best filters on the market, including the new KPT Convolver, the classic Gallery Effects set, and some exciting shareware filters that are included on the CD-ROM bundled with this book.

PART IV

Third-Party Filters

The ability to add third-party filters to Photoshop, Fractal Design Painter, Pixel Paint Pro 3, ColorIt, and other image editors has created a huge demand for imaginative plug-ins. HSC leads the charge with Kai's Power Tools and KPT Convolver, but there are hundreds of other filters available from innovators like Second Glance Software, DPA, and, even, Adobe itself with its Gallery Effects series.

This part of the book provides you with a close-up look at all the leading filter packages. I'll devote separate chapters to overviews of Kai's Power Tools and Convolver, take an exhaustive look at the Adobe Gallery Effects filters, and review the best of the other commercial and shareware filter packages. You'll be introduced to Plug-In Manager, a great utility included on the CD-ROM to enable you to install and remove sets of filters with a few clicks.

CHAPTER 10

Kai's Power Tools

The Great Value of Kai's Power Tools

I won't fall into the trap that snared one pompous fellow who began one of his pronouncements with, "As God once said, and rightly so..." as if the Almighty needed his stamp of approval. It seems silly to solemnly tell you that I think Kai's Power Tools are worth your attention. Thousands of image editor-wielding Mac owners have already turned Kai Krause's premiere brainchild into a run-away bestseller. It's a staple tool that every serious worker must have.

I can't count the number of times I've added excitement to an image with Pixelwind or created shiny globes using one of the glass lens filters. As a survivor of the 1960s, I appreciate the psychedelic effects you can get with Fractal Explorer. Kai's Power Tools are more than a set of filters, they're a new way of working with images. Oops. I think I've fallen into the trap anyway.

About Kai's Power Tools

Kai Krause is an artist who was seduced by the dark side of technology when Photoshop was introduced. As such, his perspective on digital imaging is refreshingly different from that of the software engineers who usually design the tools that more creative types have to struggle with.

Kai (no, we're not on a first-name basis, but you hardly ever see him referred to by his surname) truly loves experimenting with Photoshop, and during his tinkering he managed to come up with hundreds of tricks no one else had ever thought of. For some time, he collected these into a series of technical tips and tricks notes that were available on-line or through other sources—for free. Kai is giving away swarms of ideas at no charge! In a perfect world, Kai's technical notes would have been published in a book that would be sold at very low cost to every Photoshop owner, making Krause rich in the process.

Alas, that wasn't to be. Kai had to get rich the old-fashioned way, by developing and/or inspiring a series of products that began with Kai's Power Tools (KPT) and blossomed into a whole series of KPT products, including KPT Bryce (a 3-D rendering program that generates other-worldly, or even this-worldly, terrain images) and KPT Convolver, which we'll explore in the next chapter.

KPT remains the flagship of the product line, and if you haven't used it yet, I supply six stand-alone filters from the set on the CD-ROM packaged with this book. You can try out filters like Pixelwind or Diffuse More on your own and take advantage of the special half-price coupon at the back of the book.

This chapter contains only a few step-by-step exercises because I found that even when settings are saved as presets, it's virtually impossible to duplicate anything you do with these marvelously flexible and unpredictable tools.

What's in Kai's Power Tools?

Kai's Power Tools consists of a whole series of Photoshop-compatible plug-ins that scatter themselves automatically throughout your filters' menus, sometimes never to be seen again. To help you track down these elusive gems, I'll summarize what you get here.

In general, the tools break down into two categories: 33 stand-alone, single-step filters and four explorer/designers, which are dialog boxes that let you access more complicated features. The single-step filters are easy to use: just select an area of your image and choose the filter from the menu. There are no options or settings to worry about. The explorer/designers are the exact opposite: you have so many choices, you may not know what to do with them. I'll help clear up the confusion in this chapter.

The main categories of filters in the KPT set are:

- **Blur menu filters.** These filters include three kinds of Gaussian blurs and four varieties of smudge filters.

- **Distort menu filters.** You get three sensational glass lens filters, including a Kodak-like page-curl plug-in and an innovative effect called vortex tiling.

- **KPT menu filters.** Kai dumped seven stand-alone effects or features that didn't fit elsewhere in this menu, along with the four explorer/designer filters. These filters include Fractal Explorer, Texture Explorer, Gradient Designer and Gradients on Paths, 3-D Stereo Noise (to let you create "magic" pictures), three pixel-dithering "wind" effects, Seamless Welder, and a useful box that pops up with information about your selection.

- **Noise menu filters.** Here you'll find seven new ways to add noise to an image or selection.

- **Sharpen menu filter.** Just a single Sharpen Intensity filter is provided. Obviously, in Kai's world, extra sharpness is not the direction in which he is headed.

- **Stylize menu filters.** Variations on familiar filters like Diffuse More or Find Edges Charcoal are provided here.

- **Video menu filters.** Look for the sensational KPT Cyclone, which evolves through dozens of effects before your eyes. Just press **Shift-Return** to capture one of them.

Because 33 of the tools in this kit are single-step filters that provide no additional input on your part, I won't discuss each and every filter individually. Many of them are clustered into groups of three or four filters, which provide variations on a single theme, anyway. Such explanations are more appropriate for the 54 Adobe Gallery Effects filters detailed in Chapter 12 because they generally have dialog boxes with multiple options, sliders, and data fields. The beauty of KPT is that you don't need much instruction to use these tools effectively.

About That Interface

The first thing you'll notice about any KPT product, from the Power Tools through Bryce or Convolver, is that weird interface, sometimes described as a 1960 Chevy Impala dashboard from Mars. Mac purists are sometimes offended at this drastic departure from the locked-in-stone Mac interface. Other users are confused. Is this a good thing?

Again, I'm not qualified to put my stamp of approval on Kai's user interface, but I do think that it's a good thing. Think of it this way: the Mac interface was designed in the early 1980s and first brought to market in 1984. It was intended for a computer with 128K of RAM and one-bit black-and-white images. A screen with thousands or millions of colors and 3-D imaging was only a dream, if that. How would you like to build, say, a Space Shuttle, using only tools designed to cobble together a log cabin?

There's a big difference, after all, between easy to learn and easy to use. The Mac interface was designed to be easy to learn, largely being intuitive (to overwork an overworked term). Your desktop, all those folders, and the Trashcan were put there because you didn't have to be taught how to use them. But, were they easy to use? Not necessarily. There are many difficult-to-learn operating systems (MS-DOS), for example, that are very easy to use once you master all the arcane commands and options. It may take you a year to learn how to use DOS, but once you've gone through the agony, there are certain things you can do much faster with DOS than with a Mac.

For example, I prepared both color and grayscale versions of every figure in this book. On the Mac, I gave them names ending in TIF and TIG to differentiate them. When it came time to rename the TIG files, I had to select each file's icon and type in the new name. I didn't have to be taught how to do that, but it wasn't particularly convenient to do, and I certainly didn't want to write an AppleScript to do it for me.

At the same time, I had to transfer all the TIG files to an IBM PC so that they could be output on a high-resolution printer not available to my Macintosh. Once exported to the PC, all I had to do was type at the DOS prompt: **RENAME *.TIF *.TIG**, and half a second later several hundred files had new names. Of course, at some time in my life I had to learn how to do that, but it was easy to do.

What Kai has done with his interface is add a small amount of learning to the equation, so that you may not be able to figure out exactly how to work Kai's Power Tools on first glance. You will have to learn a thing or two. But, once you learn it, you'll find that the interface is markedly easier to use for those tasks for which it was designed. Not every application should have rolling marbles instead of sliders, but Kai's Power Tools should have them.

KPT includes things like control buttons that fade into the background when they're not in use. Compare these with radio buttons that show you every possible option available at all times, even those that you have no use for at the moment. The controls are not labeled with annoying or condescending text. You're going to have to learn KPT's explorer/designers (each has a Help button, by the way), but you'll find the investment will pay off in faster operation for the rest of the time you use these tools.

Using Kai's Power Tools

This next section goes through each of the filters and tools in the KPT set, with an overview of what they do and, where appropriate, how to use them. I'll also supply examples of images with KPT effects applied.

Blur Filters

The Blur menu includes two groups of filters: the three Gaussian blurs (Electrify, Glow, and Weave) and four smudge filters (Darken Left, Darken Right, Lighten Left, Lighten Right). The KPT components added to your Blur menu are shown in Figure 10.1.

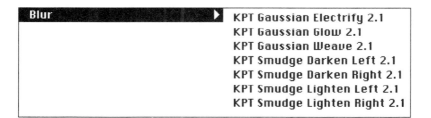

Figure 10.1 Blur filter menu with KPT components.

The Gaussian filters add a great glowing effect to your selection that you can't really achieve using normal blurring techniques. Figure 10.2 shows an image that has been blurred using Gaussian Glow. The smudge filters create directional motion blurs, which are unlike those supplied with Photoshop in that you can blur in one or the other horizontal direction only and choose to lighten or darken the affected image area as they are applied. These filters produce different effects when applied several times.

Figure 10.2 Image with KPT Gaussian Glow applied.

These filters amply demonstrate why the KPT stand-alone filters don't require dialog boxes. What Kai has done is split individual options into separate filters. Instead of choosing a Smudge filter and clicking on radio buttons to specify darken or lighten, left or right, you simply select the one filter with the options you want. It's much faster and less confusing.

Distort Filters

Pound for pound (ignoring the fact that filters are weightless) this menu offers some of the sexiest filters in the KPT set. You'll find three glass lens filters, page curl, and vortex tiling all in a single menu, shown in Figure 10.3.

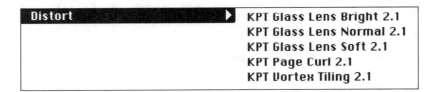

Figure 10.3 Distort filter menu with KPT components.

Glass Lens

The glass lens filters create awesomely realistic 3-D spheroids from your (preferably) circular or ellipsoidal selection. This is the real thing, folks. Instead of simply distorting the edges of the image so that they look like they're being stretched around a rounded surface, Kai goes whole hog, using ray trace algorithms that calculate the actual path of light rays bouncing off the surface of your sphere.

Even though there are no dialog boxes associated with the glass lens filters, you can still adjust the position of the apparent light source that creates the highlights by holding down specific keys on your numeric keypad as the filter is invoked. For example, hold down the **9** key, which is at the upper right of the numeric keypad, to specify a light coming from that direction. The **0** key provides backlighting, which is particularly cool.

There are three versions of glass lens—Bright, Normal, and Soft—which vary the contrast and appearance of the spheroid produced. You can use the glass lens filters to create realistic spheres—cue balls, marbles, Gypsy crystal balls, or whatever. Need to have an image reflected in a raindrop? This is your tool. These filters give you the same effects as expensive 7.5 mm and 16 mm fish-eye lenses but for a lot less money!

Figure 10.4 shows an image (included on the CD-ROM in the Spain folder as RUINS.TIF) that has been processed using an elliptical selection and the Glass Lens Bright filter. I deleted everything outside the selection to create a crystal ball effect.

Figure 10.4 Old ruins with Glass Lens Bright filter applied.

Page Curl

Many years ago, Eastman Kodak Company used an image of an edge (presumably of a photograph) curling up to reveal the Kodak name. This logo eventually fell into disfavor, possibly because Kodak decided that prints that curled up on their own weren't particularly desirable. Yet, the imagery lives on in KPT's Page Curl filter.

This filter adds an interesting 3-D effect to your images, since the curling page has a bright highlight running down the center, and it casts a shadow. Moreover, the curled page is translucent, so that you can see the image underneath.

There are several downsides to using this filter. It is unique but always produces a similar-looking curl effect, so virtually any knowledgeable graphics worker who sees a photo processed with Page Curl will immediately think, "Ah, this image was processed with Page Curl." You don't want people thinking about your technique instead of relating to your image.

On the other hand, Page Curl is a lot more flexible than you might think. I've gotten some interesting abstract effects by rolling up all four corners of an image and applying it repeatedly at various angles. Use a little imagination and you can generate effects with Page Curl that don't immediately scream out their source. Figure 10.5 shows an image that has been curled twice, using some of the following options.

Figure 10.5 Image with Page Curl applied twice.

Select a corner to curl by holding down keys on the numeric keypad at the diagonal corners of the pad (**7, 8, 1, 3**) to curl the corresponding corner of the image. Use the

CapsLock key to orient the direction of the curl. With CapsLock on, the curl will be in a horizontal direction; with CapsLock off, the image will curl vertically.

Vortex Tiling

There are no options here. Just select the Vortex Tiling filter and watch KPT go to work. Your image is repeated in smaller versions as if it were being sucked down a celestial whirlpool in a bad *Star Trek* episode. This filter doesn't seem to work well with human subjects, but it can do strange things with architectural, still life, or scenic photos. The most interesting effects are achieved if your image has one clearly defined subject surrounded by a plain background so that the vortexing can show up more clearly. Figure 10.6 shows an ancient Roman arch (inset) sucked down the vortex.

Figure 10.6 Vortex Tiling filter applied to Roman arch in the Spanish city of Medinaceli.

KPT Menu Filters

The KPT menu filters, shown in Figure 10.7, contains all the explorer/designer filters, as well as a hodge-podge of stand-alone single-pass filters. We'll go through each of these in turn.

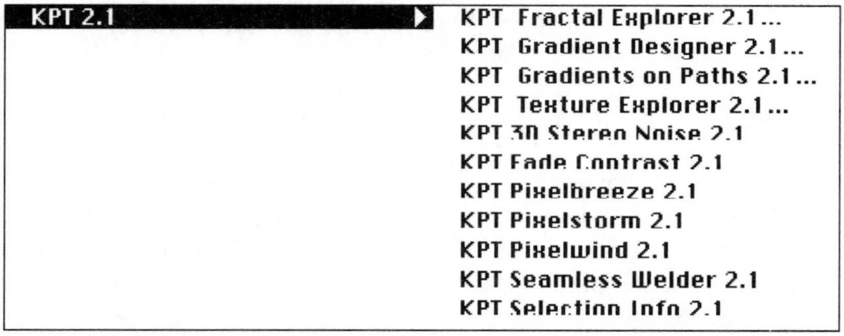

```
┌─────────────────────────┬──────────────────────────────┐
│ KPT 2.1              ►   │  KPT  Fractal Explorer 2.1... │
│                         │  KPT  Gradient Designer 2.1...│
│                         │  KPT  Gradients on Paths 2.1..│
│                         │  KPT  Texture Explorer 2.1... │
│                         │  KPT  3D Stereo Noise 2.1     │
│                         │  KPT  Fade Contrast 2.1       │
│                         │  KPT  Pixelbreeze 2.1         │
│                         │  KPT  Pixelstorm 2.1          │
│                         │  KPT  Pixelwind 2.1           │
│                         │  KPT  Seamless Welder 2.1     │
│                         │  KPT  Selection Info 2.1      │
└─────────────────────────┴──────────────────────────────┘
```

Figure 10.7 KPT menu components.

Fractal Explorer

Fractals are an interesting mathematical concept, based on shapes that are composed of an infinitely progressive series of miniature versions of their own shape. Because I'm not mathematically inclined, I usually visualize fractals by thinking of broccoli. A large bunch of broccoli is made up of smaller stalks, which look a lot like the large bunch. Of course, each smaller stalk has its own smaller stalks, and so on until you reach the tiny florets. The original idea for fractals was conceived by the scientist Dr. Seuss in *Horton Hears a Who*.

Actually, a couple of fellows named Julia and Mandelbrot did all the real work and helped computer users in the process, since fractals happen to have broad applications in imaging. It's possible to create realistic-looking images with none of the computer generated flavor (à la KPT Bryce) using fractal algorithms. Fractals can also be used to reconstruct highly compressed images by replacing missing information with fractal textures that are just as real looking as the actual thing.

None of these useful effects has any place in Fractal Explorer, however, which is used simply to create interesting-looking textures to play with. Although not random in nature, there are so many different fractal designs (an infinite number in the Julia set) that working with Fractal Explorer is often just a matter of goofing around until you find something you like.

The filter comes with four dozen presets with names like Neon Solar Flares and Polar Bear on its Side, which you can then transmute into thousands of other textures. There are multiple preview windows for things like opacity, the entire fractal map, and the effect that will be applied. You can zoom in and out of your preview, control the gradients, the spiraling, and other factors. Figure 10.8 shows the Fractal Explorer dialog box.

Figure 10.8 KPT Fractal Explorer dialog box.

The various controls are decidedly not self-explanatory. In fact, explanations won't help you much in any case. It's not as if you could set out to achieve a specific look and then go manipulate controls to achieve it. Your best bet is to load an image, fire up Fractal Explorer, and play with each control until you get a feel for what it does. Figure 10.9 shows a typical image with the fractal texture applied to the background only.

Figure 10.9 Fractal Explorer created this background.

Gradient Designer/Gradients on Paths

Gradients are cool effects that let you blend one or more colors into each other in a progressive way. The Gradient Designer and Gradients on Paths filters give you a way to create custom gradients and apply them to images in outrageous ways. The gradients themselves are sometimes very beautiful even without an underlying image associated with them. Figure 10.10 shows the Gradient Designer dialog box.

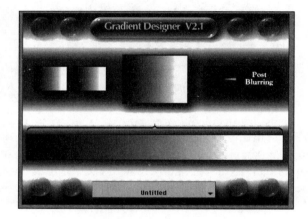

Figure 10.10 KPT Gradient Designer dialog box.

Gradient Designer is furnished with cascading preset menus with 18 main entries, and dozens of subentries within each of those categories. You can spend days just exploring all the different gradient types that are provided with Kai's Power Tools. You can also create your own gradients using the controls in the dialog box and save them as presets of your own.

To explore Gradient Designer, select one of the presets and click on the **Shuffle** button a few thousand times to view the possibilities. The **Option** button lets you choose how the gradient will be applied (lighten, darken, normal, multiply, etc.).

If you thought the ability to choose between radial and linear gradients was cool, the algorithm control box will really open your eyes. In addition to linear and radial, you can choose circular sunburst, pathbursts, radial sweeps, square bursts, and other mind-boggling effects.

The Gradients on Paths filter is a similar plug-in, which lets you wrap the gradient around any object or a free-form path that you design. Use it to create metallic tubes or shapes, complex text effects, or other interesting looks. Figure 10.11 shows the Gradients on Paths dialog box.

Figure 10.11 Gradients on Paths dialog box.

Texture Explorer

This filter is the putative "father" of KPT Convolver, which is discussed in the next chapter, because it features primitive versions of some of the previews and controls found in Convolver. Of course, primitive is a relative term. Texture Explorer is a sophisticated tool for creating custom textures using the hundreds of provided presets or those you create and save on your own. The Texture Explorer dialog box is shown in Figure 10.12.

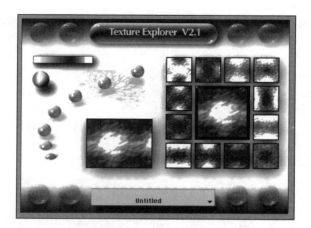

Figure 10.12 Texture Explorer dialog box.

The key components of Texture Explorer are the preview windows. The one at left shows the current texture as it will look when applied to your image. At right is another preview of the texture, surrounded by 12 derivative textures that you can select as the current texture by clicking on them.

Click on one of the mutation balls to create 12 new previews. The color mutation ball (the multicolored marble at left) varies only the colors used to change the current texture. The mutation tree balls can be clicked to vary all the other parameters at random, using either a small amount of change (at the root of the tree) to a vast amount of change (at the higher branches). Option-clicking a derivative texture preview window saves it for later use and prevents new changes. You can also select the tile size for applying the texture you've created.

Figure 10.13 shows an image created using Texture Explorer and several other filters. To create Figure 10.13, I followed these steps.

1. Select a circular area of a blank, white image.

2. Using Texture Explorer, find the texture shown in Figure 10.13.

3. Apply Glass Lens Bright to change the texturized image into a bright, shiny ball.

4. Select an eliptical area under the ball, feather it by 10 pixels, and fill it with black to create a shadow under the floating sphere.

The entire image took only minutes to construct.

Figure 10.13 Using a Texture Explorer texture.

Other KPT Menu Filters

In addition to the explorer/designers, there are seven other choices on the KPT menu. The 3-D Stereo Noise filter lets you perpetuate the "magic" picture hoax by converting your own images into fuzzy stereo noise that supposedly produce an image when you stare off into space while looking through them. My friends think I'm gullible enough to believe they actually see things in these images. Now you can fool your friends, too.

Fade Contrast, Pixelbreeze, Pixelstorm, and Pixelwind all produce interesting effects of their own that you'll want to try out. Figure 10.14 shows at left a cloud image, which has been smudged in an interesting manner using (left to right) Pixelwind, Pixelstorm, and Pixelbreeze. Use these filters to add painterly strokes to images or to create diffusion effects.

Seamless Welder takes your patterns and merges them smoothly with an image without any obvious transitions. The Selection Info "filter" actually pops up to give you information about your selection—its width and height in pixels, the number of pixels it contains, and its percentage of your total image. Figure 10.15 shows the Selection Info dialog box.

Figure 10.14 Image of clouds (left to right): unmodified, Pixelwind, Pixelstorm, and Pixelbreeze.

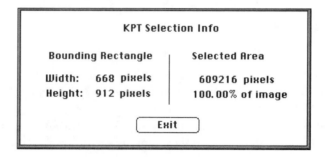

Figure 10.15 Selection Info dialog box.

Noise Menu Filters

The Noise menu includes three distinct filters—Grime Layer, H-P Noise, and Special Noise, with the latter two broken out into three separate filters each so that you don't have to bother with controls. The Noise menu filters are shown in Figure 10.16.

Grime Layer applies dark, transparent noise that is remarkably useful once you start to explore it. I created the image in Figure 10.17 using absolutely nothing but selection and layer tools, the Grime filter, and one application of Glass Lens Bright. To create the image, follow these steps:

Noise ▶	KPT Grime Layer 2.1
	KPT H-P Noise Maximum 2.1
	KPT H-P Noise Medium 2.1
	KPT H-P Noise Minimum 2.1
	KPT Special Blue Noise 2.1
	KPT Special Green Noise 2.1
	KPT Special Red Noise 2.1

Figure 10.16 Noise menu filters.

1. Select a circular portion of a blank, white image.
2. Apply the Grime filter to the selection.
3. Use the Glass Lens Bright filter to turn the grimy circle into a grimy, planetoidlike sphere.
4. Reverse the selection to create a new layer and then apply the Grime Layer filter to everything outside the original circle.
5. Set the Opacity of the new layer to about 70% and merge it with the planetoid to produce the image in Figure 10.17.

Figure 10.17 Image created entirely using Grime Layer and Glass Lens Bright filters.

The other two types of noise filters in this menu are Hue Protected (H-P) Noise and Special Noise. The H-P Noise filters are a set of three noise filters—Minimum, Medium, and Maximum—that add random noise without adding the colored speckles you get from the Photoshop Noise filter. Only the amount of noise differs among the three H-P variations.

The Special Noise filters add noise only to the selected RGB layer, without affecting the other layers. You can use these filters when you want to randomize portions of an image and add different kinds of noise to each layer. Each of these filters uses a different way of creating the noise; it's not just one filter applied to different layers.

Stylize Menu Filters

In this menu, which is shown in Figure 10.18, you'll find five interesting filters that change your image in new ways. You'll want to experiment with them to see exactly how they differ from their Photoshop counterparts.

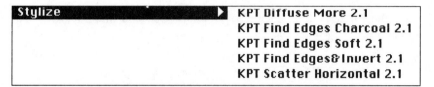

Figure 10.18 Stylize menu filters.

Diffuse More provides more diffusion (by a factor of four) than you get with Photoshop's Diffuse filter. It operates using a cell size that is four times larger, so that the effect is quite different from Photoshop's Diffuse filter, even when the latter is applied multiple times. You can hold down the number keys on the numeric keypad, from 1 to 0 to vary the amount of diffusion from least to most, as it is applied.

The three Find Edges (Charcoal, Soft, and Invert) perform variations on the Photoshop Find Edges filter. You can also use the number keys to vary the amount of any of these three effects. Find Edges Charcoal produces an effect like gray charcoal on white paper, while the Find Edges Soft filter produces a more diffuse effect. I used it for the image shown in Figure 10.19. Find Edges & Invert takes advantage of the fact that once the Find Edges filter has found all the edges, the final effect often looks better when inverted. The Find Edges & Invert filter performs the task all in one step, which means that you can undo it if you are not satisfied. I used the **WOODS.TIF** image found on the CD-ROM in the Miscellaneous folder.

Figure 10.19 Image with Find Edges Soft applied.

The Scatter Horizontal filter adds diffusion only in a horizontal direction and can be controlled, like the others in this menu, by holding down the number keys on the numeric keypad.

Video Menu Filter

KPT Cyclone is included in the video menu. It provides an awesome animated display of color variations that cycle in never-ending patterns until you apply one you like by pressing the **Return** key. You can use a variety of other controls with this filter.

- The **Left Arrow** key slows down the animated display.
- The **Right Arrow** key speeds up the animated display.
- The **Up Arrow** key throws the animation into reverse so that you can go back to an effect you liked but weren't quick enough to preserve.
- The **Down Arrow** key is a fast forward to the next color map.
- The question mark (**Shift-/**) pops up a Help screen.

- The S key saves the currently displayed map for later retrieval. File names are created automatically, using the current date and a number that corresponds to the order in which the maps were created.
- The 0 through 6 numeric keys change to different color styles.

Cyclone is a quick way to cycle through hundreds of different effects, which would be time consuming to produce by random fiddling with Photoshop's Levels, Curves, Arbitrary Map, Balance, and Hue dialog boxes. Cyclone messes with all these for you and lets you preview the results until you see one you like.

Figure 10.20 shows an image that has been manipulated with Cyclone (the original is on the CD-ROM in the Miscellaneous folder as **ROAD.TIF**). The black-and-white reproduction doesn't do this faux night scene justice. Check out the original figure on the CD-ROM.

Figure 10.20 Cyclone filter applied.

The Next Step

This hasn't been exactly a short chapter, but it still was a whirlwind tour of Kai's Power Tools. You'll find that this kit is worth exploring and that you will spend hours fiddling and playing with images just to see what you can turn up.

Now, we'll look at the latest offering from HSC and the mind of Kai Krause—KPT Convolver. It's a dream tool that gives you unprecedented control over filter parameters that you use everyday but never were able to combine or tweak before.

CHAPTER 11

Using KPT Convolver

KPT Convolver is perhaps the ultimate Photoshop-compatible filter, especially in terms of flexibility. This single plug-in gives you complete dominion over a huge range of image-tweaking parameters like relief angle, intensity, or tint. You can use it to create a variety of blurring, sharpening, embossing, and hue-bending effects.

Convolver doesn't limit you to a single effect, either. It lets you mix filters in fine increments, for example, to meld edge detection with relief effects in one-of-a-kind combinations. Add the traditional Kai Krause interface-from-Mars, and you have a plug-in that's as powerful and temporarily disorienting as a direct hit from a Maui breaker. Once you get your bearings, you'll find that Convolver can replace many of the filters you're already using.

If you're at all familiar with image editing on the Mac, you know Kai Krause, an artist who's made a living out of exploring every nook and cranny of Photoshop, turning the interface upside down, and finding new ways to use the capabilities built into the program. At the most basic level, KPT Convolver doesn't add many new capabilities to your image editor—it only makes it possible for you to get at those capabilities and combine them in ways that aren't ordinarily possible.

The most difficult thing about using KPT Convolver is getting a handle on what it is and what it does. How to use it is relatively simple once you understand those two things. Although Convolver's interface may be shocking to

Mac purists, once you begin using it, you'll find that it does make sense and has all that New Age intuitiveness its creator's brag about.

This is the only chapter in this book devoted solely to a single plug-in. I hope to help you pierce through the mental barrier your previous Mac experience may have set up and to get you right to work using this valuable tool. After you finish reading this chapter, I think you'll agree that the rewards are worth the journey.

What Is KPT Convolver?

If you don't happen to be an artist—those people who can toss around terms like "negative space" with aplomb—or live in California, where everybody talks like a space cadet, you may find the terminology that cloaks KPT Convolver a bit confusing. What are kernel matrices? Convolutions? How can you adjust values with controls that don't even have a slider? What's going on here?

In plain English, Convolver is a filter that lets you control the amount of many different parameters found in other filters. You can use it to adjust the degree of blurring, sharpening, edge enhancement, relief, saturation, brightness, and other factors applied to a selection or image. That much is easy to understand.

Convolver also lets you combine these characteristics, so that you can, say, sharpen, change hue, adjust brightness, or make other modifications in a single step. That's a powerful capability. Instead of making each change one at a time, you can tweak your image in many different ways and preview the total effect before applying the filter. Since the appearance of some changes may be modified by later filters, this is much more efficient than trying out each filter in turn and then discovering that you should have reduced brightness a little before you enhanced the edges. Using Convolver is a little like looking at a computer-generated picture of your living room with new carpet, curtains, wallpaper, and furniture all in place rather than studying separate photographs of each component.

Convolver also allows you to view different combinations of each of the factors you're controlling in a matrix. Imagine a square divided into 16 smaller squares, with the lower left-hand corner of the square as your zero point. The square in that corner contains your original image, with no modifications. Now, imagine each smaller square in the bottom row with progressively more sharpening applied—say 20% in the second square, 40% in the third, and 80% in the fourth, something like Figure 11.1.

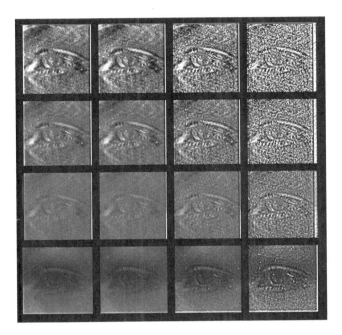

Figure 11.1 A matrix of filter effects.

Now, apply increasing amounts of embossing to the squares in the first column, as they extend from the zero point, and add combinations of the sharpening and embossing to each of the other squares in the matrix, so that the square in the upper right has the maximum amount of both. That's a simple matrix displaying combinations of two different filter effects. Convolver tilts this array on its side, as shown in Figure 11.2. But, in either case, you can preview many different combinations of filters as quickly as you can click your mouse button.

That's the basic concept behind Convolver—the ability to meld many factors to create one filter. But wait, there's more. Convolver has three different modes, each of which lets you use these capabilities in various ways. All operate so quickly that they lend themselves to wild experimentation.

Figure 11.2 KPT Convolver's main screen.

Explore Mode

In Explore mode a selection is previewed in 15 diamond-shaped slices—a matrix—plus a larger window. Click on the **Mutate Genes** button to generate 15 random versions. In this mode the individual images within the diamond grid don't have any particular relationship to one another.

The **Genetic Diversity** button controls the amount of variation in the effects in five steps, while **Genetic Influences** produces a list of effects that will be combined in each new generation: **Blur/Sharpen, Embossing, Edge Detection, Hue, Saturation, Brightness, Contrast,** and **Tint.** You can choose and investigate any combination.

What about the word Genetics? This is just an artsy term for things you already understand, using an organic analogy that makes a lot of sense if you view Convolver as a way of "growing" new images. The **Genetic Diversity** button (a cool spheroid with a right-pointing triangle like that found in conventional Mac menus to indicate that a fly-out menu is present) can be set for five different levels from **Minimum** to **Maximum,** as shown in Figure 11.3. These simply control the coarseness of the changes (or, if you're a programmer, the granularity) each generation of samples displays. Click on **Minimum** and successive sets will have only minor changes. Choose **Maximum** for some wild variations.

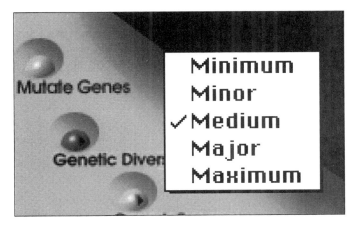

Figure 11.3 Genetic Diversity menu.

The **Genetic Influences** button produces a menu, shown in Figure 11.4, that controls which factors will be changed in each generation. You can select from **Blur/Sharpen, Embossing,** and **Edge Detection** (the so-called Texture parameters) and **Hue, Saturation, Brightness, Contrast,** and **Tint** (the Color parameters.) The choices at the top of the menu let you quickly set the check marks next to *just* the texture parameters (**Texture Only**), just the color parameters (**Color Only**), or both sets of factors (**Mutate All**), or none of them.

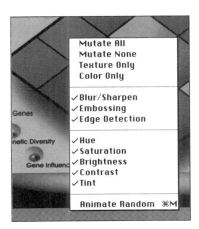

Figure 11.4 Genetic Influences menu.

In Explore mode you can zip through hundreds of variations quickly. Clicking on one of the preview boxes adds it to the currently active diamond at the top. That will be the effect applied to your image or selection when you click on the check mark icon shown at lower right of Figure 11.5. The circle with the international symbol for NOT next to it is Convolver's Cancel button.

As you look at Figure 11.5, notice that there is an arc of buttons at the right side of the screen that are grayed out. Those are features that are not available in Explore mode. One of Krause's user interface conventions is to have options not in use fade from sight where they won't obtrude. You can use them, switching modes in the process, just by clicking on them. It's clever, and it works.

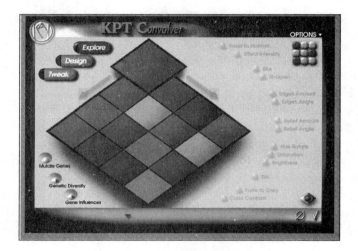

Figure 11.5 Convolver's Explore mode.

Tweak Mode

Where Explore mode randomizes the changes, Tweak mode is a production tool that manipulates parameters individually using percentages. You can also specify things like edge or relief angle and amount or color contrast. The full preview area can be used to perform image correction and enhancement on a larger portion of your image, using combinations of conventional filter effects. Unlimited Undo allows backtracking to any desired point in the process.

You get a selection of about a dozen controls, grouped into the texture and color parameters already listed. In addition, you get a button to reset the image to its original settings, another to control effect intensity (which increases or decreases the amount of all the settings you've made by the same percentage), plus fade to grey and color contrast controls. These are all shown in Figure 11.6.

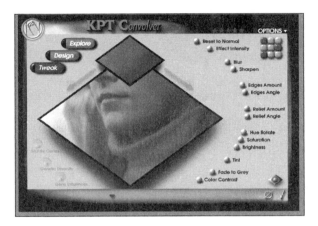

Figure 11.6 Tweak mode.

Although each button is actually a slider control, you don't see the sliding pointer found in a normal Macintosh dialog box. Instead, you click on the button with the mouse cursor and drag rightish and leftish to effect changes in a positive or negative direction. A readout in the status bar at the bottom of the window (Figure 11.7) shows the current value. Krause's interface de-emphasizes the slider idea because you're probably more interested in changing a value until the appearance you want shows up in the preview window, rather than when you achieve a particular setting. The value is shown so that you can duplicate the amount at a later time, if you wish. (Settings can be stored, however, to streamline saving and retrieving the effects that you like.)

Unlike a regular slider, you can double-click on any of these buttons to return the effect to its original state. The individual controls for **Blur/Sharpen, Embossing, Edge Detection, Hue, Saturation, Brightness, Contrast,** and **Tint** all operate on your image in ways that should be familiar to you by now, so I won't individually explain what blur, saturation, or contrast controls do.

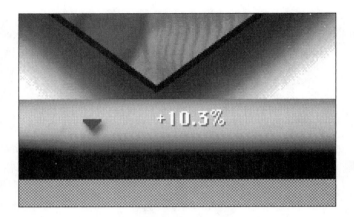

Figure 11.7 Slider status bar.

Tweak itself has three submodes, which change the way this mode operates. You can select one of the three submodes by clicking on the **Tweak** button and holding it down until the menu shown in Figure 11.8 appears. The default is **Linear Convolution**, which is nothing more than the mode used for the Explore and Tweak options we've already discussed, as well as the Design mode, which follows. The **Unsharp/Gaussian** submode lets you apply tweaking to large blurred or sharpened areas quickly. The **Blur, Sharpen, Edges Amount**, and **Edges Angle** buttons vanish in this mode and are replaced with **Gaussian, Unsharp, Radius**, and **Threshold** buttons, as shown in Figure 11.9.

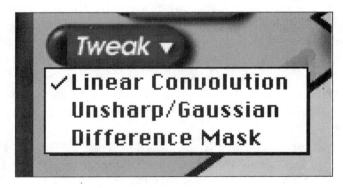

Figure 11.8 Tweak submode menu.

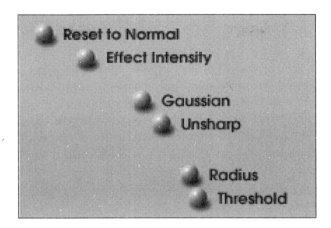

Figure 11.9 New controls appear when you use
the Unsharp/Gaussian submode.

You can set blur amounts from 0 to 100%, and specify unsharp masking in values well over 1000% (I got tired of dragging the mouse after I reached 1500%, since it was more sharpness than I could plausibly use at that point.) The radius control is used to determine the size of the area used to compute average brightness (instead of the 3 x 3 pixel radius normally used). The threshold control specifies a level of contrast below which the sharpness filter is not applied. Larger values limit sharpening to areas that are already relatively sharp; lower values extend the effect to more and more pixels.

The **Difference Mask** submode of Tweak tells Convolver to perform a difference channel operation on your modified and original images, producing a new effect. You'll want to experiment with this mode; it's difficult to predict exactly what you'll get.

Design Mode

Design mode returns to the matrix idea outlined earlier in the chapter. This mode assigns any filter parameter to one of two axes, with sample images displayed in the diamond preview area incorporating increasing amounts of the factors you've selected. Choose **Edge Detection** and **Relief**, for example, and you'll see an array of samples with combinations of both effects applied.

In Design mode you'll see two axes with the names of the currently active parameters shown. Click on the parameter name and menus appear like those shown in Figure 11.10. (In fairness, these menus are normally cool horizontal gray lists, but those didn't capture very well for this illustration, so I switched to the optional Mac-normal black-and-white menu mode.) You can choose any of the parameter sets for each axis. Double-click on one of these effect labels to change it to its complementary effect instantly; blur becomes sharpen. Drag on the arrows located beneath the large, top diamond to increase the effect along each axis. The arrow gets longer as you drag, so you always have a visual cue to what's going on.

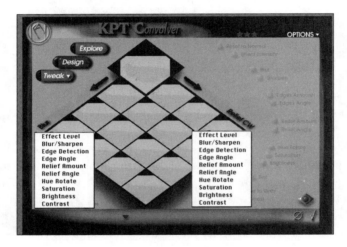

Figure 11.10 Design mode menus.

Design mode is a great way to create your own filters in a nonrandom way, using the exact parameters you specify.

Saving Your Filters

While Convolver doesn't let you save your custom settings as stand-alone filters, you can store any of the presets on disk and recall them at any time for reuse with a different image. The Preset arrow on the status bar produces the menu shown in Figure 11.11 when you click it.

You can Add a preset, using any name you choose, restore the image to the default Convolver settings, or scroll down to one of your prestored sets of parameters (all called Cool Preset followed by a number in this example).

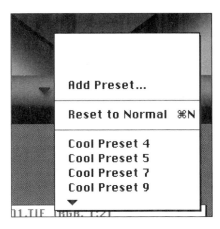

Figure 11.11 Adding and restoring presets.

Special Rewards

Convolver rewards intense use by progressively unveiling four new tools: a split-screen preview facility; a slick tint wheel that serves as a joysticklike color balancer; a set of nine memory dot scratch pads that can store effects combinations for instant recall; and an animation feature. The manual only hints at these and their functions, and the over-eager user may be frustrated at the length of time it takes for each individual new tool to appear. I know that when I upgraded from a prerelease version of Convolver to the final release, I "lost" all my bonus tools and was inconsolable until I earned them back.

I haven't found any secret sequence of steps to use to activate these tools (except for the initial, toolless bonus star), but I can relieve some of your anticipation by describing each of the bonuses. They may appear in any order, depending on what particular features of Convolver you use to trigger a particular tool.

- **Star the First.** When you use each of Convolver's three modes at least once, a dialog box, shown in Figure 11.12, pops up, and a red star appears at the top of the Convolver screen. If you haven't read the manual, this may be your first indication that Convolver has any hidden tools. You're not granted any new capabilities at this point, unless you count frustration. If you like reading the dialog box associated with any of the stars, hold down the **Option** key while clicking on the star. (This doesn't work until the star has appeared; "ghost" stars in the background don't count.)

Congratulations !

You have attained your first Star, indicating you have passed through each Convolver mode at least once.

As you continue to work with KPT Convolver, you will earn more stars along the way. With each new Star, you will be awarded a new tool to further enhance your Convolver "tool-belt." Stars are awarded according to your need, based on frequency of specific functions used. They will not necessarily appear in any particular order...

We hope you enjoy this unfolding functionality... keep an eye on the stars, and when you get to five stars, feel free to gloat!

★ teamCONVO

Figure 11.12 First star dialog box.

- **Star the Second.** The second star (which did not appear second for me) grants you a handy split-screen preview mode, which you can activate by clicking on a new button that appears in the lower right-hand corner of the Convolver screen, as shown in Figure 11.13. In this mode, the large diamond grid is turned into a single window, which displays your original image at left, and the adjacent part of the same image with the currently active filter effect applied.

  When the split screen button is activated (the button changes color to show that it is on), this preview will always be available when you are in Tweak mode. You can toggle back and forth between it and the normal diamond grid while in Explore or Design mode by clicking on the topmost tile.

- **Star the Third.** This algorithmic tint wheel appeared second for me both times I installed Convolver. It's a new button that produces a Saturn-like revolving disk that you can click on to select any of 3600 different hues and 10,000 different levels of saturation. It's a handy tool that's much faster than using conventional hue/saturation sliders. Just click and drag around the wheel to choose colors, move toward or away from the center to change saturation. Hold down the **Option** key while dragging to remove colors. The tint wheel is shown in Figure 11.14.

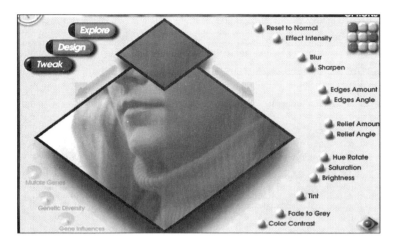

Figure 11.13 Split-screen preview mode.

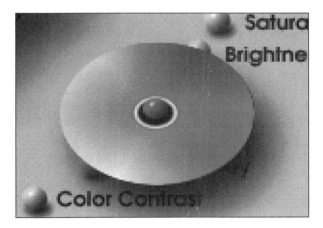

Figure 11.14 Algorithmic tint wheel.

- **Star the Fourth.** Memory dots are an array of nine 3-D dots that can be used as function buttons to store and restore any preview setting. Think of them as scratchpads: store effects that you are considering, but perhaps aren't ready to save as a full, named preset at this point. You can also save sets of memory dots and recall them at any time, giving you little groups of presets to use whenever you like.

Memory dots are very easy to use. When you have a setting you want to save, just click on one of the dots. A dot darkens from gray to brown to indicate that it is remembering a particular setting. A reddish dot indicates one that has been applied to the image. Use **Option**-click to erase the contents of a dot. Figure 11.15 shows the memory dots as they appear on the Convolver screen.

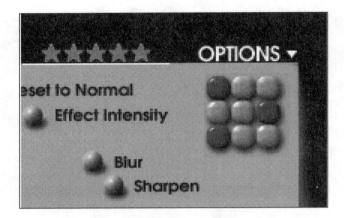

Figure 11.15 Memory dots

- **Star the Fifth.** The final star provides animation between effects, which gives you the ability to compare two settings and see all the intermediate settings between them. It's a great tool for previewing effects. You can use this tool in two modes—either to compare two effects stored in memory dots or to compare the current image and randomly generated effects produced in Explore mode.

  Activate the memory dots version by choosing **Animate Dots** from the Option menu at the upper right in the Convolver screen. The Explore mode version can be turned on in the Gene Influences menu. Use the numeric keypad to enter percentages—(from 1 (1%) to 0 (10%))—of change between frames of the animation.

Other Options

Although we've covered most of Convolver's features, there are other options you'll want to know about. This section will explain each of them.

The Kai Logo

Click on the Kai logo at the upper left of the KPT Convolver screen to shrink the display down to a small box. (See Figure 11.16.) You can use this feature to take a quick look at your image's main window. The minimized logo can be dragged to any position to give you an unobstructed view. Click again to restore the full Convolver screen. Moving the cursor within the logo produces a list of credits for the program. Figure 11.16 shows the logo.

Figure 11.16 Kai's logo can minimize the filter so that you can view the whole image.

Options:About Convolver

This is a text file you can view with an interesting message from Kai Krause about the filter. There are even a few useful tips here.

Options:Preferences

Convolver doesn't have many options here, because most of its features are always available. However, you can tell the program to **Return to Previous State**—that is, to use the most recently selected settings whenever the filter is loaded rather than Convolver's defaults. You can also replace some of the fancy 3-D menus with boring 12-point Chicago menus conforming to the Mac standards, by checking **Monochrome Design Menus**. This option may help those of you who have slower machines or who just can't let go of the Mac's original 1984 interface. The **Virtual Mouse** option lets those of you with pressure-sensitive tablets turn off Convolver's ability to drag beyond the edge of the screen. This choice appears only if you have such a tablet. I don't, so you won't find it in Figure 11.17, which shows the Preferences dialog box.

Figure 11.17 Convolver's Preferences dialog box.

Options:Kernel Matrices

This dialog box lets you look at the actual numeric values being used by Convolver to compute the current effect. In general, this information is of interest only to mathematicians or masochistic computer programmers. If you're that curious, Figure 11.18 shows a typical display.

Spatial Kernel

	X	Y	Z
X	0	0	0
Y	0	256	0
Z	0	0	0

Color Kernel

	R	G	B
R	256	0	0
G	0	256	0
B	0	0	256
Z	61	-74	13

OK

Figure 11.18 Typical kernel matrix.

Options:Comparison Grid Overlay

This viewing option is available in Explore and Design modes. It places the grid onto the entire preview image and then applies each change to a different portion of the image rather than to the same smaller section. It's a quick way to see how various permutations look on different sections of your original image.

Options:Reselect Sample

Use this option to change the portion of your image used as a preview, without exiting Convolver and returning. You can drag the Preview window around in your original image until you find a new section you want to use.

Options:Current Selection (and Cool Car, Hand Lines, Eye)

You can change between your current image selection and several sample images with names like Cool Car, Hand Lines, and Eye. You can use these to explore different effects without loading different images of your own. Figure 11.19 shows the full Options menu.

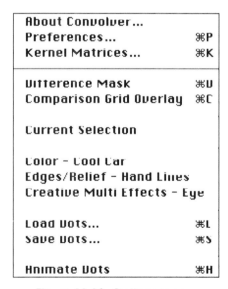

Figure 11.19 Options menu.

The Next Step

You'll want to experiment with KPT Convolver to see how combining filters you are already familiar with can produce exciting, new effects. Unsharp masking, in concert with Embossing, Hue, or Saturation changes, and other filters can give you entirely new images. Pixels that appear one way at a particular setting may vanish entirely or change dramatically when you change one setting slightly. And Convolver's Explore mode is a great way to look at hundreds of effects at random in just a few minutes.

When you're finished exploring design-it-yourself filters, we can look at some more third-party plug-ins that have their own special looks and that are themselves highly customizable. In Chapter 12 we'll start with Adobe's own Gallery Effects product line, which it acquired in the merger with Aldus.

Color 1: A blur filter turned the background of Segovia, Spain's famous castle into an interesting gradient blend.

Color 2: The Wind picture added streaks to the image at upper left, while the Extrude filter created a 3D effect at upper right. At lower right, the Facet plug-in turned a snapshot into a painting.

Color 3: Find Edges and Clouds created the weird scene at upper left. At upper left, an engraving was created with the Emboss filter. At lower right, the Wind plug-in gave an ominious look to the artificial clouds inserted in the photo.

Color 4: A custom filter designed by the author created this effect.

Color 5: Kai's Power Tools Cyclone filter generates a series of arbitrary color maps in outrageous combinations that you can preview and capture when you see a variation you like.

Color 6: Kai's Power Tools Fractal Explorer creates otherworldly landscapes out of mundane photographs.

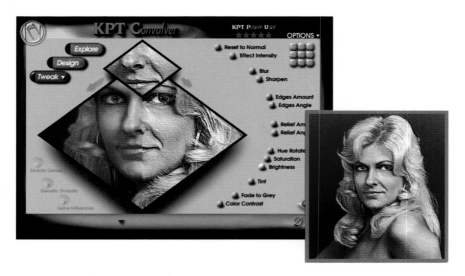

Color 7: KPT Convolver's Tweak mode lets you experiment with combinations of filter settings, and preview your results in a split-screen mode.

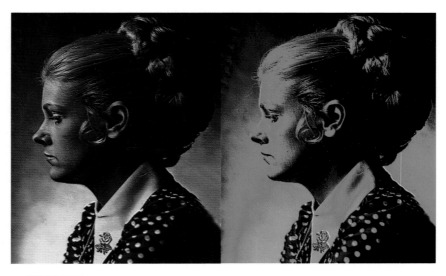

Color 8: Convolver lets you create dozens of variations in minutes.

Color 9: The Dry Brush filter added artistic brush strokes to this photo of statues in Leon, Spain.

Color 10: The Gallery Effects Film Grain filter adds a hazy, romantic quality to this portrait.

Color 11: A modernized medieval castle takes on a more appropriate look when the image is antiqued using the Ink Outlines filter from Adobe Gallery

Color 12: This unique effect was achieved by applyling Alien Skin's Swirl filter, from the Black Box collection, to each layer of an RGB image separately.

Color 13: Second Glance's Chromassage lets you spin a few control wheels to alter your image's palette of colors.

Color 14: Shareware filters can create some amazing effects, like this posterization created with Chris Cox's Skeleton filter.

Color 15: Stunning text effects created with various combinations of filters, gradients, and other tools.

Color 16: Textures can transform an image. At upper left, a rocky texture from Pixar 128 adds interest to a mountain scene. At lower right, a Chrome filter, gold tint, and pumped up contrast create a metal statue effect.

CHAPTER 12

Using Adobe Gallery Effects

It was a marriage made in heaven when Adobe acquired Aldus, which numbered among its products one of the leading packages of plug-in filters for Adobe's flagship image-editing program. Adobe Gallery Effects:Classic Art includes 48 distinctly different filters divided into three packages, each with a list price of $149. Many of the effects that you can achieve with these filters are possible with no other plug-in, so serious workers will find them an essential tool for image manipulation. All the Gallery Effects filters were recompiled to run fast on Power Mac platforms, so you'll find them to be among the speediest plug-ins you can use.

This chapter, the longest in the book, introduces each of the filters, explains how the individual controls affect the images produced, and provides an example image after manipulating each of the key settings.

How to Use This Chapter

Gallery Effects offers a bewildering variety of looks and a staggering number of different combinations of controls and settings. I've tried to make visualizing each filter's properties and selecting the one you want a little easier in the following ways:

- The discussion of each filter includes a screen shot of the controls.

- An accompanying figure includes an example of an image using the default parameters, plus typical settings for each of the other controls. You can quickly compare examples side by side. I used the same picture for all the illustrations in this chapter so that you may compare the difference between similar filters like Film Grain and Grain.

- On the CD-ROM that is bundled with this book, you'll find a special set of Photoshop 3.0 files that include the example images, which you can load and examine in detail.

- Because the example image used throughout this chapter may not always be the best one for showing off a particular effect, I included a small gallery of different images with a sampling of effects applied at the end of this chapter and in the color insert.

N O T E   Each file consists of three or more separate layers, with the effects applied to the same image in each of the layers. The layers have names like Sharpness 20 and Texture 3, so that you'll know exactly what settings were used to produce those examples.

Working with Gallery Effects

As you might expect from the name of the product, Gallery Effects:Classic Art provides artistic effects like those you might expect to see in an art or photo gallery. The filters are packaged in three volumes with 16 filters each. Volume 1 offers traditional media effects that simulate techniques that artists might use when working with chalk, charcoal, watercolor, fresco, ink pen, various brushes, and so forth. Volume 2 adds more media, such as colored pencil, rough pastels, and palette knife, along with a few higher-tech tricks, including a photocopylike effect and a clever texturizer. Volume 3 ventures more into photographic-style effects, letting you simulate exposures through blocks or sheets of glass and halftone screens and employ a darkroom technique known as reticulation. There also are quite a few new artistic filters such as paint daubs, sponge, and ink outlines.

As with most of the filters in this book, you can use Gallery Effects to enhance images in the following ways:

- Add a consistent look to a series of images that vary in appearance. You'll find that several pictures taken under varying conditions (some color, some black-and-white) all tend to become more compatible once you've put them through a heavy filter meat grinder. Applying the same filter makes a series of portraits, say, seem enough alike to share a single layout.

- Add texture to flat graphics. Even simple bitmaps or outlines become interesting when you process them with filters.

- Simulate painting or sketching effects. Add these effects to sharp photos to tone down excess detail. Use them with unsharp photos to mask the lack of detail. Take a mundane image and give it a sophisticated, artsy look.

- Reduce complex images to outlines or other simple components or isolate portions of an image so that they can communicate an idea more quickly. A photo of 2000 football fans screaming their heads off may be distracting. Zoom in on one fanatic and give him a stark appearance using, say, Poster Edges, and you'll find the concepts of enthusiasm or excitement a lot easier to get across in a quick look.

N O T E The effects of some of these filters varies, depending on what application the add-on is "plugged into." Chalk & Charcoal and Charcoal, for example, which are discussed in the next section, use the foreground and background colors to stroke your images, when applied within Photoshop or Fractal Design Painter. Some applications may just use black and white, giving you less control over the filter.

Volume 1 Filters

The Gallery Effects:Classic Art Volume 1 filters make an excellent first set for anyone who wants to get started using plug-ins. I recommend them even over Kai's Power Tools, since you'll find these add-ons easy to use with no training. Just install them and start working. We'll look at each of the filters in the package in turn.

All these Adobe filters feature similar dialog boxes, as shown in Figure 12.1. The name of the filter is listed in the upper left-hand corner of the box, just above a reduced-size version of the main image. A rectangle marks the area in the reduced image that is shown enlarged at the right size of the dialog box. Both Before and After views are shown. Click on the **Preview** button to apply the current filter settings to the preview section of the image. The preview is not continuously updated; each time you change settings you must click on the **Preview** button again.

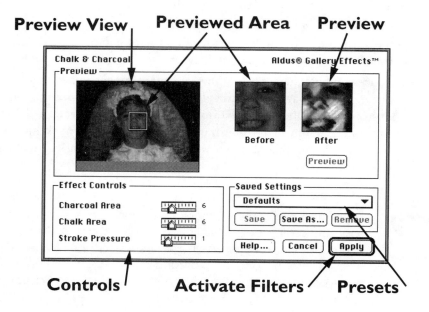

Figure 12.1 Gallery Effects' Chalk & Charcoal dialog box, which is similar to those provided with all 48 Adobe filters.

The controls for a given filter are always displayed in the lower left-hand corner, usually as sliders accompanied by a numeric readout. A few filters such as Texturizer in Volume 2 have additional dialog boxes with more controls.

At lower right is a drop-down list showing currently saved presets for the active filter and buttons that you can use to save your settings, save them under a new name, or remove presets from the list. The **Apply** button at the extreme lower right is used to exit the dialog box and implement the filter on your image or selection.

Chalk & Charcoal

Chalk & Charcoal filter gives you the effects of a mixed-media drawing using rough chalk for the midtones and highlights and charcoal for the shadows. The diagonal lines used obliterate quite a bit of image detail, so you should use this filter with pictures that have strong, bold areas. The dialog box for this plug-in is shown in Figure 12.1.

The unmodified image used for all the filter illustrations in this chapter is shown at left in Figure 12.2. At right is the same image with the default Chalk & Charcoal settings applied.

Figure 12.2 Unmodified image (left) and default
Chalk & Charcoal settings (right).

You'll find that you usually must adjust the settings from the defaults to best suit your image. Several controls are available. If Photoshop's default colors (black and white) are used, the charcoal will be black and the chalk white. However, you can choose any set of colors, even reversing their relationship (with the background darker than the foreground) to generate interesting effects. The relative amount of area devoted to the highlights and shadows can be adjusted using the Charcoal Area and Chalk Area sliders. The pressure of the strokes is also variable. Figure 12.3 shows our test image with Charcoal Area set to 20 (left), Chalk Area set to 20 (middle), and Stroke Pressure increased to 5 (right).

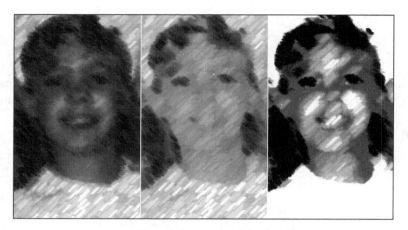

Figure 12.3 Chalk & Charcoal applied with Charcoal Area 20 (left), Chalk Area 20 (middle), and Stroke Pressure 5 (right).

Charcoal

The Charcoal filter turns your image into a charcoal drawing, using the current background color as the underlying canvas, with the charcoal strokes applied using the foreground color. You can adjust the thickness of the stick of charcoal, the amount of detail applied, and the balance between the light/dark areas of the image, as shown in the dialog box in Figure 12.4.

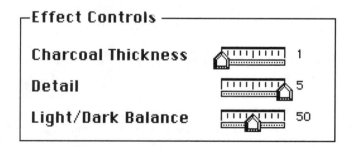

Figure 12.4 Charcoal filter controls.

In Figure 12.5 you can see examples of the test image with the default settings (left), with Charcoal Thickness expanded to a smudgy 7 (center), and, with Detail set to 4 and Light/Dark Balance moved up to 80 (right).

Figure 12.5 Charcoal applied with default settings (left), Charcoal Thickness 7 (center), and Detail 4, Light/Dark Balance 80 (right).

Chrome

If used correctly, Chrome can be a stunning and versatile filter, adding a slick metallic effect straight out of *Terminator 2*. When applied, it smoothes out the details of your image and adds a 3-D effect, making the lightest areas the "highest" in the transformed image and the darkest areas the "lowest." There are only two controls, which are shown in Figure 12.6. They adjust the amount of detail represented in the final image and the degree of smoothness.

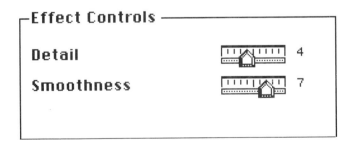

Figure 12.6 Chrome filter controls.

There are several tricks to using this filter properly. You'll rarely, if ever, want to apply it to an entire image. Your best bet is to select some object in the image, isolate it from the background, and then apply the Chrome filter to that. If there is not sufficient differentiation between the gray tones of an image or selection, Chrome turns the whole thing into a featureless gray mass. In that case, beef up the contrast using **Image:Adjust:Brightness/Contrast** and give the filter some meaty details to work with.

You can see what I mean in Figure 12.7. The example at left uses the default settings, which use a medium value for Detail and a high degree of Smoothness. In contrast, see the version in the center, which sets Detail to 10, and the example at right, with Smoothness phased down to a meager 1. Both of these settings give you a chrome effect with more character than the default.

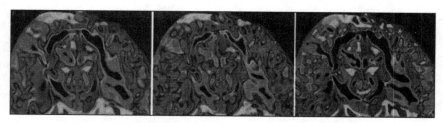

Figure 12.7 Chrome applied with default settings (left), Detail 10 (center), and Smoothness 1 (right).

Craquelure

If you want an ancient example of how a bug becomes a feature, look no farther than the Craquelure filter. In only a few hundred short years, the bane of ancient artists has become a quality that professional photographers and, now, computer image workers will actually pay for.

Paints applied to canvas or some other surface don't retain their pristine surface, broken only by carefully applied brush strokes, for very long. The paints themselves aren't stable, composed as they are of exotic substances that can include egg whites, clay, and weird chemicals or plants as pigment. Nor can you count on the substrate to keep its shape and size forever. Something as simple as fluctuations in temperature can cause paintings to develop a network of cracks. Professional photographers sometimes have this texture applied to their photographs to give them an Old Masters patina. You can achieve a similar effect, which adds a nice 3-D look, using the Craquelure filter.

As shown in Figure 12.8, you can control the crack spacing, depth, and brightness. The default crack spacing of 15 gives you a good mixture of cracks and image area. Decreasing the spacing much below 10 makes the cracks so wide that the raised, embossed portion of the image may be just a few isolated bumps. Increasing the spacing to 50 or more produces an image that resembles your original, with a sparse distribution of cracks.

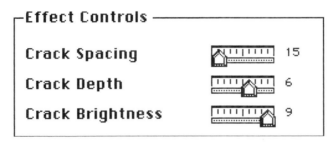

Figure 12.8 Craquelure controls.

The Crack Depth and Crack Brightness settings change the appearance of the cracks themselves. You'll find that deeper or shallower cracks can dramatically change the effect. Figure 12.9 shows the different effects you can get with this filter. At upper left is an example with the default settings applied. In upper center, the spacing has been increased to 50. At upper right, Crack Depth was increased to 10, producing the deep rifts you see. I reduced Crack Brightness to a value of 2 at lower left and then pumped it up to 10 at lower right. Changing Crack Brightness reduces or increases the amount of original image detail that shows in the cracks.

Figure 12.9 Craquelure filter applied with default settings (upper left), Crack Spacing of 50 (upper center), Crack Depth of 10 (upper right), and Crack Brightness of 2 and 10 (lower left and right).

Dark Strokes

The Dark Strokes filter has two effects on your image. First, it reduces the number of different tones in the image through a posterizationlike effect that combines similar tones in an unusual way. Instead of grouping similar colors together, Dark Strokes makes dark tones darker and light tones lighter, increasing contrast. At the same time, each tone is rendered using diagonal brush strokes—short strokes for dark tones and longer strokes for light tones. You can see the effects quite clearly in the examples in Figure 12.11.

Figure 12.10 shows the three controls available for the Dark Strokes filter. You can adjust balance between light and dark tones, as well as their respective intensity.

Even though the default settings give some interesting effects, I like to set the white intensity fairly high and reduce black intensity to cut back on the somber mood this filter can sometimes produce. It's a great filter for masking imperfect pictures that contain details that detract from, rather than enhance, their look. Figure 12.11 shows four examples made with different settings.

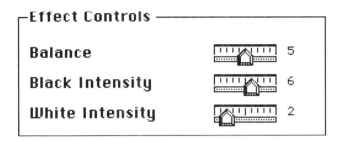

Figure 12.10 Dark Strokes controls.

Figure 12.11 Dark Strokes applied with default settings (upper left); Balance 10 (upper right); Black intensity 10 (lower left); White Intensity 8 (lower right).

Dry Brush

The Dry Brush filter mimics a natural-media effect—stroking with a brush that's almost devoid of paint—in a fairly predictable way. If I wanted to change a photograph into a painting, I would try this filter first. It doesn't obscure as much detail as the typical watercolor, stipple, or impressionistic filter found in most image-editing applications, but it still has a distinct painted look.

Dry Brush posterizes your image but produces more distinct banding than Dry Strokes. The bands of colors themselves become the strokes, as all similar colors in a particular area are reduced to one average hue. Figure 12.12 shows the controls available for this filter. You can adjust the size of the brush—larger brushes apply broader strokes. The Brush Detail control allows you to change the amount of detail in each area by modifying the roughness of the edges. The Texture control applies light, medium, or heavy texture to the image, using a series of three radio buttons.

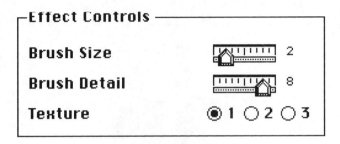

Figure 12.12 Dry Brush controls.

You can see how the Dry Brush filter works in the examples in Figure 12.13. The default settings, shown at upper left, are probably your best bet for most images. They provide a good compromise of detail and painterly effect. Increasing the brush size, as in the example at upper right, produces a more diffused look. Reducing Brush Detail to 1, as in lower left, or adding the maximum amount of Texture (lower right) makes the posterization effect more pronounced.

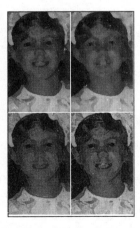

Figure 12.13 Dry Brush examples with default settings (upper left); Brush Size 10 (upper right); Brush Detail 1 (lower left); and Texture 3 (lower right).

Emboss

Why would you need another Emboss filter, since most image editors, including Photoshop, already provide one in their basic toolkit? You'll find that the Gallery Effects version is much more subtle and useful because it retains the colors in your original image rather than converting all the hues to a murky gray tinged with a slight amount of color (as does the Photoshop Emboss filter).

Where Photoshop gives you height, amount, and angle controls, the Gallery Effects Emboss filter offers only two adjustments, which are shown in Figure 12.14. They are Relief (roughly corresponding to the height and amount controls in the Photoshop version) and Light Position, which allows you to choose the direction of the light that produces the 3-D effect using descriptive terms (e.g., Top Right) rather than the more precise angles used by Photoshop.

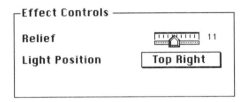

Figure 12.14 Emboss filter controls.

Figure 12.15 shows the test image with the default settings (left) and with the amount of Relief more than doubled to a value of 25 (center). For the example at right, I reduced the amount of Relief to half the default value (5) and moved the light source to the bottom left.

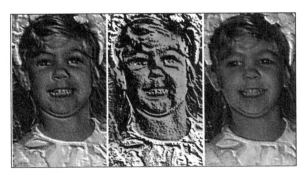

Figure 12.15 Emboss filter applied with default settings (left);
Relief 25 (center), relief 5 and, Light Source Bottom Left (right).

Film Grain

Film grain is a uniquely photographic phenomenon, rather than a painterly effect, and as such tends to lend more of a modern look to images, as opposed to the Old Masters air of some of the other filters. Grain is another bug-turned-feature that resulted when photographers found that enlarging small sections of photos, or attempting to push film's sensitivity to new heights in low-light photography, produced interesting effects. When images are abused in this way, the clumps of silver in the film (or the clumps of dye left behind when a color negative or transparency is processed) add a distinct texture to the picture.

The closest thing Photoshop provides to the Film Grain filter is Add Noise in its monochromatic mode (Uniform and Gaussian Noise also add random RGB color). The Gallery Effects filter (shown in Figure 12.16) gives you some controls not found in the Add Noise plug-in. You can achieve one really cool effect with this filter. I'll explain it in the next few paragraphs.

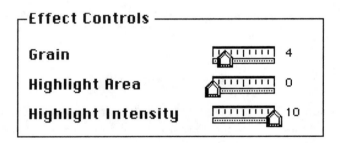

Figure 12.16 Film Grain controls.

You can adjust the amount of grain, the size of the highlight area, and the intensity of the highlights. The Grain setting controls the density of what appear to be random little black grains that are sprinkled throughout your image. The higher the value, the more details of your image are obscured by the grain overlay.

Because the Film Grain filter applies more grain to the highlights than to the shadows and midtones, two controls let you adjust how this heavier grain is applied. The Highlight Area slider determines how many tones are considered highlights; at higher values, virtually all the image is given the full treatment. The Highlight Intensity slider controls how strongly the grain is applied to the highlight areas.

Figure 12.17 shows some variations possible with the Film Grain filter, including that often-overlooked effect mentioned earlier. At top left, you can see how this plug-in's default parameters look when applied to the sample image. At top right, take a close look at the wonderful, almost cartoonlike appearance you get when the Highlight Area control is cranked up all the way to 20. I've applied this setting to dozens of images and get a different look every time.

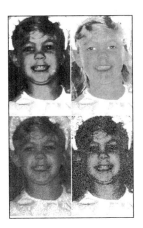

Figure 12.17 Film Grain fliter applied with defaults (upper left), Highlight Area 20 (upper right), Highlight Intensity 1 (lower left), and Highlight Intensity 10 (lower right).

Compare that sample with the image at lower left, in which highlight intensity is set to the minimum value, so that the grain is applied equally over highlight, shadow, and midtone areas. At lower right, the intensity is set at 10 (the maximum) so that the grain is applied more strongly in the highlight areas.

Fresco

Fresco is a technique in which watercolors are applied to wet plaster (*fresco* is Italian for fresh) and allowed to dry, forming a permanent image on the wall or other structure containing the plaster. If you're an artist and can work fast, fresco is a great way to produce murals.

Because the plaster is sticky and dries quickly, fresco images are distinguished by their short, jabby strokes. Gallery Effects' Fresco filter produces a similar look, using just three controls, which are shown in Figure 12.18.

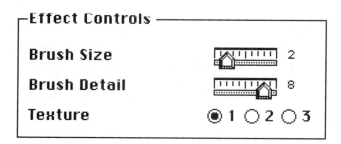

Figure 12.18 Fresco filter controls.

If these controls look familiar, that's because they are the same as those used with the Dry Brush filter discussed earlier in the chapter. Both filters add a posterization effect to your image, but Fresco lightens the highlights considerably and appears to be a little more smeared. Like Dry Brush, you can vary the brush size, amount of brush detail, and degree of texture applied to your image.

Figure 12.19 demonstrates some of the permutations you can expect when applying the Fresco filter to your image. At upper left is the image with default settings, while at upper right Brush Size has been set to 10, producing a grosser, more highly smeared image. At lower left, Brush Detail has been reduced to 1, and at lower right, Texture has been set to the maximum value of 3.

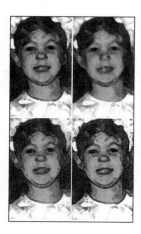

Figure 12.19 Fresco filter applied using defaults (upper left) Brush Size 10 (upper right), Brush Detail 1 (lower left), and Texture 3 (lower right).

Graphic Pen

The Graphic Pen filter obliterates the detail in your image with a series of monochrome strokes that can be applied in right or left diagonal directions as well as horizontally and vertically. It is tricky to use because it's easy to obscure all the detail in an image with overly enthusiastic stroking, lengthy strokes, or an unfortunate selection of light and dark balance. Figure 12.20 shows the controls available with this filter.

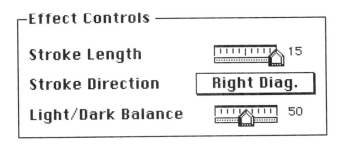

Figure 12.20 Graphic Pen filter controls.

Many users often overlook the fact that Graphic Pen applies its strokes in the foreground color, leaving the background color behind to fill in the rest of the image area. Therefore, only the details in an image actually stroked by the pen remain. If you use the default black/white foreground/background colors, you'll get a positive black and white image. If you reverse the two (white foreground, black background), you'll end up with a negative image. Some interesting effects can be produced by selecting complementary colors as foreground and background.

The Stroke Length slider controls how much detail is preserved. With the default settings (a Stroke Length at the maximum value of 15), as shown at upper left in Figure 12.21, the very long strokes break up an image into a high-contrast abstract sketch. Using shorter strokes, such as the Stroke Length of 4 used for the version at upper right, fills the screen with a hazier rendition. Adjust the Light/Dark Balance slider to select the areas of the image to which the strokes are applied: lighter settings sketch in the highlights, while darker settings use the shadow areas for the strokes.

If you don't like the right diagonal strokes applied as the default (they are a good compromise with images that have an equal mixture of horizontal and vertical components), you can change to vertical or horizontal strokes, as shown at lower left and lower right, respectively. Vertical strokes break up and show predominant horizontal lines well (say, a landscape), while horizontal strokes do the same thing for images with strong vertical strokes (such as a stand of pine trees).

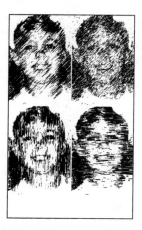

Figure 12.21 Graphic Pen filter applied using default settings (upper left), Stroke Length 4 (upper right), vertical strokes (lower left), and horizontal strokes (lower right).

Mosaic

True mosaic is an artistic process of creating pictures by inlaying small pieces of colored stone or glass in mortar. Gallery Effects' Mosaic filter, unlike the plug-in of the same name built into Photoshop, performs a fair imitation of the original technique. This filter creates irregularly shaped 3-D tiles from your image and embeds them in grout. You can vary the size of the tiles, the width of the grout, and the relative darkness of the grout, using the controls shown in Figure 12.22.

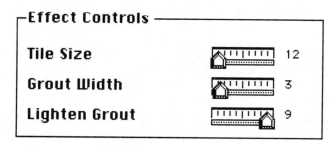

Figure 12.22 Mosaic filter controls.

In contrast, Photoshop's own Mosaic filter simply divides a photo into squares and averages the tones within those squares to produce a pixelated effect. The Gallery Effects version gives you a much more organic, human-made look with added control. Choose the photos you apply this effect to with care, since this is such a dramatic filter that it is easy for the medium to become the message, so to speak. Figure 12.23 shows some examples of different looks you can achieve. At upper left, the default settings produce medium-sized tiles with fairly wide grout. Increasing Tile Size to 32 retains more of the image detail but makes the picture look less like a true mosaic and more like a jigsaw puzzle. At lower left, Grout Width was expanded one notch to 4. You can see that making the grout much wider than that would reduce an image to a series of bumps. At lower right, the grout was darkened, generating a more abstract effect.

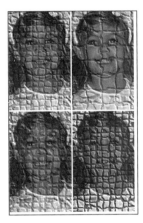

Figure 12.23 Mosaic filter applied with default settings (upper left), Tile Size 32 (upper right), Grout Width 4 (lower left), and Lighten Grout 2 (lower right).

Poster Edges

Poster edges is another classic filter that transforms your image into a poster in a clever way. It converts full-color or grayscale images into reduced color versions by combining similar colors into bands of a single hue. This is similar to the posterization effect built into all image editors (in Photoshop, use **Image:Map:Posterize**). Poster Edges goes a step further by outlining all the important edges in your image with black. In many cases, the finished photo looks as if it were an original drawing that was hand-colored in poster fashion.

Of course, the original nonelectronic poster effect was created to allow simulating continuous tone images without actually using detailed halftones. The broad bands of color could each be printed on a separate run through a sheet-fed press at a relatively low cost. Posters were often created in this way for circuses, plays, and, later, motion pictures. Even when halftoning was a common and inexpensive process, poster printing techniques were an economical way to produce very large posters on thick stocks.

Poster Edges gives you the three controls shown in Figure 12.24. You can adjust the relative thickness of the black lines used to outline the edges and specify their darkness or intensity. A third slider lets you specify the degree of posterization—that is, how many tones are used to produce the effect. Note that with this filter the value represents only a relative degree, not the actual number of tones used (which is the case with the Photoshop native Posterization effect).

The examples in Figure 12.25 show the Poster Edges filter at work using the default settings (upper left) and with heavier edges (upper right). You can see at lower left that increasing the edge intensity makes some "edges" that weren't very pronounced show up more clearly. At lower right, Posterization has been increased to 6, producing an image that is more like a drawing, with fewer poster tones.

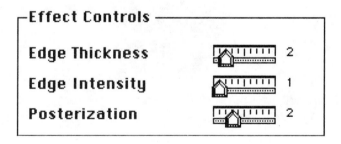

Figure 12.24 Poster Edges controls.

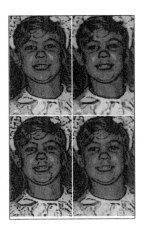

Figure 12.25 Poster Edges filter applied with default values (upper left), Edge Thickness 10 (upper right), Edge Intensity 10 (lower left), and Posterization 6 (lower right).

Ripple

It's hard to find a real-world equivalent for the effect produced by the Ripple filter. The default settings make images look as if you were viewing them through a glass block that has been distorted or melted. With other settings, the effects start to resemble water flowing over pebbles in a stream. You'll find that the Ripple filter can give you quite different looks depending on how you adjust the controls. Experimentation is fairly easy, since there are only two sliders to fiddle with, as shown in Figure 12.26.

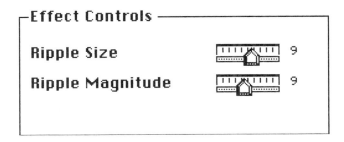

Figure 12.26 Ripple filter controls.

Talk about intuitive! It's almost an insult to your intelligence to explain what the two controls do: the Ripple Size slider adjusts the size of the ripples themselves, and the Ripple Magnitude control sets the amount of waviness in each ripple. Figure 12.27 shows, at left, medium-sized ripples of a medium magnitude, producing a glass-block effect. In the middle, the size of the ripples have been increased to 15, while at right, I set the magnitude to the maximum of 20, producing a shimmering water effect.

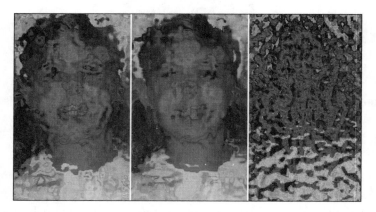

Figure 12.27 Ripple filter applied with default values (left), Ripple Size 15 (middle), and Ripple Magnitude 20 (right).

Smudge Stick

Smudge Stick is a hard filter to like, because most of the effects are so smudgy. But it does have at least one spectacular setting that I use a lot. The basic filter paints the image in strokes that blend dark areas into the lighter areas. As shown in Figure 12.28, you can control the stroke length, highlight area, and highlight intensity.

The examples in Figure 12.29 show the Smudge Stick filter applied with default values (upper left), a long Stroke Length of 10 (upper right), and an interesting variation generated when you move the Highlight Area slider up to the maximum value of 20 (lower left). The glowing image that results looks something like what you get with the Film Grain filter and the same Highlight Area setting. This use of the Smudge Stick filter is not one you would expect to get from casual experimentation. At lower right, the Highlight Intensity slider has been set to 1, producing a smudgy image with not a lot of character.

Figure 12.28 Smudge Stick controls.

Figure 12.29 Smudge Stick filter with default settings (upper left),
Stroke Length 10 (upper right), Highlight Area 20 (lower left),
and Highlight Intensity 1 (lower right).

Spatter

The Spatter filter is another easy-to-use painterly effect that reproduces a look that would be generated if an airbrush could spatter out different color hues. Although you can use the effect to soften portrait or landscape subjects, it also makes a great tool for creating endless abstract backgrounds. The only controls you have to worry about are shown in Figure 12.30.

The Spray Radius slider adjusts the number of pixels covered by the sputtering spray emitted by your imaginary airbrush. The Smoothness control modifies the evenness of the effect. I use this filter to produce background textures. Try these tricks.

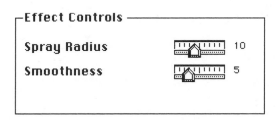

Figure 12.30 Spatter filter controls.

- Select only the background of an image and spatter it a few times to transform a busy background into an interesting abstract painted backdrop.

- Set Spray Radius on maximum and Smoothness to minimum; then apply the filter to a radial or linear gradient fill.

- Select a portion of your subject, copy to a new layer, spatter, and then merge with the original layer using different opacity settings. This filter works well even in small doses.

Figure 12.31 shows several variations of the Spatter filter. Default settings are used at left. The center example used a Spray Radius of 25, while at right, with Smoothness set to 15, the spatter effects are minimal.

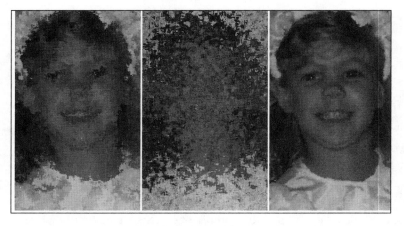

Figure 12.31 Spatter filter applied using default settings (left),
Spray Radius 25 (center), and Smoothness 15 (right).

Watercolor

Watercolors produce their distinctive pastel effect because the pigments that dissolve in water are typically not as strong or opaque as those that can be carried in oil or acrylic paints. In addition, watercolors tend to soak into the paper, carrying bits of color outside the original strokes as the water spreads. The Watercolor filter offers the same soft, diffused effect with a bit more control for the electronic artist. It's a good plug-in for landscapes, female portrait subjects, or any image that can be improved with a soft look.

Figure 12.32 shows the controls available with this filter.

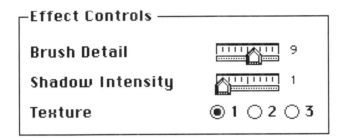

Figure 12.32 Watercolor controls.

You can specify the amount of brush detail but will find that the blending effect of this filter doesn't work well with small, detailed strokes. Use higher values to get broad strokes that show off the pastels and blended colors. At the same time, you'll often want to use low Shadow Intensity settings to avoid an overly contrasty look. Any of three levels of texture can also be applied.

Figure 12.33 shows examples of the Watercolor filter applied with default settings (upper left), Brush Detail reduced to a value of 1 (upper right), Shadow Intensity increased to 9 (I told you that neither of these extremes were a good idea!), and a texture setting of 3.

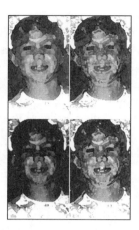

Figure 12.33 Watercolor filter with default settings (upper left), Brush Detail 1 (upper right), Shadow Intensity 9 (lower left), and Texture 3 (lower right).

Volume 2 Filters

Gallery Effects:Classic Art Volume 2 filters include a mixture of traditional artistic techniques like colored pencil and rough pastels with some more modern and nontraditional approaches, such as photocopy- and rubber-stamp-like effects. Several of the very best effects on the market are included in this package, so if you purchased Volume 1 to get some basic workhorses, treat yourself to this set for some spectacular special looks you can't get with any other filter package.

Accented Edges

The Accented Edges filter works a little like the Find Edges filter, but you have extra control over the width, smoothness, and brightness of the edges located in your image. You'll rarely use this filter all by itself. A better plan is to emphasize the edges in an image and then apply another filter to add the brushlike effects, grain, or other special effect you want. In this mode, Accented Edges provides the extra edge detail you need to keep your original image from being overcome by the second plug-in.

The controls available are shown in Figure 12.34.

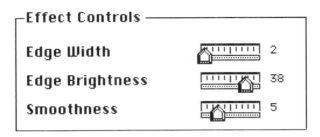

Figure 12.34 Accented Edges controls.

These controls are all fairly self-explanatory. Edge Width adjusts the relative width of the edges, Edge Brightness controls whether the edges are stroked in a dark or light tone, and Smoothness determines how closely the edges follow the actual edges in the image. Higher settings produce more gradual transitions from one angle to the next.

Figure 12.35 shows four examples of images generated with various settings. At upper left the default settings produce a contrasty, edge-enhanced view. The version at upper right has had Edge Brightness reduced to 13, while at lower left the edges have become very wide. At lower right, Smoothness was set to 10, producing a soft image that you might want to merge with a copy of the original, using various opacity settings.

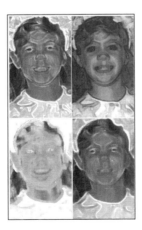

Figure 12.35 Accented Edges filter applied with default values
(upper left), Edge Brightness 13 (upper right), Edge Width 10
(lower left), and Smoothness 10 (lower right).

Angled Strokes

Angled Strokes is another filter that must be used with care because it produces such strong effects. Angled Strokes paints your image using diagonal strokes in one direction for the dark tones and diagonal strokes going in the other direction to represent the light tones in an image. The controls for this filter are shown in Figure 12.36.

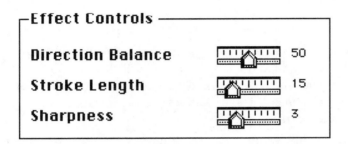

Figure 12.36 Angled Strokes controls.

The Direction Balance is a key control. Slide it to the right to shift the emphasis toward the right-angled strokes; move to the left to emphasize the left-angled strokes. If you want to watch this control at work in its most dramatic mode, change the Stroke Length slider to the maximum (50) and the Sharpness control to 10. Your entire image will be rendered in left and right strokes that you can see clearly. Adjust Direction Balance to see the different effects you can achieve.

With high-resolution files, the effects may not be as noticeable unless you either reduce the size of the image to 25–50% of its original size before applying the filter (scale it back up when you're finished) or use a high Sharpness setting. This filter can be applied to primary subjects but also makes a good tool for creating artsy background textures. Figure 12.37 shows four sample images made using the default values (upper left), Direction Balance set at 10 (upper right), Stroke Length shortened to 10 (lower left), and Sharpness increased to 10 (lower right).

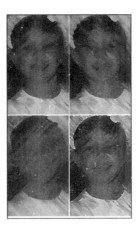

Figure 12.37 Angled Strokes applied using default settings (upper left), Direction Balance 10 (upper right), Stroke Length 10 (lower left), and sharpness 10 (lower right).

Bas Relief

The Bas Relief filter provides a quite different effect from the Emboss plug-in found in Volume 1. Bas Relief makes the image appear to have been carved from stone, a look you can enhance by applying a sandstone texture to the selection using the Texturizer filter discussed later in this chapter. Another great effect can be applied using the texture option in the Lighting Effects filter, covered in the first section of this book.

The colors in your image are lost, because the current foreground and background colors are used to create your carving. As a result, this is one filter that works just as well with grayscale images as it does with color. If you want to retain hues, use the Emboss filter, instead.

You can adjust the amount of detail retained from your original image, the position of the apparent light source used to illuminate the resulting 3-D image, and the smoothness of the surface, using the controls shown in Figure 12.38.

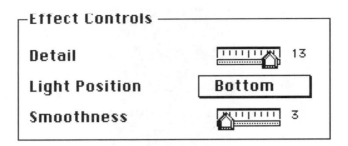

Figure 12.38 Bas Relief controls.

When experimenting with this filter, don't forget the psychology of lighting: humans expect objects to be lit from above and usually from one side or the other. You'll get the most realistic raised effects if you position the light source at top, top left, or top right. Move the light underneath, and you'll get anything from a "horror" effect to a reversal of the 3-D look—your image may appear to be depressed into the surface rather than raised above it. Figure 12.39 dramatically shows the effects of this filter. At left, the default settings have been applied. In the center, most of the detail from the original photo has been removed by setting the Detail slider to a value of 2. At right, a Smoothness setting of 15 was used.

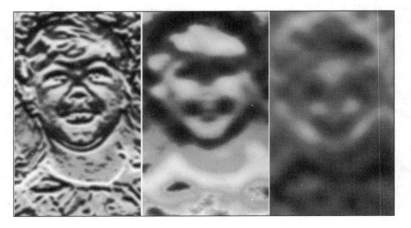

Figure 12.39 Bas Relief filter applied with default settings (left), Detail 2 (center), and Smoothness 15 (right).

Colored Pencil

If you remember the Venus Paradise colored pencil sets—essentially paint-by-numbers kits for those who could not handle damp pigments—you'll soon discover that this filter is nothing like what you remembered. Instead, Colored Pencil redraws your image, using the image's own colors, in a pencil like effect.

The strokes are applied in a crosshatch fashion to delineate the edges of your image, while the current background color is allowed to show through the less detailed portions of your image, as if it were the paper on which the drawing was made. You have the three controls shown in Figure 12.40.

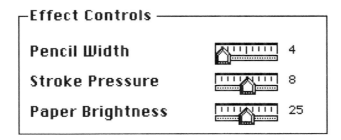

Figure 12.40 Colored Pencil controls.

The Pencil Width slider adjusts the broadness of the strokes, while Stroke Pressure modifies their intensity. Paper Brightness determines how strongly the background color shows through smooth details in your image. This is a tricky filter to use, but I've found that using the brightness/contrast controls to increase contrast once the filter has been applied can approve the appearance dramatically.

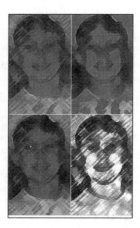

Figure 12.41 Colored Pencil filter applied with default values (upper left), Pencil Width 24 (upper right), Stroke Pressure 15 (lower left), and Paper Brightness 50 (lower right).

Diffuse Glow

You'll love the Diffuse Glow filter. It's my absolute, hands-down favorite filter from among this group. Diffuse Glow can produce in any image a radiant luminescence, which seems to suffuse from the subject and fill the picture with a wonderful lustre. At the same time, this plug-in softens harsh details. It's great for romantic portraits or for lending a fantasy air to landscapes. Diffuse Glow works equally well with color and black-and-white images.

This is a particularly easy filter to use. Almost any combination of settings, including the defaults, look good. But to get the most from Diffuse Glow, you'll want to master its simple controls, shown in Figure 12.42.

To get the most from this filter, play with the controls as follows to understand their effects.

- The Graininess slider adds or reduces the amount of grain applied to an image. A large amount obscures unwanted detail and adds to the dreamy look of the image.

- The Glow Amount control adjusts the strength of the glow, as if you were turning up the voltage on a light source. The higher the setting, the more glow spread throughout your picture.

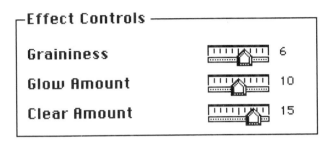

Figure 12.42 Diffuse Glow controls.

- The Clear Amount slider controls the size of the area in the image that is not affected by the glow. You can use this control with the Glow Amount slider to simultaneously specify how strong a glow effect is produced as well as how much of the image is illuminated by it.

- The current background color becomes the color of the glow. That's an important point. Beginners sometimes forget this and then wonder why their glow effect looks weird. If you want a glowing white effect, make sure the background color is white. Anything else will tint your image. You can use this feature to good advantage by selecting background colors with a very slight tint of yellow, gold, or red to add a sunny or warm glow to your image.

Figure 12.43 shows several examples with the filter applied using the defaults (upper left), with a Graininess setting of 10 (upper right), with Glow Amount pumped up to 15 (lower left), and with Clear Amount reduced to 7, so that the glow spreads to a larger area.

Figure 12.43 Diffuse Glow filter applied using defaults (upper left),
Graininess 10 (upper right), Glow Amount 15 (lower left),
and Clear 7 (lower right).

Glowing Edges

Glowing Edges adds wild colors to the edges of your image, producing a strange, abstract masklike effect that you can enhance further by inverting the image, increasing the brightness and contrast, and applying other tweaks. This filter is similar to the Find Edges plug-in, but with a great deal more control over the results. You can easily spend a couple days playing with the different abstract effects possible with Glowing Edges. None of the images will look realistic, but they'll all be interesting!

The controls at your command, shown in Figure 12.44, are the same as with Accented Edges, which operates in a similar manner, but without reversing the tones of your image.

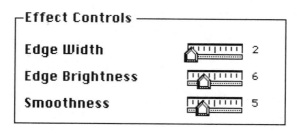

Figure 12.44 Glowing Edges controls.

Edge Width adjusts the relative width of the edges, Edge Brightness controls whether the edges are stroked in a dark or light tone, and Smoothness determines how closely the edges follow the actual edges in the image. Figure 12.45 shows four examples of images generated with various settings. At upper left, the default settings produce a contrasty, edge-enhanced view. The version at upper right has had Edge Width increased to 14, a much higher value than you'll realistically need.

At lower left Edge Brightness was raised 20, while at lower right, Smoothness was set to 20, producing a soft, ghost like image.

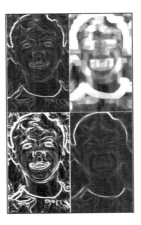

Figure 12.45 Glowing Edges filter applied using defaults (upper left), Edge Width 14 (upper right), Edge Brightness 20 (lower left), and Smoothness 15 (lower right).

Grain

Do we really need another grain filter, when Volume 1 of Gallery Effects already provides a Film Grain effect? Absolutely! This version is quite different, having the added option of 10 different varieties of grain. Although you could argue in favor of having all the Adobe grain effects combined in a single filter, I don't mind having these choices spread among two plug-ins.

While the Film Grain filter lets you adjust the amount of grain and how the granules are applied to highlights, the Grain plug-in works with contrast (the darkness of the grain in relation to the image area surrounding it) plus the shape of the granules. You can also control how much grain is added, using the adjustments shown in Figure 12.46.

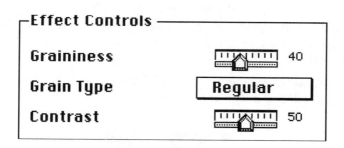

Figure 12.46 Grain filter controls.

I use this filter quite a bit. When I'm combining image elements from two different photographs, I often find that the images don't match in several important ways. The electronic paste-up job is as obvious as a sore thumb. The Grain filter makes it possible to match the grain characteristics of two image components. With the pasted-in object still selected, I adjust the graininess and contrast controls until the object matches the background as closely as possible.

The 10 available types of grain cover several varieties often seen in photographs, plus some new ones that offer imaginative artistic effects. You can choose from Regular, Soft, Sprinkles, Clumped, Contrasty, Enlarged, Stippled, Horizontal, Vertical, or Speckle grain patterns. You may have to examine the results to see the difference between, say, Clumped and Speckle. The Stippled effect uses foreground and background colors, while Sprinkle uses just the foreground color.

Figure 12.47 offers six examples of different grain effects, using the defaults (upper left), a super-grainy setting of 90 (upper center), Sprinkles (upper right), Stippled (lower left), Horizontal (lower center), and Contrast increased to 100 (lower right).

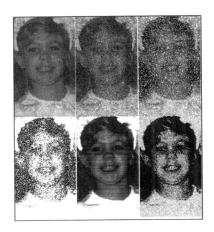

Figure 12.47 Grain filter applied using defaults (upper left), Graininess 90 (upper center), Sprinkled grain (upper right), Stippled grain (lower left), Horizontal grain (lower center), and Contrast 100 (lower right).

Note Paper

Note Paper is a cool plug-in if you know how to make it work! If you tried the Note Paper filter before (it's available as a try-out "freebie" on the CD-ROM bundled with this book to induce you to purchase Gallery Effects) and had no luck, I'll let you in on its secret in a moment.

This filter creates the look of embossed paper, but with a flatter image than you get with Emboss or Bas Relief. It really does look as if the image were created out of paper. There are three controls at your disposal: Image Balance, Graininess, and Relief, as shown in Figure 12.48. This plug-in changes your color or grayscale image into a high-contrast black-and-white image (if you're using the default black/white colors) or into an image using another color pair. Experiment with color combinations to get the best effect.

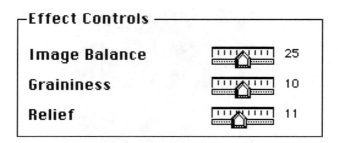

Figure 12.48 Note Paper controls.

The key to using Note Paper is the Image Balance slider. Very small changes with this control dramatically modify how much of your image appears embossed. Figure 12.49 shows the test image with the default settings applied (upper left). Not too many details of the original appear. However, by adjusting the Image Balance control carefully (using Preview to see what the image looks like), you can adjust the contrast to provide a recognizable image, as in upper right. I used a value of 16 in this case—believe it or not, 20 was way too much and 14 was not nearly enough—but you'll need to juggle the controls to find the exact setting that provides the best image.

Figure 12.49 Note Paper filter applied using default settings (upper left), Image Balance 16 (upper right), Graininess 20 (lower left), and Relief 25 (lower right).

You can also increase the amount of grain in the image (I doubled it to 20 at lower left) or adjust the degree of relief applied. When Graininess is set to zero, a useful carved-from-plastic look results. You can also take an image given the no-grain treatment and apply a texture of your choice using the Texturizer filter.

Palette Knife

If you take the knife that artists use to apply paints to their palette and paint with it, you'll end up with a highly abstract image composed of irregular globs of pigment. That's the effect you get with the Palette Knife filter. The controls are shown in Figure 12.50.

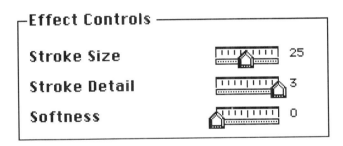

Figure 12.50 Palette Knife controls.

The Stroke Size slider adjusts the size of the "knife" you're using, while the Stroke Detail control can be used to specify how much of the detail in your original image is retained. The Softness control increases or decreases the roughness of the edges of the palette strokes.

Although you can use this filter alone, it works well with other plug-ins, either as a first step to reduce the amount of detail before you apply a second filter, such as Watercolor or Grain. Textures, particularly Canvas, can add to the painterly effect of this filter. Figure 12.51 shows four examples of images processed with Palette Knife. At upper left is a sample using the default settings; at upper right, Stroke Size was decreased to 6. At lower left, extra detail was added by using a Stroke Detail setting of 1. At lower right, a Softness setting of 10 blurred the image dramatically.

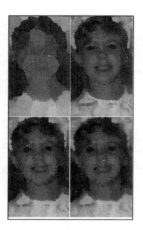

Figure 12.51 Palette Knife filter applied with default settings (upper left), Stroke Size 6 (upper right), Detail 1 (lower left), and Softness 10 (lower right).

Photocopy

Return with us now to those thrilling days of yesteryear, when photocopiers produced washed out, high-contrast images of any photograph you deigned to submit to the xerographic process. Since low-tech has become chic again (witness all the broken "typewriter" fonts in the trendier magazines), even this high-tech way of achieving the photocopy look can be useful. Your desktop publications will take on a casual air when you make all your photographs appear as if you had to copy them on an old Xerox machine. All the black tones in your image will be outlined, while midtones will turn either black or white, depending on how you have the Darkness slider set. You can also adjust the amount of detail in the processed image, using the other control shown in Figure 12.52.

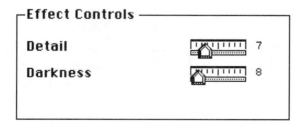

Figure 12.52 Photocopy filter controls.

For several effects you can't achieve with any other filter, try these tricks.

- Split a 24-bit color image into red, green, and blue channels, then apply Photocopy to each channel separately, using different Darkness settings. Merge the three channels to achieve a great cartoon effect.

- Apply other filters, such as Diffuse Glow or Grain to the separated channels before re-combining them. I found you can use a different filter with each channel to create some outrageous effects.

- Use different foreground and background colors. If your foreground color is lighter than the background color, Photocopy produces a "negative" image.

Figure 12.53 shows samples with the Photocopy filter applied using default values (left), Detail 24 (center), and Darkness 50 (right).

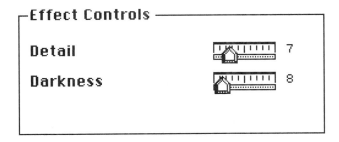

Figure 12.53 Photocopy filer applied using defaults (left), Detail 24 (center), and Darkness 50 (right).

Rough Pastels

The Rough Pastels filter transforms your image into a rough chalk drawing, using the default canvas texture as a background, or an alternate texture, such as brick, burlap, sandstone, or your own PICT file. The least amount of texture is applied to the brightest areas, while darker areas take on more of the underlying texture. You can picture how this filter works by imagining a canvas with chalk applied: the thicker the chalk, the less of the canvas texture shows through.

Figure 12.54 shows the controls at your disposal. You can specify stroke length, the amount of stroke detail, and a specific texture to be used.

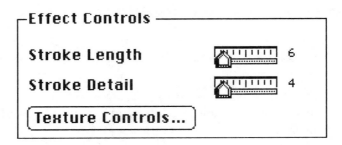

Figure 12.54 Rough Pastels controls.

You may find that this filter modifies your image too strongly and prefer to apply it to a duplicate layer and then merge with the original using some opacity value less than 100%. As you can see in Figure 12.55, the unadulterated filter is strong medicine. At upper left, I used the default settings; at upper right, the Stroke Length setting was set to 24. At bottom left, Stroke Detail was increased to 20, and Relief (available in the Texture Controls dialog box) was bumped up to 50 at lower right.

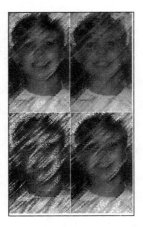

Figure 12.55 Rough Pastels filter applied with default values (upper left), Stroke Length 24 (upper right), Stroke Detail 20 (lower left), and Relief 50 (lower right).

Sprayed Strokes

The Sprayed Strokes filter uses angled, sprayed strokes of wet paint. You can adjust the stroke length, direction, and radius of the spray emitted, using the controls shown in Figure 12.56.

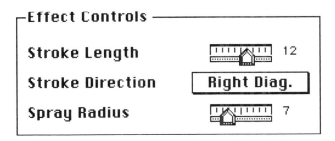

Figure 12.56 Sprayed Strokes controls.

This is a good filter to use to create painterly images and artsy backgrounds or to add a painted effect to pictures that have been processed with other filters. You can see the effects available in Figure 12.57, which shows four samples with the filter applied using the default setting (upper left), Stroke Length of 20 (upper right), vertical strokes (lower left), and an outrageously wide Spray Radius of 18 (lower right).

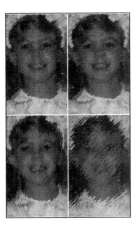

Figure 12.57 Sprayed Strokes applied with default settings
(upper left), Stroke Length 20 (upper right), vertical strokes
(lower left), and Spray Radius 18 (lower right).

Stamp

The Stamp filter recreates the effects you get with rubber or wooden stamps. Artists and artisans have often produced interesting, repeatable patterns by carving an image in a block of wood or in a piece of rubber or linoleum glued to a block of wood. Since world supplies of linoleum dried up when all the linoleum mines in Macronesia were closed down, the electronic equivalent provided by the Stamp filter has been the closest we can get to the original effect.

The controls used by the Stamp filter are shown in Figure 12.58.

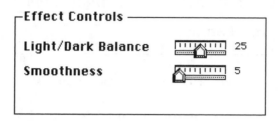

Figure 12.58 Stamp controls.

You can adjust Light/Dark Balance and should do so carefully to ensure that the important outlines of your image are represented in your finished stamp. The Smoothness control can adjust how rough the stamp's outlines appear. This filter uses the foreground and background colors you've selected, transforming your photo into a two-tone, stencil like image.

In Figure 12.59, I applied the default settings at left and then adjusted the Light/Dark control for the center image, so that the facial features showed up better. Smoothing, as shown at right, blurs the image and makes it look even more abstract.

Figure 12.59 Stamp filter applied using defaults (left), Light/Dark Balance 3 (center), and smoothness 24 (right).

Texturizer

The Texturizer filter should be one of your basic tools for applying textures to images or selections, but by no means should you make it your only surface-modifying tool. Most of what you can do with Texturizer you can also accomplish by loading a texture into a separate layer, but this filter is fast, highly automated, and already includes basic textures that will satisfy most of your needs.

The Texturizer controls are shown in Figure 12.60. You can select from the type of texture to be applied, using a drop-down list. Brick, Burlap, Canvas, and Sandstone are supplied, and these are suitable for a remarkable number of different images. However, you can also work with any PICT file you have. You can create custom textures by scanning common household objects and surfaces. Don't worry too much about the size of the custom texture: if the image is too small to texturize your entire selection, it will be automatically tiled. Don't try to get away with too small of a texture file, however: tiny tiled images can add a repeating pattern to your image that you probably won't like.

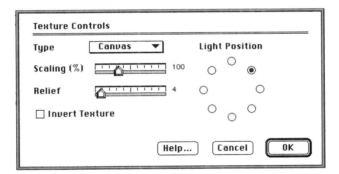

Figure 12.60 Texturizer controls.

If your texture is fairly abstract, but still too small to avoid repeating patterns during tiling, you can "enlarge" the texture using the Clone tool. Place the textured area that you do have into a larger, empty image (or use Photoshop's **Image:Canvas Size**.) Then clone portions of the original texture to fill up the new, larger window. Select a new origin point frequently so that your final texture itself won't have repeating patterns and save this texture as a PICT file for use with Texturizer.

You can also use any custom texture PICT files with the Rough Pastels filter already covered or the Underpainting, Conté Crayon, and Glass filters described later in this chapter.

Textures are applied more strongly in those areas of your image where the brightness changes, so the results are not identical to what you'd get if you merged your image with another layer containing the texture. You can choose a light position for the imaginary light source used to produce the 3-D texture's raised effect. Select a position at right angles to the "grain" of your texture, rather than parallel to it, in order to accentuate the 3-D look.

The scaling control specifies how large the texture is compared to the original image, and you can also set the amount of relief—the degree the texture is raised from the surface of the image. The texture can be inverted if you like.

When Not To Use Texturizer

Although the Texturizer filter is convenient, you'll find that there are many times when you should use other techniques to apply textures to images. In those cases, you should load a texture into a separate layer and then combine that layer with the background image using opacity settings to control how much of the texture will appear in the finished selection. For example, the Texturizer filter does not work well in the following situations.

- When you want to use multicolored textures, such as marble, rich woods, or other surfaces, Texturizer ignores the color information in your texture and applies only the grayscale data.

- Textures applied in layers can be attenuated by using layer masks. You could load a texture and mask out portions of it using a radial or linear gradation as a layer mask, so that the texture is applied more strongly to some areas of the image when you flatten the layers.

Figure 12.61 shows some examples of the Texturizer, applied using the default texture, (a good canvas like surface) and Brick.

Figure 12.61 Texturizer applied using default texture (Canvas) at left and Brick texture at right.

Underpainting

The Underpainting filter produces the effect you might get if you texturized an image in one layer and then combined it with an unaltered version of the same image in a layer applied on top of the first. It's otherwise similar to the Texturizer filter, but with the addition of Brush Size and Texture Coverage controls, as shown in Figure 12.62.

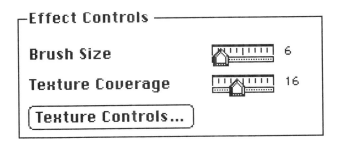

Figure 12.62 Underpainting controls.

Figure 12.63 shows three examples of images texturized with this filter. At left, the default settings were used. In the center, Brush Size was increased to 16, and a Texture Coverage setting of 16 was used at right.

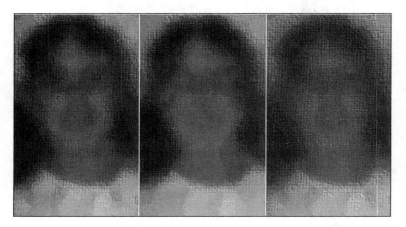

Figure 12.63 Underpainting filter applied using default settings (left), Brush Size 16 (center), and Texture Coverage 16 (right).

Volume 3 Filters

Aldus, which created these filters before the merger with Adobe, certainly wasn't scraping the bottom of the barrel when it came up with this final set of 16 filters. You'll find the usual mix of artistic effects like Conté Crayon or Paint Daubs, combined with photographic effects like Halftone Screen and more modern tricks like Plastic Wrap.

Conté Crayon

Georges Seurat supposedly developed the soft, smudgy, atmospheric effects that made Conté Crayon popular in the 19th century. The Gallery Effects version gives you deeply rendered dark tones, textured midtones, and clean whites. These crayons are commonly available in different colors, from black to sepia, and you can use the foreground and background colors of your application to control the hues to simulate actual commercial crayons. The original colors of your image are lost. This is a combination texturizing/painting filter, as you can see from the controls in Figure 12.64.

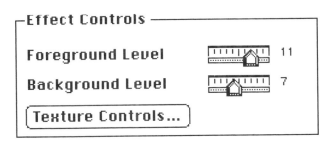

Figure 12.64 Conté Crayon controls.

The Foreground and Background Level controls can be used to adjust the amount of the foreground and background colors, respectively, used in the image. You may have to fiddle with these to find the right combination to represent your image without overpowering it. In addition, you can apply a texture using the standard controls already discussed for the Texturizer filter. Figure 12.65 shows two examples using the default canvas texture, with Foreground Level set to 11 and Background Level set to 7 at left, and Foreground Level set to 2 and Background Level set to 15 at right.

Figure 12.65 Conté Crayon filter using the default settings (left)
and Foreground Level 2 and Background Level 15 (right).

Crosshatch

Crosshatch adds a cross pattern of pencil like strokes to your image, adding texture without destroying all the original colors and detail of the original. It's a good arty effect with an unusual degree of control. Not only can you specify the stroke length and sharpness, but you can also specify the number of times in succession the filter is applied. The more repetitions, the stronger the effect. Figure 12.66 shows the controls for this filter.

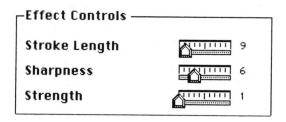

Figure 12.66 Crosshatch controls.

Figure 12.67 provides a few examples of the different looks you can achieve, applying the filter using the default settings (upper left), a Stroke Length of 24 (upper right), a Sharpness setting of 20 (lower left), and three iterations of the filter (lower right).

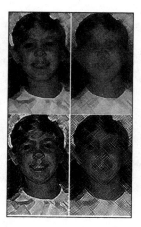

Figure 12.67 Crosshatch filter applied using defaults (upper left),
Stroke Length 24 (upper right), Sharpness 20 (lower left), and
Strength 3 (lower right).

Cutout

The Cutout filter is an unusual posterizing technique in which the image shapes are seemingly built up from similarly colored cutouts of paper. Adobe notes that you can combine this filter with Emboss, discussed earlier in this chapter, to make the shapes look as if they were actually cut out of paper.

Figure 12.68 shows the controls available with the Cutout filter.

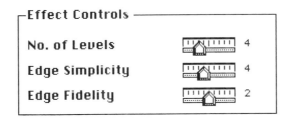

Figure 12.68 Cutout controls.

The Number of Levels control specifies the number of tones used to posterize the image. Edge Simplicity controls the complexity of the cutout shapes, while Edge Fidelity adjusts how well the shapes match the actual outlines of the underlying image. Figure 12.69 shows three examples, using the default settings (left), eight different levels (center), and Edge Simplicity Setting of 1.

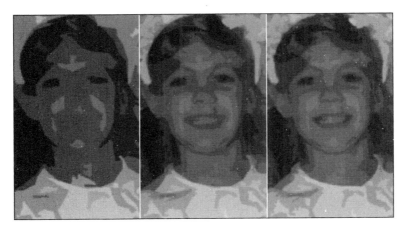

Figure 12.69 Cutout filter applied using defaults (left),
No. of levels 8 (center), and Edge Simplicity 1 (right).

Glass

This is a multipurpose filter that you can use to produce glass-block effects, warping, watery ripples, and dozens of other looks. The flexibility comes from the multitude of combinations you can achieve using just five different controls, shown in Figure 12.70.

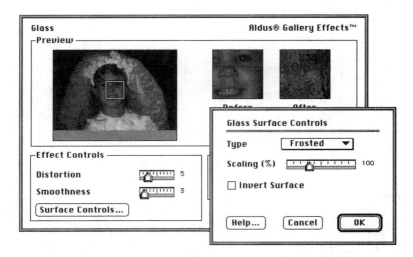

Figure 12.70 Glass filter controls.

You can specify the amount of distortion (choose a high number for some wild effects) and smoothness of the glass. A separate Surface Controls dialog box allows you to choose from glass blocks, frosted glass, tiny glass lenses (to recreate a fly's eye-view), and even canvas. You can also apply a PICT file texture of your choice to the image.

For images with individual features (e.g., tiny lens), you can select a scaling to control the relative size of the image and the underlying texture. The texture can be inverted, too. Figure 12.71 shows six examples, each very different from the last. At upper left is the standard rippled glass effect you get from the default settings. At upper center, I moved the Distortion slider all the way up to 15 to produce a highly distorted, abstract image. A great deal of distortion also results from setting the Smoothness control to 20 (upper right). In the bottom row, I applied different textures, ranging from glass block (lower left) and tiny lens (lower center) to canvas (lower right).

Figure 12.71 Examples of Glass filter.

Halftone Screen

The Halftone Screen is a versatile effect, changing your image into a black-and-white halftone screen and replacing all the original colors with shades of gray—or another set of colors, since Halftone Screen uses your application's current foreground and background colors. Only the three controls shown in Figure 12.72 are required.

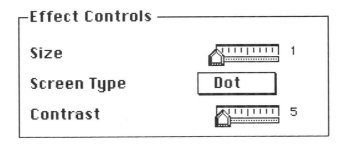

Figure 12.72 Halftone Screen controls.

All these settings are simple enough to understand. The Size slider controls the size of the halftone dots used. These are fake dots, composed as they are of grayscale pixels rather than hard-edge, single-tone pixels as you'll find in a digital image. You can select the type of screen, from dot, line, and circle, and adjust the contrast of your image as the filter is applied.

Figure 12.73 shows several examples of images processed with this filter. At upper left, I used the default settings, generating a simple halftone effect. Enlarging the dot size only a little—to a value of 2—produces a more pronounced halftone look. You'll find that, except for high-resolution images, any dot size larger than 5 or 6 will be too gross for anything other than highly stylized effects. At lower left and right you'll find the same image processed with circle and line dot types, respectively.

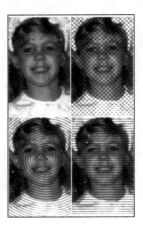

Figure 12.73 Halftone Screen filter applied using default settings (upper left), Size 2 (upper right), Circle Dot pattern (lower left), and Line Dot patterns (lower right).

Ink Outlines

Adobe calls Ink Outlines a "corroded" ink drawing. It produces an image with the outlines and edges enhanced, but without losing the original colors. You can use it to create a cartoon like appearance or combine it with other filters to generate a more painterly effect.

The controls are shown in Figure 12.74. You can adjust the length of the strokes, dark intensity, and light intensity. Moving the Light Intensity control all the way to the right can produce an especially interesting effect.

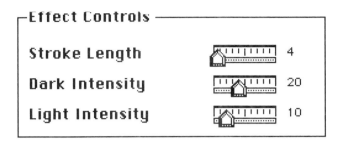

Figure 12.74 Ink Outlines controls.

See for yourself in the samples shown in Figure 12.75. At upper left, I used the default settings. A Stroke Length Setting of 25 (upper right) produces more pronounced lines, while a somber effect is generated when you set a high Dark Intensity, as I did at lower left. A pumped-up Light Intensity provides the glowing effect shown in lower right.

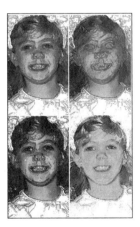

Figure 12.75 Ink Outlines applied using default settings
(upper left), Stroke Length 25 (upper right), Dark Intensity 24
(lower left), and Light Intensity 36 (lower right).

Neon Glow

Neon Glow is similar to the Diffuse Glow filter discussed earlier in this chapter, except that the grainy diffusion is replaced by a colored glowing effect. It makes the object appear as if it were radiating light of the color you select (the default is blue, but you can choose any color using a pop-up picker). The effect doesn't work too well with humans, but it looks great with text or other objects. The controls are shown in Figure 12.76.

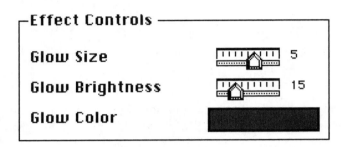

Figure 12.76 Neon Glow controls.

These controls work a little differently from those you may be used to. The Glow Size slider has both positive and negative values (from 0 to +24 or –24) with the center as the zero point. Positive values set the glow to the outside of dark objects and the inside of light objects, while negative values do the reverse. The higher the number, the larger the glow.

The Glow Brightness control modifies the luminance of the glow. A preview box shows the current glow color. Click on it to pop up a color picker you can use to select another glow color. The current foreground and background color are also used: this filter gives you a two-color image with a third hue used for the glow. Although black-and-white illustrations don't do justice to this filter (check out the original examples on the CD-ROM), Figure 12.77 shows how the glow affects your image using the default settings, Glow Size 24, and Glow Brightness 36.

Figure 12.77   Neon Glow filter applied using defaults (left), Glow Size 24 (center), and Glow Brightness 36 (right).

Paint Daubs

Yes, Paint Daubs is another brush strokes filter! It offers six different brush types, a selection of brush sizes, and some sharpness controls, as shown in Figure 12.78.

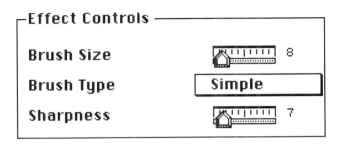

Figure 12.78 Paint Daubs controls.

You can choose from Simple, Light Rough, Dark Rough, Wide Sharp, Wide Blurry, or Sparkle Brush types. Figure 12.79 offers examples using the default settings (upper left), a Brush Size of 3 (upper right), Sharpness of 4 (lower left), and a typical brush—Light Rough (lower right).

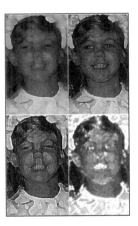

Figure 12.79 Paint Daubs filter applied using default settings (upper left), Brush Size 3 (upper right), Sharpness 4 (lower left), and Light Rough brush (lower right).

Plaster

I'm not sure that the Plaster filter really gives you a plaster look, but it certainly does produce an outrageous and useful 3-D effect. In some cases, your images will take on a molten plastic look, while in others you'll see more of a sunken effect.

Dark areas of the image are raised, while light areas are flattened or sunk into depressions. The foreground and background colors of the application are used to transform your image. You can work with three different controls, shown in Figure 12.80, which operate much like their counterparts in the Bas Relief filter.

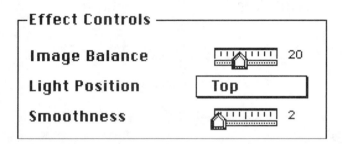

Figure 12.80 Plaster controls.

The Image Balance slider is important, since you can use it to control how much of the important detail in your original image shows up. You'll find that even small adjustments can make a dramatic difference. Select a Light Position and Smoothness value to fine-tune your image. The three examples shown in Figure 12.81 provide a good representation of this filter's effects using the default settings (left), light source moved to the bottom (center), and Smoothness set to 10 (right).

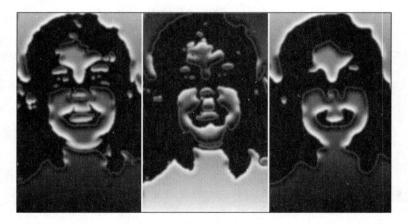

Figure 12.81 Plaster filter applied using default settings (left); Light Position Bottom (center), and Smoothness 10 (right).

Plastic Wrap

You'll love this filter! It provides an amazingly true representation of a subject image wrapped in bright plastic. If you ever need a shrink-wrapped subject, this is the filter that can provide it for you.

Actually, Plastic Wrap works much like the Chrome filter included with Volume 1. If you apply Chrome to an image and then merge that image with a copy of the original using various opacity settings, you can duplicate the plastic wrap look quite closely. This filter lets you do the same thing in a single step, with some useful controls to modify your image. The three sliders are shown in Figure 12.82.

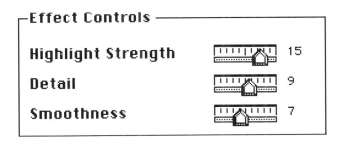

Figure 12.82 Plastic Wrap controls.

The Highlight Strength control changes how the glowing plastic reflections at the edges of certain details are represented. In Figure 12.83 the illustration at upper left was created using the default settings, which includes a Highlight Strength of 15. At upper right, Highlight Strength was increased to 20. The Detail slider controls how "clingy" the plastic wrap will be to the subject. At lower left, the Detail setting was increased to 15. At lower right, Smoothness was more than doubled, to a value of 15.

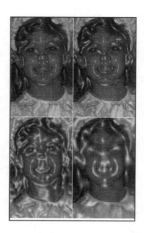

Figure 12.83 Plastic Wrap applied using defaults (upper left),
Highlight Strength 20 (upper right), Detail 15 (lower left),
and Smoothness 15 (lower right).

Reticulation

Reticulation is an old photographic effect. As you may know, photographic film consists of a silver-rich photosensitive gelatin coated on a plastic or acetate base material. If you happen to change the temperature of the film rapidly during development, when the gelatin is soft, it can "wrinkle," producing the effect duplicated by this filter.

Reticulation was originally an undesirable effect, until photographers discovered that it added an interesting texture to their images. Even so, it was a drastic step, since the process abused original camera negatives in a way that couldn't be reversed, and it was unpredictable to boot. The first few times I tried it, I managed to boil the emulsion right off the film and ended up with a sticky mess rather than a cool picture.

The Adobe **Help** button for this filter says that reticulation is produced when "film emulsion shrinks and distorts" in a controlled fashion. While experimentation can help you predict roughly what will happen when you mistreat your film in this way, I can assure you that it's not that well controlled. This filter lets you play with the effect safely, and reversibly. Figure 12.84 shows you the controls that digital image workers do have.

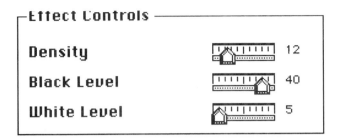

Figure 12.84 Reticulation controls.

You can adjust the density of the light grains and the amount of both black and white levels. Figure 12.85 shows four examples of reticulation applied using default settings (upper left), a Density setting of 40 (upper right), a Black Level setting of 14 (lower left), and a White Level setting of 40 (lower right).

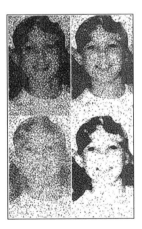

Figure 12.85 Reticulation filter applied using defaults
(upper left), Density 40 (upper right), Black Level 14
(lower left), and White Level 40.

Sponge

Real artists can paint with anything—even sponges. The effect is highly textured, with contrasting splotches of color. Those of us who need a little help with such a sloppy tool will like this Sponge filter, which creates images a dab at a time, using some controls (shown in Figure 12.86) that should be fairly familiar to you by this time.

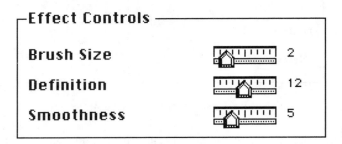

Figure 12.86 Sponge controls.

You can adjust brush size, definition, and smoothness using these sliders. The wide variety of effects you can get are showcased in Figure 12.87. I applied the filter using the defaults (upper left), which provide a fairly detailed spongey effect. At upper right, Brush Size was increased to 9 to produce a more abstract image. In the version at lower left, Definition was moved up to 24, while at lower right, the Smoothness setting was reduced to 1 to give the roughest image.

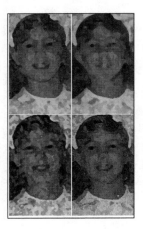

Figure 12.87 Sponge filter applied using defaults (upper left), Brush Size 9 (upper right), Definition 24 (lower left), and smoothness 1 (lower right).

Stained Glass

If you dream of a filter that can convert any image into a beautiful stained glass window or Tiffany lampshade, dream on. This filter does create some great effects, but the irregularly shaped chips of "glass" created out of your image don't really mimic true stained or leaded glass very well. Instead, the effect is more of an image viewed through a stained glass window. Even so, this is an unusual filter that you'll have fun with.

The current foreground color is used for the leaded inserts between the glass pieces, but the other colors come from your image itself. You can control the size of the glass pieces (cells), the thickness of the leading, and the intensity of the light source behind the window that transilluminates your image. The controls are shown in Figure 12.88.

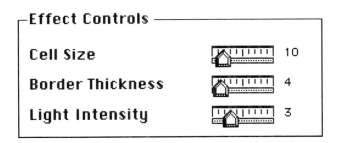

Figure 12.88 Stained Glass controls.

Even the thinnest borders will intrude on the image too much for a realistic rendition. Large cell sizes produce abstract images that have no resemblance to your original subject. Small cell sizes generate images that aren't especially stained-glass-like. You can use this filter to create interesting backgrounds or abstract studies. Other filters, including Diffuse Glow, Paint Daubs, or Dry Brush, can further break down the image to produce some truly outrageous abstracts. Figure 12.89 shows our test image with Border Thickness set to 1 (left), Light Intensity reduced to 0 (center), and Cell Size set to the smallest possible setting—3 (right).

Figure 12.89 Stained Glass filter applied using Border Thickness 1 (left), Light Intensity 0 (center), and Cell Size 3 (right).

Sumi-e

Take a wet brush, load it with ink, and draw on highly absorbent rice paper and what do you get? "Ink painting," or, in Japanese, sumi-e. This filter doesn't convert your image to monochrome, however, but it does add the effect of painting on blotter paper with ink.

Shown in Figure 12.90, the controls—Stroke Width, Stroke Pressure, and Contrast—are simple to master. .

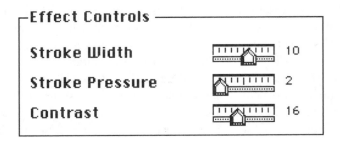

Figure 12.90 Sumi-e controls.

This filter works best with landscapes or abstracts, because it tends to blur portrait subjects into unrecognizability. Figure 12.91 shows four examples using default settings (upper left), a Stroke Width of 3 (upper right), a Stroke Pressure of 15 (lower left), and Contrast 32 (lower right).

Figure 12.91 Sumi-e filter applied using defaults (upper left),
Stroke Width 3 (upper right), Stroke Pressure 15 (lower left),
and contrast 32 (lower right).

Torn Edges

The Torn Edges filter gives you image (what else?) torn edges. It converts color images to two-color, using the current foreground and background hues. As with previous "picky" filters, the Image Balance control (shown in Figure 12.92) is the most important, because it governs how much of your original image will be viewable in the final version.

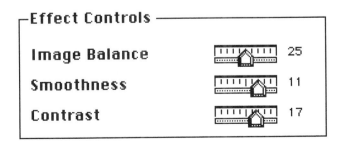

Figure 12.92 Torn Edges controls.

You can also adjust smoothness and contrast and may need to experiment to get the best settings because even small adjustments in any of these three controls can produce dramatically different images. Figure 12.93 shows four examples, generated using the default values (upper left), Image Balance 20 (upper right), Smoothness 15 (lower left), and Contrast 25 (lower right).

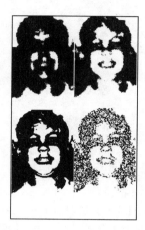

Figure 12.93 Torn Edges filter applied using default values (upper left), Image Balance 20 (upper right), Smoothness 15 (lower left), and Contrast 25 (lower right).

Water Paper

Water-based paints applied to wet paper tend to migrate along the fibers, producing a blurry effect. The Water Paper filter gives you control over the length of the fibers, the brightness, and the relative contrast of the image, using the three sliders shown in Figure 12.94.

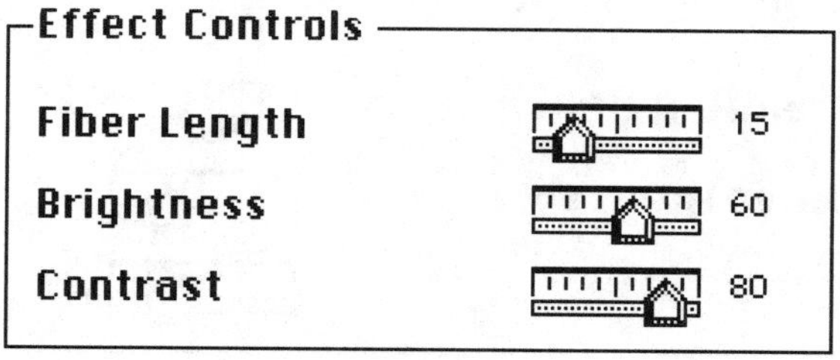

```
┌─Effect Controls ──────────────
│
│  Fiber Length      [▲        ]  15
│
│  Brightness        [    ▲    ]  60
│
│  Contrast          [      ▲  ]  80
│
└───────────────────────────────
```

Figure 12.94 Water Paper controls.

The effects you can get with this filter vary considerably as you manipulate the controls. The examples in Figure 12.95 show the divergent looks that this plug-in can produce. At upper left, the default settings were used. At upper right, a Fiber Length of 50 was applied, stretching out the strokes sharply. A Brightness of 74 (lower left) and Contrast of 95 (lower right) generated two other different effects.

Figure 12.95 Water Paper applied using defaults (upper left), Fiber Length 50 (upper right), Brightness 74 (lower left), and Contrast 95 (lower right).

A Gallery Effects Gallery

I promised you a few images processed with Adobe Gallery Effects to show what can be achieved when you select photographs that lend themselves to a particular effect. Here are four examples using some of the more commonly used filters in this set.

A Dry Brush Renaissance

The original photograph (shown in the inset in Figure 12.96) of statuary in a cathedral in Leon, Spain, lacked strong colors, and the ultrasharp rendition of these worn medieval figures was a sharp contrast. I softened the image by converting it into a painting using the Dry Brush filter. This plug-in deemphasized the minor defects in the carvings in favor of the strong lines. A color version is shown in the full-color insert as Color 9.

Figure 12.96 Image processed with Dry Brush filter.

Adding a Haze with Film Grain

Although I used a diffusion filter with the original portrait, I wanted to further mute the details in this picture. My first choice was Diffuse Glow, but I tried it and didn't like the results. There really weren't enough bright highlights to apply the glow, which concentrated itself around the model's shoulder. So, I applied the Film Grain filter, using a relatively large Highlight Area setting. The result, shown in Figure 12.97 and in the color insert as Color 10, has a hazy, dreamy quality.

Figure 12.97 Portrait diffused using the Film Grain filter.

Antiquing an Image with Ink Outlines

This ancient castle north of Palencia, Spain, looked far too modern with its paved roads and the cars parked out front. The photo still looked like a Disney World prop after I retouched the cars out, as shown in the inset in Figure 12.98. The medieval look returned when I applied the Ink Outlines filter. You can see the color version of this picture, Color 11, in the color insert.

Figure 12.98 Castle antiqued with Ink Outlines.

Using Mosaic

This high-key figure study needed something extra, so I added a texture using the Mosaic filter. I set the Tile Size to 3 and the Grout Width to 1 and made the grout very dark to produce the cracked effect shown in Figure 12.99.

Figure 12.99 Adding texture to a figure study with the Mosaic filter.

The Next Step

This was easily the longest chapter in this book. However, since Adobe Gallery Effects, along with Kai's Power Tools, make up the basic third-party filter set that every serious image worker must have, he time we've spent looking at each filter individually was worth while.

CHAPTER 13

Other Commercial Filters

The world of filters doesn't begin and end with HSC Software and Adobe, by any means. I devoted entire chapters to Kai's Power Tools, KPT Convolver, and Adobe Gallery Effects because those collections give you the most bang for your buck. All three packages offer a full range of basic and advanced filter tools for a reasonable price. If Photoshop, PixelPaint Pro, or Fractal Design Painter are your hammer, saw, and rule, think of the HSC and Adobe add-ons as your power drill and electric sander—not absolutely essential, but you wouldn't want to work without them.

Now, let's look at the best of the rest. These are all commercial filters that offer effects that you can't readily achieve on your own. Once you've explored every nook and cranny of your image editor's filter capabilities and purchased one or more of the add-on packages already discussed, the filters in this chapter will give you something new to work with.

If you have upgraded to Adobe Photoshop 3.0, the CD-ROM furnished with the package includes a good selection of try-out filters from Kodak, Andromeda, Alien Skin, HSC, and others. I have put more on the CD-ROM packaged with this book, for use by both Photoshop users and those who have another image-editing package.

What's Included

There is available a rather large group of filters that I won't mention in this book; they are specialized production plug-ins designed solely to interface with a particular scanner or other piece of equipment, including high-end drum scanners. My reasoning is simple. It's ludicrous to imply that someone who would spend $50,000 or more on a scanner would need to buy this book to find out what kind of software is needed to link it up with a Macintosh.

Most color separation houses that might need, say, ScanPrep from ImageXpress (which automates complex prepress operations on digital files) don't need any recommendations from me. The same reasoning applies if you happen to be production manager or photo editor at a newspaper equipped with an AP/Leaf Picture Desk and are now wondering how you'll going to receive photos over phone lines like that slick-talking salesman said you could. You know there is a Photoshop plug-in to accomplish this task.

So, if you do happen to have one of those specialized needs, don't be terminally disappointed if you don't find one of several dozen high-end plug-ins mentioned in this chapter. We needed to limit the number of pages in this book to accommodate the 8-page color insert, and I didn't want to waste pages on filters that most readers could care less about.

Instead, I took the most exciting general-purpose filters on the market and collected them for discussion in this chapter. Only the best, most cost-effective, and easiest-to-use plug-ins are given the full treatment. You'll be pleased with any of the filters discussed here.

Surprisingly, some vendors did not want to be included in this book. One company I spoke with claimed that they were "too small" to cooperate with authors who wanted to review their products. (Now we know why they have been small for such a very long time!) I'd hate to try to get technical support from them. Others simply never responded to our questions or had telephones that had been disconnected. It's hard to keep current in the fast-moving computer software industry. Happily, several new packages were introduced or upgraded as this book was being prepared, so most of the coverage is up to date.

Intellihance Filters

If you manipulate many photographs (say for a regular newsletter, newspaper, or other publication) that aren't always, let us say, ideally exposed, you need the Intellihance filters. Those of you who produce catalogs, yearbooks, or other projects and want all the images to have similar characteristics will also love this set. Try out the sample versions on the CD-ROM and see if you don't agree with me.

The Intellihance filters automate much of the manual tweaking and fiddling that you need to do to improve the appearance of scanned images. As a result, they can improve a whole batch of photos in the time it might take you to do one. Indeed, Intellihance is quite adept at improving scanned images, doing a much better job than all but the most experienced image manipulator.

Intellihance is a product of DPA Software, by the way. DPA stands either for Digital Prepress Applications or David Pfeiffer and Associates (the parent company), depending on your viewpoint.

Let's look at this set of photographs using the image shown in Figure 13.1. It's a side-lit portrait that has a few non-compositional problems that Intellihance can help. The image lacks sharpness and is relatively high in contrast. In fact, what should have been a subtle hair light at the model's back has managed to wash out all the detail there. At this point, the only option is some judicious cropping and, perhaps, a few alibis from the photographer about all the work that went into achieving this particular fuzzy, high-contrast look.

Figure 13.1 Original photo, before Intellihance was applied.

Intellihance actually is a set of three filters, one each for grayscale, RGB, and CMYK images. To use any of the filters, you first enter some general preferences into a dialog box like the one shown in Figure 13.2. This one happens to be for the Pro version of the grayscale filter, with additional technical options on the right-hand side of the box. The try-out lite edition (LE), the version supplied on the CD-ROM, has four of the six settings shown at left. I'll explain them all.

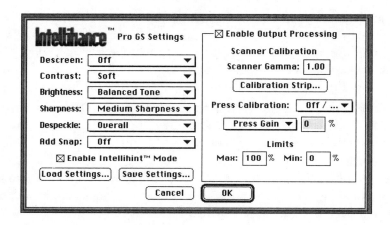

Figure 13.2 Intellihance Pro GS settings.

You choose settings from a drop-down list of choices. A list of the options that can be manipulated follows.

- **Descreen.** This option, available in the Pro version only, allows you to remove, to the extent possible, the halftone dots from a scanned image of a picture that has already been screened (perhaps you scanned it from a magazine or book). Intellihance can do a better job if you can estimate the approximate line ruling used to make the halftone. That's usually simple to do from eyeballing the image and determining where it was printed first. Many laser printers use a 53-lpi screen, while newspapers may rely on 85- to 100-lpi screens. A photo cut from a magazine might have been screened at 133 lpi or higher, while the top setting of 180 lpi or more is best reserved for lithographs and other works printed on sheet-fed presses.

- **Contrast.** When you decide how your finished image should look in terms of contrast; you can select soft, normal, snappy, or hard contrast.

- **Brightness.** This list allows you to emphasize shadows, midtones, or highlights, depending on where the important detail is. Or you can request balanced tones favoring none of these.

- **Sharpness.** Intellihance can sharpen only blurry pictures (leaving sharp images alone), mildly sharpen, or add extra sharpness.

- **Despeckle.** Intellihance can remove noise from your image, either overall, in dark tones only, or in light tones only.

- **Add Snap.** Found only in the Pro version, this option lets you add additional gentle, medium, or hard snap, or contrast.

- **Enable Intellihint Mode.** Check this box to activate a second dialog box of settings. If you don't check it, when you click **OK**, Intellihance will proceed to process the image using the settings you already entered.

- **Other choices.** The dialog box shown in Figure 13.2 also has several other choices only available in the Pro version. These options let you adjust for the basics of a particular scanner or press's biases by setting the gamma to accommodate the results of a calibration strip you interpret. You can also specify corrections for dot gain (the tendency of the halftone dots to spread or enlarge on the press).

Intellihint Mode

If you check the Enable Intellihint Mode box, a dialog box like the one shown in Figure 13.3 will pop up when you click **OK** in the previous dialog box. The tool palette and readouts at left are not available in the LE or demo version of the filter.

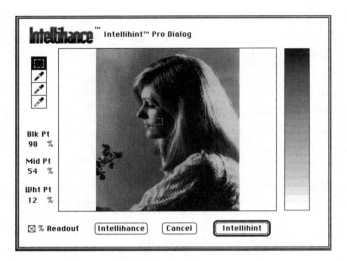

Figure 13.3 Intellihint dialog box.

Intellihint lets you better work with images that have very bright or dark backgrounds. Intellihance generally averages the entire image to produce its tone, curve, sharpness, and other information. In the LE version, you can help the program out by dragging a selection box with the mouse to highlight the area of the image of most interest. Click on the Intellihint button, and the filter will commence processing the image using the selected area for its calculations. If you decide to go ahead and process the image using the entire picture, click on the Intellihance button instead.

The Pro version has a tool palette with the selection marquee for choosing an area of interest, plus three eyedroppers, which are full of black, gray, and white tone, representing the blacks, midpoint, and white points of you image. Use each eyedropper to select the points in the image that you want to correspond to each of those values.

This capability is pretty cool. Select the black eyedropper, for example, and click on various dark gray and black values in the image. As you click, all the corresponding tones that will be registered as black will glow red. You can also decide what should be the midpoint and white in your image. With a little practice, you can show Intellihance how to ignore very deep shadow details that you don't care about (by telling it to consider them black), to allow more tones in the important highlight areas. Or you can move both whites and blacks closer together to compress the grayscale.

Figure 13.4 shows our test image both before Intellihance processing (left) and after (right). Even Intellihance couldn't restore the detail that had been in the hair, so the picture was cropped.

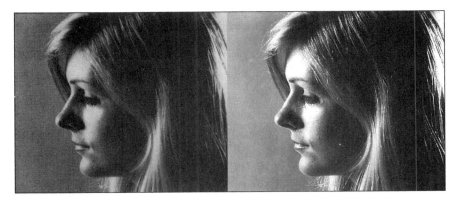

Figure 13.4 Image before (left) and after (right) Intellihance processing.

The RGB and CMYK modules operate in much the same way. Figure 13.5 shows the RGB filter dialog box. Again, the options on the right-hand side aren't available in the LE version. Both additions have a Remove Cast list, which lets you purify grays, remove a slight color cast, or aggressively go after color tinges. The Pro RGB filter has settings for calibrating for both your scanner and output device (generally a CRT screen with RGB images).

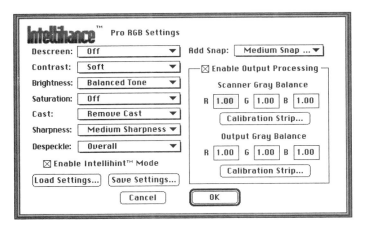

Figure 13.5 Intellihance Pro RGB filter dialog box.

The CMYK filter dialog box (shown in Figure 13.6) has additional settings for controlling dot gain (something you don't need for RGB images).

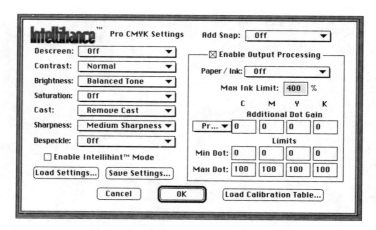

Figure 13.6 Intellihance Pro CMYK filter dialog box.

As noted at the beginning of the chapter, I tended to shy away from highly technical and specialized filters in this section, but the Intellihance filters offer some useful functions from which even those who don't get directly involved in color separation or production can benefit. These are filters that help your images look their best, with little work or input from you.

Alien Skin Filters

Alien Skin produces a variety of effects, some of which are marketed by other companies (such as the Alien Skin Textureshop sold by Virtus) and the Black Box filter set described later in this chapter.

The myriad possibilities of Textureshop are best applied from the stand-alone application version of the program, so I won't cover that in great detail here. It lets you specify realistic lighting and shadows to create 3-D textures with vivid patterns overlaid. You can store these one-of-a-kind textures for use with Photoshop. The module is available as a Photoshop plug-in, so I can justify mentioning it in this book.

I'll put most of my emphasis, however, on the Black Box set of six plug-ins that deliver effects that are either time-consuming to achieve or impossible using conventional image editor functions. For $89 (list) you get a version that works with both 680x0 Macs and Power Macintoshes.

None of the Black Box filters come with previews, so you'll have to apply them to see what they do to your image. Luckily, they aren't particularly slow (and are positively speedy on a Power Mac) so you won't waste a lot of time with trial and error.

Drop Shadow

Drop shadows are one of the most frequently used special effects, and they're easy to achieve. Just select the object you want shadowed, copy the selection to another layer, feather the selection or blur it with a Gaussian blur, fill with your choice of shadow color, and then merge it behind the object being shadowed. Alien Skin's Drop Shadow filter does all those things for you. Best of all, you get complete control over all the parameters. You can try a version of this filter from the CD-ROM.

To use Drop Shadow, just select the object to be shadowed. It's a good idea to save your selection because selection is lost during the shadowing process due to the vagaries of the Photoshop filter interface. Photoshop doesn't allow filters to modify anything outside the boundaries of the current selection. Four of the six Black Box filters add a bevel or some other effect outside the selection and so couldn't perform their work under normal circumstances. The Alien Skin programmers found a safe way around this restriction (safe in the sense that you can Undo the effect after it's been applied; true multistep processes can't be undone), but an unavoidable side effect is that your selection is lost.

You'll need to save your selection, especially if you want to work with an object that you just pasted into the image or with text you've just created. Both types of selections float above the background image, and Drop Shadow won't work on floating selections. So, you need to save the selection, defloat, reload the selection, and apply Drop Shadow.

Figure 13.7 shows Drop Shadow's dialog box, which consists of just a couple sliders and buttons that aren't particularly hard to visualize. One set of two sliders control the x (toward the right) and y (downward) offset of the shadow, which you can set in positive or negative values to move the shadow up, down, left, or right in relation to the shadowed object.

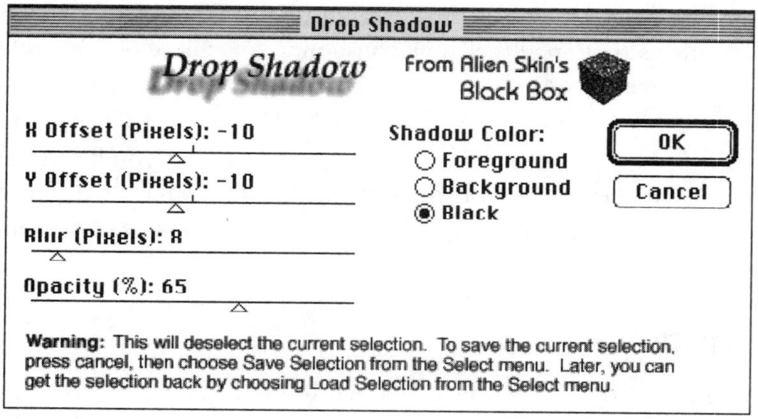

Figure 13.7 Drop Shadow dialog box.

Another slider specifies the width of the blurring around the shadow edges, from 0 to 100 pixels, while the remaining slider lets you adjust the transparency of the shadow, from 0 to 100% (80% is the default). The only other parameter to select is one radio button to color the shadow with background or foreground colors or black. Figure 13.8 shows some text that has been shadowed using this filter.

Figure 13.8 Text given the Drop Shadow effect.

Glass Filter

The Glass filter places a beveled layer of glass over your selection. (Use the Emboss filter if you actually want to raise the selection above the surface.) You can select the width of the bevel in pixels, the smoothness of the bevel, and its shape (rounded, a flat 45° angle, or mesa—a sharp curve with almost vertical sides). Figure 13.9 shows the dialog box for this filter.

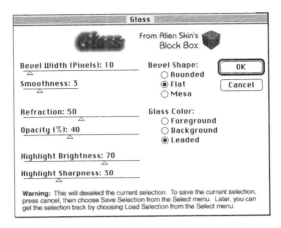

Figure 13.9 Glass filter dialog box.

You may set the amount of refraction (distortion) produced by the edges or bevel of the glass overlay. A wider bevel shows off the refraction effects best. You can control the opacity, which in any event will be stronger in the area of the selection and weaker in the bevel. The highlight brightness and sharpness controls give you command of the contrast and acutance of the image underlying the glass. Glass color can be set to the foreground or background color or leaded (dark gray). Figure 13.10 shows an example of some text raised up from the surface of a brick I created.

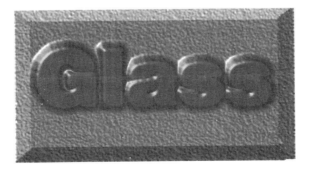

Figure 13.10 Glass effect.

Glow Filter

The Glow filter is another filter with effects you can easily duplicate on your own, but, again, Black Box saves you a lot of time and adds a little something you can't duplicate exactly. In this case, it's a sharpness at the corners of your selections, and the effect is full strength throughout. Figure 13.11 shows you the controls offered for this filter.

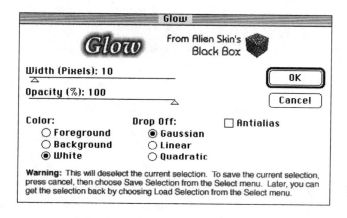

Figure 13.11 Glow filter controls.

Glow is a flexible filter. You can specify the width for the glowing effect as well as its opacity and select either a color from the foreground or background or white. The drop-off effect of the glow can be set for the usual Gaussian blur (equivalent to a rounded bevel with other effects), an even linear blur (which is similar to a flat bevel in effect), or one calculated using a quadratic algorithm (think mesa—there's some code being reused here.) There's also a check box that you can use to specify antialiasing so that the blur effect will merge more smoothly with the surrounding image. Figure 13.12 shows some text that has been given the glow treatment.

Figure 13.12 Text with glow effect applied.

HSB Noise

There are many add-on noise filters out there, and HSB Noise is another one. This version lets you control the hue, saturation, and brightness factors (hence the HSB name) so that you can match your noise carefully to the look and feel of a particular image. It's a great improvement over the "random" noise provided with Photoshop. Figure 13.13 shows the dialog box, which, as you might expect, features separate sliders for hue, saturation, and brightness.

Figure 13.13 HSB Noise filter dialog box.

I applied the HSB Noise filter to the text shown in Figure 13.14. The black outline around the characters was added later using the Stroke function (one pixel wide) to differentiate the area in which noise had been added from the rest of the brick (which itself was created using Gallery Effects' Texturizer filter, with the edges darkened and lightened to produce the 3-D look). Noise was included in this package to give you a filter that can apply some tooth to images that will be modified using one of the other plug-ins.

Figure 13.14 HSB Noise filter applied to text.

Swirl Filter

You'll love the Swirl filter from the Black Box set. It creates outrageous swirly effects unlike those provided by any other filter available. The dialog box is shown in Figure 13.15.

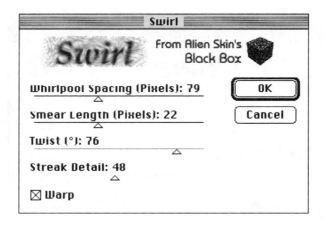

Figure 13.15 Swirl filter dialog box.

You can control the spacing, in pixels, between the miniwhirlpools that Swirl sets up in your image. Wide spacing gives you smooth, painterly looks. Smaller spacing fills your image with many interesting whirlpools. Change the smear length to produce long strokes or short ones, as you prefer. The degree of twist and amount of detail in the swirl can also be specified. Small angles produce a fountain effect, since the swirling emanates from each whirlpool in relatively straight lines. As you near 90° of twist, the smears become more like actual whirlpools. A check box lets you determine whether the image will be "warped." Figure 13.16 shows an image swirled with this filter.

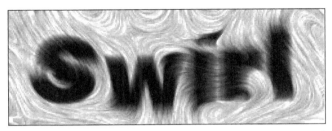

Figure 13.16 Swirl filter applied to text and background.

The Boss

The Boss filter has absolutely nothing to do with Bruce Springsteen. Surprise! It's actually an embossing filter with some extra controls that you don't normally get with such plug-ins. You can specify the height of the embossing effect (which isn't that unusual) and control the width of the bevel, its shape, and its smoothness (the latter being a sort of do-it-yourself antialiasing effect). Highlight brightness and sharpness is also under your control, as shown in the dialog box in Figure 13.17.

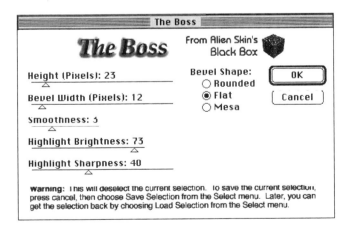

Figure 13.17 The Boss dialog box.

Unlike Photoshop's own embossing filter (which turns your entire image gray and splotchy) and the Gallery Effects embossing effect (which adds a rough texture to the selection, even though the colors are retained), The Boss does nothing more than emboss your selection.

If you think this filter just might be an illegitimate offspring of the Glass filter, you're not too far off the mark. The effects are closely related, but they are different enough to justify a separate filter for each. This filter is really cool when applied to an existing image because it produces the effect of pressing or embossing the selection out of the underlying image. Figure 13.18 shows an example of The Boss at work.

Figure 13.18 Embossing with The Boss.

Second Glance Filters

Second Glance produces a whole series of great Photoshop plug-ins for general-purpose use as well as more specialized color correction, separation, and preseparation applications. Chromassage has the broadest application for readers of this book, so I'll describe it in more detail than the others.

Chromassage

Chromassage can give you a virtually unending stream of variations on a single picture, through simple tools like jog wheels, which let you dial in the colors you want. To use this plug-in, you just load your image into Photoshop and select Chromassage from the Filters menu. Your original image is presented in a new window, flanked by two color palettes, a small toolbox, and vertically and horizontally oriented jog wheels. You create special effects by switching colors from the upper, new palette into the lower, current palette. There are several ways to do this.

First, Chromassage has a menu of 26 designer palettes with names like Art Deco, Fire, Pastels, or Sea and Sunset. Each is a custom set of 256 colors heavily biased toward the scheme you might expect from its name. The Fire palette, for example, has many variations on warm tones, while Pastels contains softer colors.

If you like, you can select an entire palette and substitute it for the current palette of your image. The results may be very startling. You can also select a range of tones or use a hypodermic like tool to select individual colors from the working palette and inject them into colors of your choice in the current palette. Use the jog wheels to shift the entire current palette through a range of hues.

Chromassage is great for experimentation. You can cycle through 100 different color combinations and special effects in less than a minute and choose the one you like best. Changes aren't made to your original photo until you click the **Apply** button. Figure 13.19 shows the dialog box for Chromassage.

Figure 13.19 Chromassage allows you to create a variety of color effects by spinning several jog wheels.

PhotoSpot

PhotoSpot is a set of filters that reduces the number of colors in an image, producing spot color separations that can be further manipulated in page layout programs such as QuarkXpress and Adobe PageMaker or vector drawing programs such as Adobe Illustrator and MacroMedia FreeHand. Three color reduction filters are included in the package:

- PaintThinner gives you a different kind of control over color reduction/posterization. Working with a preview of the original and a palette of 256 reduced colors, you can select the range of image colors that will be assigned to a single spot color in your final version. The interactive mode makes it simple to perform this task.

- Acetone rapidly reduces colors in an image by remapping the tones to the colors specified for separation. It includes a color wheel interface that allows the user to nudge a color range towards another hue.

- Turpentine creates an eight-color diffusion tone image, said to create process color images with more vibrant colors than cyan, magenta, yellow, and black colors can provide alone.

Figure 13.20 shows an image that has been posterized using PhotoSpot.

Figure 13.20 Image posterized with PhotoSpot.

LaserSeps

LaserSeps creates process color separations (as opposed to the spot color separations generated by Photospot. The resulting separations can be output to a standard laser printer or saved to a file that can be imported into PageMaker, QuarkXpress, or other programs.

Chromapoint

Chromapoint is a filter designed to optimize output on relatively low-resolution laser color printers, color ink-jets, or similar printers that use the PostScript page description language. You'll find that these files print much faster than those intended for high-resolution output devices. The color halftone screens produced by Chromapoint are said to be sharper than the default screens produced by the PostScript interpreter.

ScanTastic

ScanTastic provides Photoshop users with direct access to Apple, Epson, Hewlett Packard, and Umax scanners. It offers a live, zoomable preview and automatic balance of tones. You may like it better than the Photoshop plug-in furnished with your scanner.

Xaos Tools Filters

The fine folks at Xaos (pronounced "chaos") first made their name with Paint Alchemy, a stunningly capable natural-media tool disguised as a Photoshop plug-in. Since then, they've added another plug-in miracle-worker, Terrazzo, which creates endless kaleidoscopelike patterns from a selected area of your image. The company also offers Fresco, which is a package of useful textures that you can use with your image editor.

I moved the discussion of Terrazzo to Chapter 16 to make more room here for Xaos' latest offering—a brand-new, redesigned Paint Alchemy, Version 2, which sports a shiny new interface and significantly enhanced features.

Not to slight Adobe Gallery Effects, which, after all, deserved a chapter of its own, but if you want to move into the big leagues of painterly brush-stroke effects, you really need Paint Alchemy 2. Everything you can do with the strokelike filters in Gallery Effects, you can do with Paint Alchemy, and much more besides.

Paint Alchemy 2 is a user-configurable brush-stroke filter that is furnished with dozens of predesigned brushes and preset styles such as Pointillist, Screen Door, Ripple, or Sponge Print. In addition, any grayscale PICT file can be imported as a brush.

Parameters such as coverage color, size, angle, and opacity are available from the slick pop-up dialog boxes. Brush strokes can be varied according to the hue, saturation, or brightness of the pixels being painted over. If you like you can paint a scenic image's blue skies with one type of brush and amber waves of grain with another.

If you've used Paint Alchemy 1, prepare to be surprised. The old dialog box, arranged in a tabbed file-folder arrangement (very similar to the "new" dialog boxes just being introduced to Microsoft Windows 95) has been scrapped. Thanks, perhaps, to competition from Kai's Power Tools' space cadet interface, Xaos has itself departed a bit from the standard Macintosh conventions enough to offer a handsome, full-color 3-D dialog box set with shiny buttons and other innovative features. Don't expect whirling marbles and other KPT-like innovations, though. Underneath it all, Paint Alchemy 2 is a fairly conventional, if extensive, upgrade from the first version. Paint Alchemy's new interface is shown in Figure 13.21.

Figure 13.21 Paint Alchemy 2's new user interface.

Paint Alchemy is based on the concept of *styles*, which consist of a brush-stroke shape (a grayscale image that can be saved as a PICT file), along with the options that specify the color, size, angle, transparency, and number of brush strokes. As you can see from Figure 13.22, a list of predefined styles is arranged into cascading menus. You can select from 100 different styles, divided into categories such as Abstract, Molecule, and Oil Tip.

Buttons on the right-hand side of the dialog box give you access to coverage, color, angle, size, and opacity palettes with their own set of slider controls and previews. You can view the original image and an advance look of how it will appear with the current settings in a split window.

Figure 13.22 Paint Alchemy's cascading style menu.

What's New in Alchemy 2

Paint Alchemy is a fairly processor-intensive set of filters and has always worked fastest on systems with a floating-point processor. This latest version has been updated for faster operator on 680x0 Macs and runs fully native on Power Macintoshes. You'll find that the new version offers faster previews (which can be interrupted if you decide, as they form, that what you're seeing is not what you want to get).

A larger preview window is provided. You can use a marquee to select which portion of the image to preview and zoom between a 1:1 view of the selection only or the entire image. A new eyedropper tool allows you to sample colors to use as the background or stroke color. Xaos has also added the capability to drag and drop brush designs onto the brush selection area of the main window to create new brush palettes.

This plug-in is particularly valuable for those of you creating QuickTime movies because you can select random effects in the Brush Control Card that will vary from frame to frame. If you want animated brush strokes that squirm through your animation, Paint Alchemy 2 offers and easy way to achieve this effect.

This package is highly recommended!

FotoMagic

This modest collection of eight filters from Ring of Fire, Inc., has a characteristic that can be important for those of you who want to process images without losing any resolution. FotoMagic differs from most other filters in two ways: it won't change the relative position of pixels or add/subtract pixels. All processing changes are made by modifying the brightness/darkness or hue of existing pixels. The last phone number in the United States that I had for this Japan-based company was disconnected, and I couldn't track them down, so I hope they're still in business.

The package includes filters for creating color noise, modifying the value of colors, converting color images to monochrome in a more flexible way than Photoshop's Change Mode command, and performing various other color reductions.

Andromeda Filters

Some users have many good things to say about this venerable set of filters, most of which have been around for quite awhile. I find them incredibly overpriced—for a list price of more than $400 you get roughly 12 different filters divided into three sets. Granted, several of the filters can generate a whole array of effects, but for the same money you can find a mail order house that will sell you Kai's Power Tools, Convolver, all three Aldus Gallery Effects packages, and perhaps have enough left over for Black Box, Paint Alchemy, or Terrazzo. Those packages can duplicate most—but not all—of the effects possible with the Andromeda set.

Series 1 Filters

The Series 1 filters duplicate many filter effects that photographers will find familiar. Included are the cMulti and sMulti filters for kaleidoscopic effects in ways that are quite different from those found in Xaos Tools' Terrazzo. An example of cMulti's effects is shown in Figure 13.23.

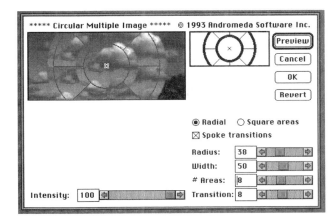

Figure 13.23 cMulti from Andromeda's Series 1 collection.

Designs creates interesting patterns using bends and warps and includes a 104-pattern library; there's also a Mezzo variation of this filter, which converts continuous tone images to a mezzo line screen effect. You'll also find Rainbow, Prism, and Diffract for spectral effects; Halo for controlled highlight diffusion; Reflection for clear pool reflections; Star for adding glints and sparks to night lights or glossy surfaces; and Velocity for unique motion trails.

Series 2 Filter

The Series 2 filter lets you wrap an image onto a shaded 3-D surface. You may shift, scale, rotate or tile the image. The variable viewing angle and distance provide many perspectives. You can work with a resizable predefined sphere, cylinder, plane, or box in any color or render the image transparent. The filters feature a movable light source and high-quality antialiased 3-D images. I really prefer to use a full-fledged 3-D program (Ray Dream Designer in particular) to generate such images, but if you want a plug-in, this one does the job. Figure 13.24 shows an example of this filter at work.

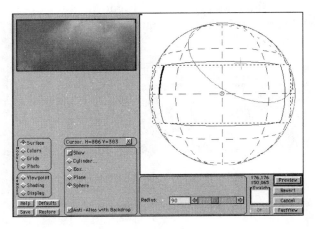

Figure 13.24 Andromeda Series 2 3-D filter.

Series 3 Filter

If you do a lot of mezzotints and can afford to spend $159 on a single filter that does just one thing, and only with grayscale images at that, the Andromeda Series 3 filter, Mezzo is for you. It creates a wide variety of mezzo effects, using 15- to 400-lpi screens, using ellipses, lines, spokes, and other variations. This is truly a mezzotint filter on steroids; if only the price wasn't bloated, too, many more users would find it helpful.

Alaras Filters

Alaras offers three filters that I couldn't resist mentioning, even though they are probably out of the needs and price range of most of the readers of this book. Each of the three work so smoothly and quickly that if you need to send files to and from high-end prepress equipment (particularly Scitex gear), you'll want to look at these products.

Alaras Apertura

Apertura is an Acquire module that lets you work with small portions of large images quickly, reducing the headaches Photoshop causes by demanding a scratch disk larger than the entire image you're working with—even if the changes you're making are only to a small portion of that image. This is a modular plug-in that can be "activated" by telephone to work with only the image file formats you need, from TIFF and HandshakeCT ($149.00) to high-end professional formats (in its full configuration, this filter costs $4990!).

Alaras Tropix

Tropix can be used to transfer jobs between Scitex and Macintosh workstations, usually twice as fast as through conventional Gateway Tools solutions.

Alaras Mixxer

Mixxer allows you to create and manipulate color separations in Photoshop, giving you the capability to change CMYK values while maintaining shape and detail.

Knoll Software CyberMesh

Any filter from one of the designers of the original Photoshop program has to be good. This one lets you convert grayscale images into 3-D wireframe models in DXF file format, for use with computer-aided drafting (CAD) programs. You can generate wireframes using cylindrical, rectangular, or spherical coordinate systems.

This specialized filter is a way of creating 3-D effects from grayscale pictures for use with maps, terrain builders, and other applications.

Pattern Workshop

MicroFrontier, the makers of the ColorIt image-editing program often bundled with programs like Kai's Power Tools or KPT Convolver, also offers this plug-in, which creates patterns that can be used to fill your selection. You can divide the patterns you create with the Pattern Edit plug-in into libraries of 64 x 64 pixel textures, each with 16 different patterns, and then use the Pattern Fill filter to apply any of these. They'll be automatically tiled to fill your selection.

If you purchased either of the HSC products I mentioned, you already have all the functionality of Pattern Workshop built into the ColorIt software included with your package. You can use ColorIt's editor to modify the patterns bundled with that program or to create new ones, and its own Pattern Fill capabilities to apply them. Of course, if you'd rather work within one program and not keep switching back and forth, you'll want the filter version of this feature set and will have to spend some money to buy Pattern Workshop. I recommend that you try out the capabilities in ColorIt first and then upgrade to the filters if you like what you see.

Filter Helper

Even with a fast Macintosh or Power Mac, using the filters discussed in this chapter with multimegabyte color image files can be painfully slow. Specular Collage eases the agony by performing many image compositing, filtering, masking, and sizing functions on a screen-resolution "proxy" of your original at warp speed.

Preview layout and special effects until you're satisfied and then "render" the image to a final, high-resolution version. The program lets you work quickly and efficiently, instead of watching as your image editor struggles to move swarms of bitmaps around on the screen every time you make a small change. In most cases, when you work with proxies, you can perform in a few minutes operations that might take an hour if you had to work with the original file.

For example, imagine applying a complex filter like Pixelbreeze (from Kai's Power Tools) to an entire image in 3 seconds instead of 30 seconds or previewing five or six special effects in the time it might to experiment with one. By working with proxies instead of the original image, you can briskly manipulate 20-MB files that normally strain your Mac to—or beyond—its RAM limits.

Think of Specular Collage as a QuarkXpress–like layout tool for image files. You can't paint or modify individual pixels or create masks or selections. You'll still need your original image editor for that; Specular Collage is compatible with Photoshop, Fractal Design Painter, PixelPaint, or any other program that can save PICT, noncompressed TIFF files or Photoshop 2.5 format.

Specular Collage comes into play after you finish basic editing. Create a blank canvas in any desired size and import one or more image files. Specify as many files as you like, one after another, and then click on the **Done** button. The program then creates 72-dpi images of each file, which you can drag onto the canvas and size, rotate, crop, or skew.

The low-resolution images look identical to what you'd see on the screen in your image editor at 1X magnification, except that manipulating them is virtually instantaneous. Each image is treated as a separate layer, which can be moved, overlapped, sent behind, grouped with other layers, or given a drop-shadow effect.

The real payoff comes when you decide to use a Photoshop-compliant plug-in. Not every third-party filter is compatible with Collage, but those we tried from the Xaos Tools' Paint Alchemy or HSC's Kai's Power Tools utility kits worked fine. You may also process an alpha channel mask (TIFF or Photoshop Channel #4). The only restriction is that a filter must be applied to an entire file element or its mask.

You can add text, merge images (so that overlapping pixels are calculated by adding, subtracting, or multiplying their brightness values), or specify the relative opacity/transparency of any element. One image can be feathered into another or enhanced with a customizable drop shadow. Built-in rulers and guides allow you to position and align images accurately. Figure 13.25 shows Specular Collage's main window.

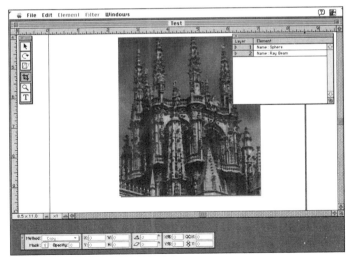

Figure 13.25 Specular Collage lets you apply filters to a low-resolution image at high speed.

The final image with your layout and effects applied can be rendered at the full resolution of the original files—leaving them untouched. Or a low-resolution, "for position only" version can be generated, for placement into your Quark or PageMaker document.

Those of you creating complex documents that incorporate images need a specialized image-compositing utility in your toolkit alongside your page layout software, word processing program, and image editor. Specular Collage fills the bill and is also a candidate for the greatest image-processing accelerator since the PowerPC.

The Next Step

We looked at most of the leading third-party filters on the market, except for a group for another source—shareware products. You'll find that many of these are just as good as some individual commercial filters, and a few are even better. I surveyed all the filters available and bring the best of them to you in the chapter that follows. I even got permission to include some of them on the CD-ROM bundled with this book.

CHAPTER 14

Shareware Filters

This chapter introduces you to the shareware concept and describes some of the leading shareware filters and tools, including Plug-In Manager, and filters from Chris Cox and Paul Badger, which are included on the CD-ROM bundled with this book.

What is Shareware?

Several years ago, I came to the conclusion that many software vendors would do just as well giving away the initial copies of their software and charging only for upgrades. After all, over the long run, upgrades can end up costing more than the original software. Making the original copies free would provide a broader base of users to pay for those lucrative upgrades.

After all, truly valuable software continues to be valuable, and users want to preserve their investments while gaining enhanced features (and bug fixes) for continual, affordable fees.

Wouldn't it be nice if software were provided to you free initially, followed by a regular program of upgrades for relatively low fees? You wouldn't mind spreading out the payments for software that allowed you to try-before-you-buy at little risk, would you?

Actually, there is a classification of software with exactly those features. It's called shareware. Shareware has been with us since the late Andrew Fluegelman introduced the communications program PC-Talk in 1982. He asked users who found it helpful to send contributions. When the Macintosh arrived on the scene, Mac shareware and freeware immediately became an important source of software for this new machine. Indeed, there were no commercial communications programs available for the Mac at first. I wrote a tiny program in Microsoft Basic that let me log onto CompuServe and download a file (that's all the program did), which was MacTEP (terminal emulation program), my original gateway to nearly all of the shareware I now own.

Today, shareware programs like Plug-In Manager and the shareware filters in this chapter resemble their traditionally marketed counterparts in many ways. Both are often (but not always) developed by teams of professional programmers. It is difficult to discern shareware from conventional retail software simply on the basis of features, functionality, user interface, or overall quality. Shareware is just commercial software that is distributed on a try-before-you-buy basis.

Millions of people are trying before they buy—on the sly—with retail software. The difference with shareware is that the practice is aboveboard, and nobody gets stuck with expensive software that doesn't fit his or her needs.

Shareware happens to be upgraded more frequently than most commercially distributed software. The upgrade fees are lower, too. You may get a free upgrade or two with your initial registration and then pay a very nominal fee for additional upgrades as the software is enhanced further. If you like the shareware I provide, or other programs or filters that you download from America OnLine, CompuServe, or elsewhere, please encourage the authors to produce more great products by sending in the small fee.

This next section introduces some of the best shareware filters on the market.

Chris Cox's Filters

Chris Cox is a recent college graduate who unleashed this fairly complete set of filters on the shareware market as a way of demonstrating his programming prowess. Although he'll probably have secured a job by the time this book is published (are you reading this, HSC?), you can still show your appreciation by registering this package with him at the address shown in the README file on the CD-ROM in the Chris's Filters folder.

Or if you need a Macintosh or RISC workstation programmer with UNIX experience, give Chris a call. Write him at ChrisCox on America OnLine. Mention this book, too, because I had to talk him into giving me permission to use these filters!

All Chris's filters should work on any Mac, but he provides separate versions for both 68000 and 68020 or higher Macs. The filters in this package include:

- Average (Blur menu). Fills selection with the average color in the selected region. Chris recommends selecting odd-sized regions and averaging them to create a stained glass effect.

- Checkers (Other menu). Puts a checkerboard pattern over your image or selection, using the foreground or background color. You can specify the width and height of the squares. Applied in small sizes, it makes an interesting dither pattern. Figure 14.1 shows an image with the Checkers pattern applied.

Figure 14.1 Checkers filter applied to an image.

- Bitshift (Other menu). Rotates the bytes of an image a specified number of bits, from 1 to 8, to create some interesting effects. Try it, you'll like it.

- Grid (Other menu). Places a grid over your image, using the spacing and line width you specify. Use this filter applied over a plain background for those times when you need an ordinary grid and don't want to draw one by hand. This should have been a built-in Photoshop function!

- Add More Noise (Noise menu). Lets you specify how much noise to add to each RGB channel. You can never be too thin or have too many noise filters.

- Total Noise (Noise menu). Entirely replaces the selection with random noise. For those times when you need even more noise than Add More Noise supplies. Total Noise supplies all noise, all the time.

- Fractal Noise (Noise menu). Fills the current selection with noise generated using fractal algorithms.

- Plaid (Noise menu) An effect discovered by Cox by mistake, this filter adds symmetrical patterns to each available color channel. Chris says, "Well, Plaid is...well, Plaid," but you may yet discover a use for this unusual filter.

- Dilate (Custom menu). Enlarges dark regions of an image. Figure 14.2 shows an image with the Dilate filter applied.

Figure 14.2 Dilate filter applied to an image.

- Psycho (Stylize menu). A solarization or psychedelic style filter with lots of possibilities. Watch it turn your color image into your worst nightmare!

- UnAlias (Blur menu). Blurs only the edges and corners of a selection. A useful filter.

- Edge 3 x 3 (Custom menu). A great Find Edges-style filter with a different effect—plus it's faster. Figure 14.3 shows this filter at work.

Figure 14.3 Edge 3 x 3 filter applied to an image.

- Erode (Custom menu). Reduces the dark regions of an image. Figure 14.4 shows an image with Erode applied.

Figure 14.4 Image with Erode filter applied.

- Skeleton (Custom menu). Thins dark areas to a centerline, producing a skeleton of the original image. Can be applied repeatedly for different effects. Figure 14.5 shows an image with the Skeleton filter applied.

Figure 14.5 Image with Skeleton filter applied.

- ColorKey (Video menu). Creates a mask using the current foreground color, using a tolerance value you specify.

- ChromaKey (Video menu). Another mask generator, using a different technique.

- FastKey (Video menu). Creates a mask based on a single RGB value, with no tolerance.

Paul Badger Filters

Paul Badger is currently commuting to work between Ohio and the East Coast but still has time to update his great filter set from time to time. His VectorGraph filter is one of the most unusual filters I have ever seen. The full set of three has the following characteristics.

VectorGraph creates weird effects that look like sharply embossed metal, as if the image were carved out of aluminum. It operates more cleanly on grayscale images, but it creates interesting effects when applied to color images, leaving behind strange color artifacts. Figure 14.6 shows this filter applied to an image.

- Radar adds a radarlike radial sweep to your image, causing the picture to fade out as the radar scan moves from one point to another like a clock's second hand sweeping around the dial. You can adjust the angle of the sweep for each image, so this could make a good tool for animators looking to add a radar effect to their images. It also does some interesting things to stills. Figure 14.7 shows the Radar filter applied to an image.

Figure 14.6 VectorGraph creates great carved metal looks from your images.

Figure 14.7 Radar filter applied to an image.

- Lumpy Noise creates lumpy noise that is quite unlike what you can get with any other filter. Use it to make interesting backgrounds, add painterly strokes to images, or perform other effects. Figure 14.8 shows Lumpy Noise in action.

Figure 14.8 Lumpy Noise applied to an image.

Other Shareware Filters

America OnLine's Photoshop forum has a large group of interesting filters that you can download. Here are some brief descriptions of some of the better ones you may find there.

- **Dither Filter Package.** These two filters from David Hull convert grayscale images into dithered black-and-white patterns that can be output on laser printers. Of course, your software will dither images automatically, but using these filters lets you preview the images ahead of time. In addition, dithered images produced by these filters can be viewed on older, black-and-white Macs as-is, with no additional Mac conversion. Figure 14.9 shows an image that was converted using the PNDither filter. The companion VGDither filter uses a different algorithm and produces a different look, which you may prefer.

- **Frame.** This filter from Kas Thomas creates interesting borders around pictures and selections, using your own values for width, brightness, gradient, and other effects.

- **Warm Contrast.** Another filter from Kas Thomas, this one warms up an image and adds contrast in a single step.

Figure 14.9 Image with PNDither applied.

- **ResDoubler.** This filter, developed by Nathan Mariels, doubles the resolution of a grayscale or monochrome image and includes cute Happy Face dialog boxes (the Happy Face being the State symbol of the author's California home).

- **Frank's Filters.** Frank's filter set includes a Colorize, Change Color, and Remove Color filter.

- **BackSwap.** This filter from Jeff Burton replaces all occurrences of the background color in the image with the foreground color—not an easy thing to accomplish otherwise!

Plug-In Manager

Plug-In Manager, while not a plug-in itself, is a great tool to help you manage your growing collection of filters. You can view a list of all your available filters and check off which ones you want active at any particular time. Filters can be collected into sets, so that you can turn particular groups on and off all at once.

Collecting this utility for this book reminded me of how much I love modern technology. I discovered Plug-In manager on the Internet one Friday evening, and spent the following Saturday playing with it. Saturday night, I sent a message over the web to the author, Jonas Wallden, who just happens to live in Sweden! When I got up Sunday morning, there was a response, giving me permission to include this product on the CD-ROM bundled with this book. Try that with postal mail! And compare that exchange with the cost of even a telephone call (assuming that Jonas was even out of bed by the time I decided to send my message).

Plug-In Manager should be installed on the same hard disk volume as the folders containing the filters it manages. That's because the program doesn't copy files but only moves them from your Plugins folder to a "disabled" folder, without copying them.

The Plug-In Manager dialog box, shown in Figure 14.10, displays a scrolling list of all your filters. Double-click on files to add/remove the checkmark, which indicates whether the file is enabled. You can use standard selection methods, including the **Shift** key to extend selections or the **Command** key to select nonadjacent filters. A second pop-up menu lets you link a set of filters to a particular application.

Figure 14.10 Plug-In Manager dialog box.

Instructions for registering this utility (it costs just $10) are in the README file provided on the CD-ROM.

The Next Step

If you want to look for other shareware filters, try America OnLine, CompuServe, local electronic Bulletin Board Systems that cater to Macintosh users, user groups, and clubs or national shareware distribution firms.

With this chapter, we wrapped up our look at the best filters on the market, both commercial and shareware. In the last section, we'll put some of those filters to work with text and textures.

PART V

Putting Filters to Work

In this final section we'll use some of the filters described in the earlier chapters to create some interesting special effects. You'll learn how to simulate shiny metal, liven up your text for presentations, and add textures to selected portions of an image. We'll use many built-in filters, and we won't hesitate to dip into the third-party plug-ins we've also learned about. Chapter 15 shows you how to use text to jazz up your illustrations. Chapter 16 shoes you how to work with textures.

Using Filters with Text

In this chapter we'll see how some outrageous ways filters can be used to liven up the text you use in illustrations, desktop publishing, presentations, or other media. Even if your Mac is already equipped with a special effects text tool, like Pixar Typestry, you'll discover that the filters you already own can do a lot more than you expected. It's easy to create 3-D text, add metallic textures, and perform other magic if you just know how.

Working with Text

The TrueType and Adobe Type 1 fonts installed on your Macintosh are scalable fonts; that is, you can take any particular font outline and size it to virtually any type size that will fit on your screen. This means that you can add type to images as small as a few points or as large as several hundred points, depending on the resolution of your image. If this doesn't seem slick to you, then you're lucky enough not to have used the Mac back in the bad old System 6 days when fonts were all bitmapped and available in just a few fixed sizes.

However, you'll still find yourself dealing with bitmapped, nonscalable fonts. Once you've created some text and pasted it down into your image it becomes a part of that image (even if pasted into a layer) and is converted into a bitmap, which, as in days of old, can't be resized without scaling up the pixels used to draw the letter. Ordinarily, enlarging anything produces jaggies, but with text the resizing will be particularly noticeable, since the diagonal strokes found in many characters are the first to succumb to staircasing.

The other thing to keep in mind—although it's obvious to image-editing veterans—is that text is pasted into your image *as a selection*. Once you've positioned the text where you want it (or placed it into a separate layer so it can be moved around later) the first thing you should do is save the selection. Saving makes it possible to do other things with the text, such as fill it with color, gradients, or textures and make copies to create drop shadows.

Although I've written a whole book on using fonts for the Macintosh, I'm not what you'd call a fan of indiscriminate use of wildly transformed fonts. In fact, I try to keep my use of different fonts to a minimum in all my work. One 16-page newsletter I edit and produce each month has just three main fonts—for headlines, bylines, and body text—plus another used for fine print on the back cover. I probably use fewer than a dozen different fonts for 90% of my work.

Yet, there are times that the difference between the right font and the almost right font, as Mark Twain might have said, is like the difference between lightning and a lightning bug. When you're creating illustrations using an image editor, you'll find that selecting the perfect font for your text can take as much time as realizing the rest of the picture. And there are times when special effects like those in this chapter can add just the right touch to finish off an image.

So, while you'll not want to go whole-hog and transmogrify every font you ever apply to an image, you shouldn't be shy about using the power of plug-ins when needed.

Pursuing the Power of Plug-Ins

The exercises in this chapter all use common techniques that you've probably used many times, so I'll provide only overview descriptions of how to accomplish each effect.

Creating a Metal Look: Part One

You'll often want to create text with a metallic sheen, especially when you want a futuristic or industrial look. Metal also enhances illustrations with mechanical things or robots and can be used to simulate silver or gold. This first effect, shown in Figure 15.1, produces an icy-blue metal surface. You can easily reproduce this look if you have Adobe Gallery Effects library #1, which includes the Chrome filter, or have another chromelike filter with your image editor. Although this illustration is in black and white, you can check out the original image on the CD-ROM to get the full effect.

Figure 15.1 Blue metal look achieved with gradient fills and Chrome filter.

To produce this text, follow these steps.

1. Place the word *Metal* in a new image, using the Copperplate font. This is a very common all-caps font with an engraved look that is favored for advertising because of its elegance.

2. Save the selection so that you can work with the text separately from the background.

3. Fill the text with a medium gray (use **Edit:Fill** and enter 50% into the Opacity box) and then add about 30 pixels worth of noise to give the text some texture.

4. Apply the Gallery Effects Chrome filter to produce the swirling metallic look you see in Figure 15.1.

5. With the Rectangular marquee tool, hold down the **Command** key and drag across the bottom half of the characters to deselect the lower part of the text.

6. Save this new selection.

7. Fill the upper half with a gradient, ranging from dark blue at the center to light blue at the top.

8. Use Load Selection to reselect all the text and then load the upper-half selection you just saved, checking the **subtract from selection** radio button. You will have just the lower half of the text.

9. Fill the lower half with a gradient, ranging from dark blue at the center to light blue at the bottom.

10. Deselect the text and use the Smudge tool to blend the two gradients in the middle.

Carving Text from Blocks of Ice

You can use a similar technique to simulate text carved from a block of ice. Just follow these steps.

1. Add the word *Snazzy* (or any other text of your choosing). I selected the font Schneidler, because it has flowing curves and rounded serifs that already look as if they were molded from ice.

2. Save the selection and then fill with random noise. In this case, I used Adobe Gallery Effects Film Grain to produce the look you see in Figure 15.2.

Figure 15.2 Film Grain added to text.

3. Use the Layers palette's fly-out menu to Duplicate the current layer.

4. Working with the copy, apply the Chrome filter.

5. Outline the letters with **Edit:Stroke** set at 100%. Make sure black is the current foreground color. The new layer will look like Figure 15.3.

6. Set the Opacity setting for the chromed layer to about 60%, or any other blend that gives you the desired icy texture.

7. Flatten the image. You'll end up with characters like those shown in Figure 15.4.

Figure 15.3 Chrome filter applied and the letters outlined with Stroke.

Figure 15.4 Final icy-block letter image.

Cutting Out Letters with Tin Snips

Here you get two effects for the price of one. I wanted a rough look, almost as if the characters were cut out of metal with tin snips. One of the intermediate steps looked pretty good on its own. So, you can learn two different type effects with a few simple steps.

1. Enter the text of your choice (I used the word *Filters*) in a suitable font. I found Lithos to be the perfect choice, because it already includes some odd angles for its strokes.

2. Save the selection.

3. Apply the Difference Clouds filter to the text. With the thin strokes of the characters, the clouds end up looking like metallic reflections rather than actual clouds. It makes the text look like uneven metal.

4. Create a new layer with the Layers palette and then load the text selection.

5. Use **Select:Feather** and a setting of 8 pixels to feather the selection.

6. Fill the feathered selection with 100% black (**Edit:Fill.**)

7. Load the selection again and press the **Delete** key. This cuts out the area occupied by the original text but leaves the feathery shadow, as shown in Figure 15.5. This actually makes an interesting effect on its own, something like the overspray left behind when you airbrush a block stencil.

8. Copy and save this layer or flatten the image to generate the final text effect, shown in Figure 15.6.

Figure 15.5 Drop shadow with original text area cut out.

Figure 15.6 Final rough-cut metal effect.

Icy Frozen Granite

Let's take what we've learned a step further and create an icy frozen granite look. I added a background gradient in the final image that looks pretty cool. Be sure to check out the original image on the CD-ROM.

1. Type the word *ICY*. I used Arial Black, because its broad sans-serif strokes resemble a solid wall.

2. Save the selection.

3. Apply a sandstone or granite texture to the letters. I used Adobe Gallery Effects' Texturizer.

4. Increase the contrast sharply to make the texture stand out, using **Image:Adjust:Brightness/Contrast.**

5. Using the Lasso, hold down the **Command** key and deselect the lower part of the characters. Create a wavy boundary to simulate snow caps.

6. Apply a light blue-white fill at 10 to 20% to the remaining tops of the characters to simulate snow.

7. Create a new layer and load the text selection.

8. Create a drop shadow as in the last exercise, feather the selection, and fill with black; then reload the original selection and delete it to produce a cut-out.

9. Create another layer, load the text selection, and then invert it to produce a selection of everything except the text.

10. Fill the selection with a blue-to-white gradient.

11. With all three layers visible, set the Opacity of the gradient layer to produce a pleasing background effect.

12. Flatten the image. Your file should look like Figure 15.7.

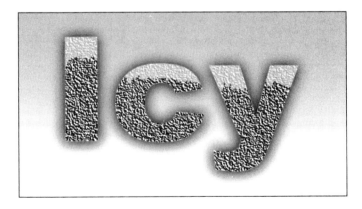

Figure 15.7 Icy frozen granite, topped with snow.

Clouding Up Your Text

I wanted some puffy white text floating in a layer of clouds, along with some subtle color effects. You can achieve this etherial result quite easily; just follow these steps.

1. Enter your text (I used *Clouds*, with Arial) and save the selection.
2. Fill with a rough texture. I used Adobe Gallery Effects and Burlap, but the exact texture doesn't matter as it will be heavily masked by the later effects.
3. Apply Difference Clouds to the text.
4. Duplicate the layer.
5. Working with the new layer, load the text selection and feather it with a setting of 4 pixels.
6. Use Gaussian Blur and a radius of 4 pixels to blur the selection.
7. Fill it with white at 80% opacity. You'll have a layer that looks like Figure 15.8.
8. Choose **Edit:Stroke** and a pixel radius of 3 to outline the characters.

Figure 15.8 Puffy cloud layer.

9. Create a new layer and fill with the Clouds filter. I used a medium blue and white as the foreground and background colors and then added a gradient fill from right to left to vary the density of the background cloud layer.
10. Adjust the Opacity of each of the layers until you get an effect you like; then flatten the image. The final version is shown in Figure 15.9.

Figure 15.9 Puffy clouds on a heavenly field.

Global Text

This next exercise illustrates how to wrap text around a globe or other surface. We'll use a whole bunch of filters for this one, but none of the steps are particularly difficult. Just follow these steps:

1. Create a perfectly circular selection by choosing the Elliptical marquee tool (**Option**-click on the Rectangular marquee tool if it is showing). Hold down the **Option** and **Shift** keys while you drag to create a perfect circle. Save the selection.

2. Type your text in a size that fits inside the selection. I used Goudy Old Style because it has thin strokes that would show the bending as we spherize it.

3. Use the **Distort:Spherize** filter at 100% to mold the lettering onto a sphere created from the circular area. Your image will look like Figure 15.10.

4. Fill the text with yellow and save the text selection.

Figure 15.10 Text mapped onto a sphere.

5. Create a new layer and load the circular selection.

6. Fill the circle with a radial fill, offset from the center to create a highlight at the upper left-hand corner. I wanted a shiny globe, so instead of using Spherize, I applied Kai's Power Tools' Glass Bright effect to produce the orb in Figure 15.11.

Figure 15.11 Glassy orb.

7. Create yet another layer and load the circular selection. Draw several 2-pixel straight lines vertically and one across the middle.

8. Apply the Spherize filter to change the straight lines into arcing lines of longitude and latitude.

9. Go to the Globe text layer, load the text selection, and copy the text. Paste it back on top of the arcing lines so that the lines are in back. Your layer should look like Figure 15.12.

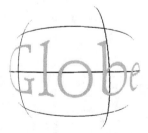

Figure 15.12 Text and latitude lines.

10. Create another layer and load the circular selection. Invert it and apply clouds to the background area.

11. I added a lens flare at the upper left boundary where the clouds meet the globe. You can barely see it in the illustration, but it looks really cool in the final image.

12. Flatten the image to produce the final effect shown in Figure 15.13.

Figure 15.13 Globe on a field of clouds.

Shining Up Your Corporate Image

Here's an impressive-looking corporate logo, suitable for a title slide, product packaging, or other application in the business world. You've already used all the tools required, so I can describe how to achieve this effect fairly quickly:

1. Enter the text into a new file. I used the name of Kitchen Table International, the world's largest fictitious producer of computer hardware, software, and limpware. I selected the Peignot font and centered the text.

2. Create two copies of the text on different layers. Fill one with a linear gradient, starting with white at the left and black at the right. You can also use another combination of light or dark colors.

3. Fill the second copy with the same gradient, going the opposite direction.

4. With both layers visible, use the cursor arrow keys to move the second copy up and to the right by a few pixels, until you get the three-dimensional effect shown in Figure 15.14.

5. Create another layer and fill it with a contrasting radial gradient bursting out from the center to dark edges. I used shades of red.

6. Apply the Lens Flare filter to the center of this layer to backlight the text.

7. Adjust the opacity of the individual layers to your taste and then flatten the image.

Figure 15.14 Glorious Kitchen Table International logo, ready for your presentation.

Book Cover with Rich Gold Inlay

I've done the production work for about a dozen of my books, but I have not done a cover for any of them. I leave that up to the artist–specialists who know what sells books. However, I wanted to prepare a cover–like image to show you what can be done. The technique used in the last section works fine, with a few enhancements.

If you check out the original image on the CD-ROM, or in the color section of this book, you'll see that the lettering has a rich, gold-plated look. It wasn't hard to achieve. The castle background I used is on the CD-ROM, so you can duplicate this image if you like. Just follow these steps:

1. Load the background castle image.

2. Create a new layer for the text.

3. Enter the text. I used an Olde English font and centered the text.

4. Move the text to the desired position on the background; then save the selection.

5. Apply a dark-to-light, left-to-right linear gradient to the text. I used a black-to-white gradient and tinted the text with yellow to give it a gold appearance.

6. Duplicate the layer and invert. This technique produces an inverse gradient, as with the last exercise, but is a faster way of doing it. (The former method lets you vary the gradient between examples; this one doesn't.)

7. Use the cursor arrow keys to offset the second copy to produce a shadow effect.

8. Go back to the castle image and invert that.

9. Select the sky and save the selection.

10. Now fill the sky with clouds, using the Clouds filter. Use a dark blue and white to generate appropriately moody clouds.

11. Load the sky selection and invert.

12. Use **Image:Adjust:Hue/Saturation** and change the hue of the castle. I used a dark brown that complemented the gold lettering.

13. Flatten the image. Your final effect will look like Figure 15.15.

Figure 15.15 Castle in Spain, letters in gold.

The Next Step

I tried to use several different kinds of filters in this chapter—distortion filters like Spherize, rendering filters, and noise filters—but there are many other things you can do to text with the other filters we've discussed in this book. This chapter was intended to show you that you don't need a special type of utility to create exiting text. Often, filters and some imagination are all you need.

In Chapter 16 we'll look at some additional ways of applying filters to your work.

CHAPTER 16

Working with Textures

In this chapter, I'll explore some more of the things you can do with textures, using the tools we've already discussed in previous chapters. I'll include a few sample images and tell you exactly how I achieved the effect. This discussion will give you a chance to look at some texturizing tricks in a little more detail.

Terrazzo

Terrazzo is an image-enhancing filter and pattern factory, disguised as an Adobe Photoshop plug-in filter. It can quickly generate a never-ending array of kaleidoscopic patterns from portions of an image, while allowing the digital artist to control opacity, transitions, saturation, and dozens of other parameters. Figure 16.1 shows the kind of texture you can create with Terrazzo.

If you want to generate tileable patterns, spice up your images with wondrous textures, create imaginative textile designs, or just play with abstract geometry, you'll add Terrazzo to your plug-in library. It's a product of Xaos Tools, which also markets Paint Alchemy, another industrial-strength filter toolkit. As with most Adobe-standard plug-ins, Terrazzo works with any compatible program, including Photoshop, Fractal Design Painter, PixelPaint Pro 3, and Deneba Canvas.

You can apply Terrazzo's transformations to an entire image or just a selection. In either case, the filter's dialog box allows you to choose a portion of the original image—or another file, if you wish—to be reflected and twisted based on one of 17 different kaleidoscopelike symmetrical patterns. Warping an existing image is a slick way to generate patterns that are automatically color-coordinated.

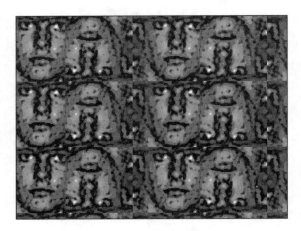

Figure 16.1 Typical Terrazzo texture.

Your tiles are built by reflecting, rotating, and repeating the portion of the image you select. Choose from Pinwheel, Whirlpool, Sunflower, or another arrangement and then play with Terrazzo's controls in real time to preview thousands of effects in minutes. Xaos warns that this "continuous preview" can slow down some color Macs, but on my Quadra 650 the display was updated instantaneously.

You can feather the boundaries between portions of the pattern to produce a smooth transition and adjust opacity so that the underlying image shows through to varying degrees.

A Mode menu, which operates similarly to the Mode menu in Photoshop, lets you control how the pattern is applied to a selection. The overlay can modify the image through Lighten, Darken, Hue, Saturation, Color, Luminosity, and other parameters.

Terrazzo can save patterns as PICT files that can be tiled seamlessly, for use as desktop wallpaper or as backgrounds in presentations or other images. Programs like Photoshop and Fractal Design Painter can use these PICT files as instant textures.

The program is accompanied by a full-color manual that leads you through the process of creating stunning patterns and textures and that has generous gallery of examples.

Figure 16.2 shows Terrazzo's dialog box and controls.

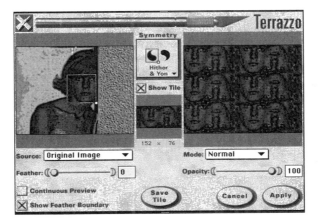

Figure 16.2 Terrazzo dialog box.

Pixar 128

Pixar 128 is a Photoshop plug-in that comes on a CD-ROM with 128 different textures in both high- and low-resolution versions. To install it, just drag the filter to your plug-in folder. Then you can import any of the textures directly into your image using the dialog box shown in Figure 16.3.

If you need to use one of the textures with a filter that works only with PICT files (Pixar provides TIFF files), you can load the texture and save it to your hard disk in PICT format.

I took a mountain scene and applied a rocky texture to it, as if it were printed on a stone wall. The texture file is shown in the inset in Figure 16.4. To do something similar, just follow these steps:

1. If you have Pixar 128, load the Contractor's Rocks TIFF file and save as PICT. You can substitute a rocky image of your own choice.

2. Using a texturizer, such as the one found in Gallery Effects Volume 2, specify the rocky PICT as the texture.

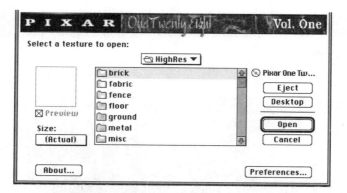

Figure 16.3 Pixar 128 dialog box.

3. Adjust the lighting angle so that the illumination appears to be coming from the same direction as the light in the photograph.

4. Apply the texture.

Figure 16.4 Mountain scene texturized with rocky background.

Kai's Power Tools Texture Explorer

Don't forget that you can create thousands (millions) of textures using the tools in KPT Texture Explorer. It's easy to preview your effects in the boxes surrounding the main window (shown in Figure 16.5).

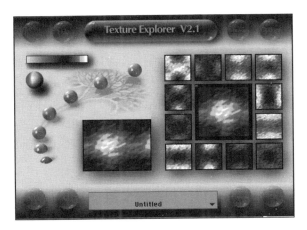

Figure 16.5 Kai's Power Tools Texture Explorer.

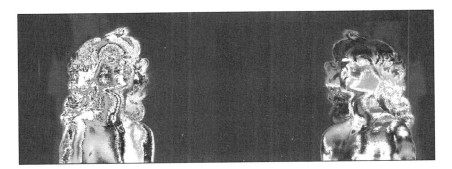

Figure 16.6 Texture applied using Kai's Power Tools Texture Explorer.

To illustrate the application for KPT Texture explorer, I added a texture to mirror images of the same study. The model had been posed on a plain background, so it was easy to select the background and then inverse the selection, so that I could apply the texture only to the model.

I found several textures I liked and applied them to two versions of the same image. Then I flipped one to produce the mirror image. KPT Texture Explorer makes browsing through the thousands of presets provided easy, but you must remember to save any of the variations you like if you expect to use it again.

Underpainting

The Adobe Gallery Effects Underpainting filter is a wonderful effect. I used it in an unusual way to produce the picture shown in Figure 16.7. I duplicated the original image layer and then applied the underpainting effect to the copy. After that, I created a Layer Mask, using the Layer palette's fly-out menu, and I applied a diagonal linear gradient to the mask, such that the underpainted image was masked out at the left side of the model's face and hair. Finally, I flattened the image. The mask made it possible to retain detail in her face, while keeping the heavy texture of the underpainting filter everywhere else in the image.

Figure 16.7 Texture added using Gallery Effects Underpainting filter.

Using Your Own PICT File

For the next exercise, I wanted to demonstrate how to create textures entirely from scratch. I recycled an old picture of B.B. King and added a noteworthy background texture. To do something similar, just follow these steps.

1. Create some freehand musical notes, as shown in the inset of Figure 16.8. It doesn't matter if you're not a professional artist, just sketch out something rough and save it as a PICT file.

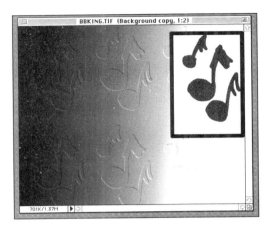

Figure 16.8 Hand-drawn notes (inset) and texturized layer.

2. Add a layer to the B.B. King TIFF file and use a linear gradient fill to color it from black to white.

3. Use the Gallery Effects Texturizer filter and your own notes PICT as the texture file.

4. Merge the layers, using an 80% Opacity setting, so that the background notes overpower the B.B. King photo in the background.

5. Add text using a rough-hewn font.

The finished image is shown in Figure 16.9.

Figure 16.9 Finished texturized photo of B.B. King.

Producing a Statue

For this next exercise, check out the original image on the CD-ROM. It really looks like a metal statue cast in bronze. This one, shown in Figure 16.10, was easy to produce. Just follow these steps:

1. Duplicate the image layer with the model.

2. Apply the Gallery Effects Volume 1 Chrome filter. I used Detail 10 and Smoothness 1 to produce an image that contained as many details as possible of the original.

3. Merge the chromed layer with the original background, adding back some of the skin detail and color.

4. Use the Brightness/Contrast controls to darken the image while boosting contrast, until you get a bright metal statue with strong highlights.

Figure 16.10 Metal texture produced with Chrome filter.

Heavy Canvas

This final example uses the Gallery Effects texturizer and a burlap texture to provide a heavily roughened image of the Court of the Lions at the Alhambra. The original photograph that I scanned also had a heavy texture, so using this technique masked the roughness of the paper. In this case, I boosted the contrast of the final image, using the Brightness/Contrast controls, to make the canvas texture even more noticeable.

Figure 16.11 Court of the Lions at the Alhambra, with heavy texture applied.

The Next Step

We've explored quite a few different filters in this book, and I hope I've given you a good feel for how individual filters work and what you can do with them. The next step, as always, is up to you. I hope you'll look through the additional examples on the CD-ROM bundled with this book, try out the software I've selected for you, and experiment with my photos or your own.

Glossary

In this glossary, you'll find definitions of most of the specialized terms and jargon that you'll run across when working with filters, scanners, and imaging software. You can use this word list to refresh your memory or find explanations of topics that aren't completely clear to you.

While many of these terms are defined in the chapters in which they first appear, this complete list should prove quite helpful to you. Check here first if you need a definition of a new or obscure word.

Achromatic color A color with no saturation, such as a light gray.

Additive colors The primary colors of light—red, green, and blue—which, when combined, produce white light.

Airbrush An atomizer used for spraying paint. Image-editing software usually has an airbrush like tool that can apply a fine spray of a given tone to a specified area. Fully controllable airbrushes allow you to adjust the size of the airbrush spray, its density or concentration, and the speed at which the spray flows.

Alpha channel An optional grayscale "layer" of an image that you can create to store selections and other modifications and that you may save with the image in TIFF or an image editor's proprietary format. See also *Channel*.

Ambient lighting The overall nondirectional lighting that fills an area. When using lighting effects filters, you can place specific lights around your subject and use ambient lighting to fill in the dark areas not illuminated by one of the main lights.

Anamorphic image An image that has been enlarged or reduced more in one direction than another. The image looks "squashed" or "stretched" in a given dimension.

Antialiasing A process that can be used to remove jaggies or stair-stepping in an image. Antialiasing smoothes out diagonal lines by placing dots of an in-between tone in appropriate places.

Applications program Software, such as a word processing program, spreadsheet, or database manager, that performs useful work not directly related to the maintenance or operation of the computer. Photoshop and PageMaker are applications programs.

Applications program interface (API) A common interface that allows software engineers to write programs that will operate with a broad range of computer configurations.

Archive To store files that are no longer active. Programs like STUFFIT combine and compress files into an archive file for more compact, easier storage.

Aspect ratio The relative proportion of the length and width of an image. For example, if you scan an original that measures 4 x 6 inches will have an aspect ratio of 4:6 or 2:3. To maintain the same proportions, you must place it in your desktop publishing document with dimensions that conform to the same ratio. That is, it could be sized at 2 x 3 inches or 1.5 x 2.25 inches. CRT screens and printers also have aspect ratios.

Attribute Characteristics of a page, character or object, such as line width, fill, underlining, boldface, or font.

Automatic document feeder (ADF) A device that is attached to a scanner and that automatically feeds one page at a time, allowing the scanning of multiple pages.

Autotrace A feature that allows you to trace a bit-map image and convert it to an outline or vector format. Aurtotrace is found in many object-oriented image-editing programs or stand-alone programs like Adobe Streamline.

Background The ability to run unattended while another program is executing. On the Mac, background printing and telecommunications are most often used. In Photoshop, the background is the bottom layer of an image.

Backlighting A lighting effect produced when the main light source is located behind the subject. If no frontlighting, fill, or ambient lighting is used in conjunction with backlighting, the effect is a silhouette. You can simulate backlighting with filters.

Back up To make a copy of computer data as a safeguard against accidental loss. The copy that is made is called the backup.

Baseline An imaginary line on which all the characters in a line rest.

BBS Bulletin Board System. A computer system that has been set up to function as a clearing house for the exchange of information among other computer users via modem. Service bureaus often set up a BBS to allow transmitting PostScript files for output directly to the bureau.

Bézier curve A cubic polynomial in mathematical terms or, simply, a way of representing a curve that allows great flexibility in manipulating the curve. Bézier curves are adjusted using endpoints and anchor points.

Bilevel In scanning, a binary scan that stores only the information that tells whether a given pixel should be represented as black or white.

Binary Base-two arithmetic, which uses only 1s and 0s to represent numbers. 0001 represents 1 decimal, 0010 represents 2 decimal, 0011 represents 3 decimal, and so on. In scanning, a black-and-white image.

Bit A binary digit—either a 1 or a 0. Scanners typically use multiple bits to represent information about each pixel of an image. A 1-bit scan can store only black or white information about a pixel. A 2-bit scan can include four different gray levels or values—00, 01, 10, or 11. Other values include:

4 bits	16 gray levels/colors
5 bits	32 gray levels/colors
6 bits	64 gray levels/colors
7 bits	128 gray levels/colors
8 bits	256 gray levels/colors
15 bits	32,767 colors
16 bits	65,535 colors
24 bits	16.7 million colors

Bit map A representation of an image in row and column format in which each individual pixel is represented by a number. A single bit (up to as many as 32 bits) can be used with each increment representing a larger amount of gray or color information about the pixel.

Black The color formed by the absence of reflected or transmitted light.

Black printer The plate used for the black ink in the four-color printing process. It provides emphasis for neutral tones, detail in shadow areas of the image, and a deeper black than can be provided by combining cyan, magenta, and yellow alone. Black printers can take two forms. A skeleton black adds black ink only to the darker areas of an image. A full-range black printer adds some black ink to every part of the image.

Bleed An image that continues to the edge of the page. It is often accomplished by extending the image past the edge and then trimming the page to the finished size.

Blend To create a more realistic transition between image areas. Image-editing software often allows you to merge overlapping sections of images to blend the boundary between them.

Blur To soften part of an image, making it less distinct.

Boot To start up a computer.

Brightness The balance of light and dark shades in an image. See also *Luminance*.

Buffer An area of computer memory set aside to store information meant for some sort of I/O, such as printing or writing to disk. Using a buffer allows the device supplying the information to feed it into memory faster, if necessary, than the device meant to accept the information can handle it. A printer buffer, for example, allows an applications program to dump a document for printing quickly and then go on to something else. The buffer can then feed the information to the printer at a slower rate. In scanning, buffers are often used to store images awaiting processing.

Bug An error in a program that results in some unintended action.

Burn In photography, to expose part of a print for a longer period, making it darker than it would be with a straight exposure. In lithography, to expose a printing plate.

Bus A hardware interface used to connect a computer to peripherals or other computers. For example, the SCSI bus and NuBus, are both used by Macintosh computers.

Byte Eight bits, which can represent any number from 0000000 to 11111111 binary (0 to 255 decimal).

Cache A fast memory buffer used to store information read from disk or from slower RAM to allow the operating system to access it more quickly. Cache programs use various schemes to make sure that the most frequently accessed sectors, as well as the most recently accessed sectors, remain in the buffer as long as possible. A disk cache stores data that would otherwise be retrieved from a floppy disk, hard disk, optical disk, or CD-ROM, while a processor cache stores instructions and data that the microprocessor needs to work with. A processor cache can be built into the microprocessor or provided in the form of an add-on board plugged into the Mac's processor direct slot (PDS).

CAD Computer-Assisted Design. Also called Computer-Aided Design and Computer Aided/Assisted Drafting/Design (CADD). A technique for creating engineering drawings and similar materials on a computer using line-oriented techniques.

Calibration A process used to correct the variation in output of a device like a printer or monitor when you compare it to the original image data you get from the scanner.

Camera ready Artwork printed in hardcopy form that can be photographed to produce negatives or plates for printing.

Cast A tinge of color in an image, particularly an undesired color.

CCD Charge-Coupled Device. A type of solid-state sensor used in scanners and video capture devices. Compared to older imaging devices such as video tubes, CCDs are more sensitive and less prone to memory problems that can blur images.

CD-ROM Compact Disk—Read-Only Memory. An optical disk device that uses pits that are written on the disk by laser to convey bits of information. CD-ROMs are encoded with information during manufacture and cannot be written to by the user. They provide a means of distributing large databases on a compact medium.

CDEV A Control Panel device, such as General, Keyboard, and Monitors, used to configure your Macintosh. Prior to System 7, CDEVs were all accessed from a single desk accessory with individual scrolling icons for each. Under System 7 you can access each Control Panel directly.

Channel One of the layers that make up an image. An RGB image has three channels: one each for the red, green, and blue information. A CMYK image has four channels: cyan, magenta, yellow, and black. A grayscale image contains just one channel. Additional masking channels, or alpha channels, can be added to any of these.

Chooser The desk accessory used to select from devices such as printers and direct their communications through either the printer or modem port.

Chroma Color or hue.

Chromalin The DuPont trademark for a type of color proof used for representing how color halftones will appear on the printed page.

Chromatic color A color that has at least one hue, with a visible level of color saturation.

Chrome In photography a color transparency, from film names like Kodachrome or Ektachrome.

Clip art Artwork that is purchased or otherwise available for scanning or other uses in desktop publishing with few restrictions.

Clipboard A memory buffer that can hold images and text so that they can be freely interchanged within and between Macintosh applications.

Clip To compress a range of values into a single value, as when a group of highlight tones are compressed to white or a set of shadow tones are represented as black. See also *Threshold*..

Clone In image editing, to copy pixels from one part of an image to another.

Color See *Hue*.

Color correction Changing the color balance of an image to produce a desired effect, usually a more accurate representation of the colors in an image. It is used to compensate for the deficiencies of process color inks, inaccuracies in a color separation, or undesired color balance in the original image. Color correction is done using one of several available color models, including RGB (red-green-blue) and LHS (luminance-hue-saturation).

Color key A set of four acetate overlays, each with a halftone representing one of the colors of a color separation and tinted in that color. When combined, color keys can be used for proofing color separations.

Color separation The process of reducing an image to its four separate color components—cyan, magenta, yellow, and black. These separations are combined using an individual plate for each color on a press. To create a color, percentages of the three primary colors and black are combined.

Color wheel A circle representing the spectrum of visible colors.

Comp A layout that combines type, graphics, and photographic material. Also called a composite or comprehensive.

Complementary color Generally, the opposite hue of a color on a color wheel, which is called the direct complement. For example, green is the direct complement of magenta. There are two other types of complements: the split complement (a color 30° away from the direct complementary color) and the triadic (a color 120° in either direction from the selected color).

Composite controls A Photoshop 2.5 command that determines how pixels of a floating selection will be pasted into an underlying image. This function is now carried out using Layer Options under Photoshop 3.0 and later.

Compression Packing of a file or image in a more efficient form to improve storage efficiency. Compression and decompression take some time, so it takes longer to save and open compressed files.

Concatenate To add together.

Constrain To limit in some way, as to limit the movement of a selection by holding down **Shift** as you begin to move the selection with the mouse.

Contiguous In reference to hard disks, contiguous sectors are those that are arranged consecutively on the disk. Your system software tries to allocate sectors to a file contiguously so that the disk drive can read as many sectors of a file as it can with a minimum of read/write head movement. However, as a hard disk fills, the unallocated sectors gradually become spread out and fragmented, forcing the operating system to choose more and more noncontiguous sectors. Fragmented files can be much slower to access.

Continuous tone Images that contain tones from black to white with an infinite range of variations between.

Contrast The range between the lightest and darkest tones in an image. A high-contrast image is one in which the shades fall at the extremes of the range between white and black. In a low-contrast image, the tones are closer together.

Control character A nonprinting character used to send information to a device, such as the control characters used to communicate special formatting commands to a printer.

Convolve To twist, roll, or twine together. When applied to imaging, the term describes the way filters use the values of surrounding pixels to calculate new values when generating a special effect.

Copy dot Photographic reproduction of a halftone image in which the halftone dots of a previously screened image are carefully copied as if they were line art. The same technique can be used in scanning to capture a halftoned image. If the original dot sizes are maintained, the quality of the finished image can be good.

Creator code A four-letter code used by your system software to keep track of which application was used to generate a given document. This code allows the Mac to launch the right application when you double-click on a file.

Because many applications can create several different types of files, a second code, called a type code, is used to differentiate among them.

Crop To trim an image or page by adjusting the side or boundaries.

Crop mark A mark placed on a page that is larger than the finished page to show where the page should be trimmed to final size.

Cursor A symbol that indicates the point at which the next action the user takes—text entry, line drawing, deletion, and so on—will begin; the current screen display position.

CMYK The abbreviation for cyan, magenta, yellow, and black.

CYMK color model A model that defines all possible colors in percentages of cyan, magenta, yellow, and black.

Daisy-chain To connect peripheral devices in series, as with the SCSI bus. You can also daisy-chain Apple Desktop Bus (ADB) devices, such as the keyboard and mouse.

Darken A feature that allows gray values in selected areas to be changed, one value at a time, from the current value to a darker one. It is found in many image-editing programs. This feature is equivalent to the burning procedure used in conventional darkrooms.

Data compression A method of reducing the size of files, such as image files, by representing the sets of binary numbers in the file with a shorter string that conveys the same information. Many image editing programs offer some sort of image compression as an optional mode when saving a file to disk.

Default A preset option or value that is used unless you specify otherwise.

Defloat To merge a floating selection with the underlying image. The defloated portion of the image is still selected, but if you move or cut it, the area it previously covered will be filled with the background color.

Defringe To remove the outer edge pixels of a selection, usually to merge the selection with the underlying image more smoothly.

Densitometer A device that measures the density of an image.

Desaturate To reduce the purity or vividness of a color. Desaturated colors appear washed out and diluted.

Descender The portion of a lowercase letter that extends below the baseline. The letter *p* is an example of a character with a descender.

Diffusion The random distribution of gray tones in an area of an image, often used to produce a mezzotint effect.

Digital signal processor (DSP) A special coprocessor designed to work in tandem with the computer's main CPU. It applies large amounts of numeric calculations to data in real-time. and is especially useful for digital audio or video applications.

Digitize To convert information such as that found in continuous tone images (or music), usually analog information, to a numeric format that can be accepted by a computer.

Displacement map A file used to control the shifting of pixels in an image horizontally or vertically to produce a particular special effect.

Dithering A method of simulating gray tones by grouping the dots shown on your CRT display or produced by your printer into large clusters of varying size. The mind merges these clusters and the surrounding white background into different tones of gray.

Dodge In photography, to block part of an image as it is exposed, lightening its tones.

Dot A unit used to represent a portion of an image. A dot can correspond to one of the pixels used to capture or show an image on the screen, or groups of pixels can be collected to produce larger printer dots of varying sizes to represent gray.

Dot etching A technique in photographic halftoning in which the size of the halftone dots is changed to alter tone values.

Dot gain The tendency of a printing dot to grow from the original size when halftoned to its final printed size on paper. This effect is most pronounced on offset presses using poor quality papers, which allow ink to absorb and spread.

Dots per inch (dpi) The resolution of an image, expressed in the number of pixels or printer dots in an inch.

Download To receive a file from another device. For example, soft fonts are downloaded from your computer to your printer.

Driver A software interface used to allow an applications program to communicate with a piece of hardware such as a scanner.

Drop cap The first letter of a paragraph, set in a larger point size than the rest of the text. It may rise above the first line or extend below it, in which case the drop cap is inset into the text block.

Dummy A rough approximation of a publication, used to gauge layout.

Duotone A printed image, usually a monochrome halftone, that uses two different colors of ink to produce a longer range of tones than would be possible with a single ink density and set of printer cells alone.

Dye sublimation A printing technique in which solid inks are heated directly into a gas, which then diffuses into a polyester substrate to form an image. Because dye sublimation printers can reproduce 256 different hues for each color, they can print as many as 16.7 million different colors.

Dynamic RAM (DRAM) Type of memory that must be electrically refreshed many times each second to avoid loss of the contents. All computers use DRAM to store programs, data, video information, and the operating system.

Emboss To change an image or selection so that it appears to be raised above the surface, in a 3-D effect.

Emulsion The light-sensitive coating on a piece of film, paper, or printing plate.

Emulsion side The side of a piece of film that contains the image, usually with a matte, nonglossy finish. This side is placed in contact with the emulsion side of another piece of film (when making a duplicate) or the printing plate. That way, the image is sharper than it would be if it were diffused by the base material of the film. Image-processing workers need to understand this concept when producing images oriented properly (either right-reading or wrong-reading) for production.

Encapsulated PostScript An outline-oriented image format that represents graphics and text in terms of descriptions of how to draw them. Desktop publishing programs like PageMaker, QuarkXpress, FrameMaker, and Ready, Set, Go can import these files, while vector-oriented draw programs can often modify them.

Export To transfer text or images from a document to another format. Some applications provide a **Save As...** option to save the entire file in the optional format, while others let you save a selected portion of the image or file in another file format.

Extrude To create a 3-D effect by adding edges to an outline shape as if it were clay pushed through a Play-Doh Fun Factory.

Eye Dropper An image-editing tool used to "pick up" color from one part of an image so that it can be used to paint or draw in that color elsewhere.

Feather To fade the edges of a selection to produce a less-noticeable transition.

File: A collection of information, usually data or a program, that has been given a name and allocated sectors by operating system.

File format A set way in which a particular application stores information on a disk. This standardization makes it possible for different applications to load each others' files, since they know what to expect from a predictable file format. PICT, TIFF, and StartupScreen are all file formats found on the Mac.

File name The name given to a file. It can be quite long in the Macintosh environment but is, in contrast, limited under MS-DOS to just eight characters and a three-character extension.

Fill To cover a selected area with a tone or pattern. Fills can be solid, transparent, or have a gradient transition from one color or tone to another.

Filter In scanning, image filters are used to process an image—to blur, sharpen, or otherwise change it. Programs like Adobe Photoshop have advanced filters that will spherize, change perspective, and add patterns to selected portions of the image.

Finder The part of the system software that takes care of opening, closing, renaming, moving, and erasing files and folders from your desktop. The Finder also formats (initializes) and ejects disks.

Fixed disk Another name for a hard disk drive, so-called because such disks are not commonly removed from the computer while in use.

File-oriented backup Any backup system that stores information in files, just as they are stored on the disk. Such systems allow easier access to and restoration of a particular file.

Flat A low-contrast image. Also, the assembled and registered negatives or positives used to expose a printing plate.

Floating selection A selection that has been pasted into an image from another image or layer is said to be floating. It's above and not part of the underlying image; that is, you can move it around without affecting the image beneath. Once it has been defloated, the selection becomes part of the underlying pixels and cannot be moved or cut without leaving a "hole."

Font A group of letters, numbers, and symbols in one size and typeface. Garamond and Helvetica are typefaces; 11-point Helvetica Bold is a font.

Format To initialize or prepare a disk for use by writing certain information in magnetic form. Formatting divides the disk into tracks and sectors and sets up a directory structure, which is shown in the Macintosh world as folders and icons.

Four-color printing Another term for process color, in which cyan, magenta, yellow, and black inks are used to reproduce all the hues of the spectrum.

FPO For Position Only Artwork that is used to help gauge how a page layout looks but that is not good enough for reproduction.

Fractal A kind of image in which each component is made up of ever smaller versions of the component. Sets of fractal images can be calculated using formulas developed by mathematicians such as Mandelbrot and Julia and used as textures in images with tools like KPT Fractal Explorer. More recently, fractal calculations have been used to highly compress image files: when the image is decompressed, fractal components are used to simulate portions that were discarded during the archiving process.

Frame grabber A device that captures a single field of a video scanner or camera.

Frequency The number of lines per inch in a halftone screen.

Frisket Another name for a mask, which is used to shield portions of an image from the effects of various tools applied to other areas of the image.

Galley A typeset copy of a publication used for proofreading and estimating length.

Gamma A numerical way of representing the contrast of an image, shown as the slope of a line showing tones from white to black.

Gamma correction A method for changing the brightness, contrast, or color balance of an image by assigning new values to the gray or color tones of an image. Gamma correction can be either linear or nonlinear. Linear correction applies the same amount of change to all the tones. Nonlinear correction varies the changes tone by tone, or in highlight, midtone, and shadow areas separately to produce a more accurate or improved appearance.

Gamut A range of color values. Those colors that are present in an image but that cannot be represented by a particular process such as offset printing or CRT display are said to be out of gamut.

Gang scan The process of scanning more than one picture at a time. Gang scans are used when images are of the same density and color balance range.

Gaussian blur A method of diffusing an image by using a bell-shaped curve to calculate which pixels will be blurred, rather than blurring all pixels in the selected area uniformly.

Gigabyte A billion bytes of information; a thousand megabytes. Only ten 8.5 x 11-inch full-color images scanned at 600 dpi would fill up a gigabyte of disk space.

Graduated fill A pattern in which one shade or hue smoothly blends into another; also called a gradient fill.

Graphics tablet A pad on which you draw with a pen like device called a stylus. The graphics tablet is used as an alternative to a mouse.

Gray balance The proportion of ink in each of the three process colors (cyan, magenta, and yellow) that will combine to produce a neutral gray color.

Gray component removal A process in which portions of an image that have all three process colors have an equivalent amount of their color replaced by black to produce purer, more vivid colors.

Gray map A graph that shows the relationship between the original brightness values of an image and the output values after image processing.

Gray scale The spectrum of different gray values that an image can have.

Gutter The inner margin of a page, which must be included to allow for binding.

Halftoning A method for representing the gray tones of an image by varying the size of the dots used to show the image.

Handles Small squares that appear in the corners (and often at the sides) of a square used to define an area to be scanned or an object in an image-editing program. The user can grab the handles with the mouse cursor and resize the area or object.

Hardware The physical components of a computer system, including the CRT display, keyboard, microprocessor, memory, and peripherals.

HFS Hierarchical File System. The file storage system introduced with the Mac Plus in 1986. It allows you to arrange files, applications, and folders in a hierarchy; that is, you can place files in folders, and folders in other folders, just as with a real hardcopy filing system.

High-level language A language that allows machine-level operations to be represented by mnemonic keywords rather than 1s and 0s. BASIC, COBOL, Pascal, C, and FORTRAN are high-level languages.

Highlight The brightest values in a continuous tone image.

Histogram A barlike graph that shows the distribution of gray tones in an image.

HPGL Hewlett-Packard Graphics Language. Language that is used to define images to be printed with plotters.

HSB color model A model that defines all possible colors by specifying a particular hue and then adding or subtracting percentages of black or white.

Hue A pure color. In nature, there is a continuous range of hues.

Icon A small graphic that represents an object or function on the computer screen.

Image acquisition Capturing a digitized version of a hardcopy or real-world image, as with a scanner or video camera.

Image editor A program like Adobe Photoshop, PixelPaint, or Fractal Design Painter that is used to edit bit-mapped images.

Imagesetter A high-resolution PostScript printer that creates camera-ready pages on paper or film.

INIT A startup document, called an extension under System 7, that becomes part of your operating system when your Mac boots. These documents often provide some special functions, such as added sound capabilities, extra function keys, font management (Adobe Type Manager is an INIT/extension), or Oscar The Grouch popping up each time you empty the trash. Many scanner drivers are installed as INITs.

Ink-jet A printing technology in which dots of ink are sprayed on paper.

Input Incoming information. Input may be supplied to the computer by the user or to a program by either the user or a data file.

Instruction cache A type of high-speed memory used to store the commands that the microprocessor used most recently. A cache "hit" can eliminate the need to access slower RAM or the hard disk, thus increasing the effective speed of the system.

Instructions The basic set of capabilities of a microprocessor, which allows the chip to load information into a register, move it to another register, increment the data, add or subtract data from a register, and so forth.

Intelligent Having sufficient programming builtin to carry out certain tasks independently. An intelligent disk drive can accept requests from the operating system, locate the data, and deliver it without detailed instructions on how to do the physical I/O.

Interactive Allowing user input during run time.

Interlacing A way of displaying a video image in two fields: odd-numbered lines first and then even-numbered lines, thereby updating or refreshing half the image on the screen at a time.

Interpolation A technique that is used when resizing or changing the resolution of an image to calculate the value of pixels that must be created to produce the new size or resolution. Interpolation uses the tone and color of the pixels surrounding each new pixel to estimate the correct parameters.

Interpreter A program that interprets and carries out each line of another program written in a high-level language like BASIC or COBOL. These languages can also be compiled so that the computer can carry out the commands directly. PostScript interpreters for printers perform the same function with the instructions found in PostScript files.

Invert To change an image into its negative; black becomes white, white becomes black, dark gray becomes light gray, and so forth. Colors are also changed to the complementary color: green becomes magenta, blue turns to yellow, and red is changed to cyan.

I/O Input/Output. Description of the process whereby information flows to and from the microprocessor or computer through peripherals such as scanners, disk drives, modems, CRT screens, and printers.

Jaggies Staircasing of lines that are not perfectly horizontal or vertical. Jaggies are produced when the pixels used to portray a slanted line aren't small enough to be invisible, because of the high contrast of the line and its surrounding pixels. Jaggies are typically found at the edges of letters.

JPEG compression Reducing the size of an image through algorithms specified by the Joint Photographic Experts Group. The image is divided into blocks, and all the pixels within the block are compared. Depending on the quality level chosen by the user, some of the pixel information is discarded as the file is compressed. For example, if all the pixels in a block are very close in value, they may be represented by a single number rather than the individual values.

Justified Text that is aligned at both the right and left margins.

K Kilobyte. In computer terminology, 1024; 16K represents 16,384, 64K equals 65,536, 512K corresponds to 524,288, and so on.

Kern To adjust the amount of space between two adjacent letters.

Knockout Area on a spot color overlay in which an overlapping color is deleted so that the background color shows through.

Landscape The orientation of a page in which the longest dimension is horizontal. Also called wide orientation.

Lasso A tool used to select irregularly shaped areas in a bit-mapped image.

Launch To start a Macintosh application.

Layers Separation of a drawing or image into separate "transparent" overlays, which can be edited or manipulated separately, yet combined to provide a single drawing or image.

Leading The amount of vertical spacing between lines of text from baseline to baseline.

Lens flare In photography, an effect produced by the reflection of light internally among elements of an optical lens. Bright light sources within or just outside the field of view cause lens flare. Lens flare can be reduced by the use of coatings on the lens elements or with the use of lens hoods, but photographers (and now digital image workers) have learned to use it as a creative element.

LHS color correction A system of color correction based on the luminance, hue, and saturation of an image.

Ligature A combination of two characters squeezed together to form a composite character. Ligatures can confuse OCR programs that use pattern matching until the software has been trained to recognize each ligature combination.

Lighten An image-editing function that is the equivalent to the photographic darkroom technique of dodging. Gray tones in a specific area of an image are gradually changed to lighter values.

Line art Usually, images that consist only of black and white lines.

Line screen The resolution or frequency of a halftone screen, expressed in lines per inch. Typical line screens are 53 to 150 lines per inch.

Lines per inch (lpi) The "yardstick" used to measure halftone resolution.

Lithography A reproduction process in which sheets or continuous webs of material are printed by impressing them with images from ink applied to a rubber blanket on a rotating cylinder from a metal or plastic plate attached to another cylinder. Also called offset printing.

Logical Any feature not physically present but defined anyway for convenience. The physical sectors on a hard disk are arranged contiguously. Logically, they may be arranged in alternating fashion through interleaving.

Luminance The brightness or intensity of an image. Determined by the amount of gray in a hue, luminance reflects the lightness or darkness of a color. See also *Saturation*.

LZW compression A method of compacting TIFF files using the Lempel-Zev-Welch compression algorithm. It produces an average compression ratio of 2:1, but larger savings are produced with line art and continuous tone images with large areas of similar tonal values.

Magic Wand A tool that selects either contiguous pixels with the same brightness value or another range of your choice.

Map To assign colors or grays in an image.

Marquee The selection tool used to mark rectangular areas.

Mask To cover part of an image so it won't be affected by other operations.

Mass storage Permanent storage of computer information. Magnetic disk is the most frequently used medium, but magnetic tape, optical disk, bubble memory, and other nonvolatile storage media are also used

Mechanical Camera-ready copy with text and art already in position for photographing.

Memory buffer An area of RAM used to store a file or an image between certain operations, such as printing, storing to disk, or displaying in an image-editing program.

Mezzotint An engraving that is produced by scraping a roughened surface to produce the effect of gray tones. Image editing and processing software can produce this effect with a process called error diffusion.

Microprocessor The computer-on-a-chip that is the brains of a personal computer.

Midtones Parts of an image with tones of an intermediate value, usually in the 25 to 75% range.

Millisecond One-thousandth of a second.

Moiré In scanning, an objectionable pattern caused by the interference of halftone screens. It is often produced when you rescan a halftone and a second screen is applied on top of the first.

Monochrome Having a single color.

Monospaced Text in which each character takes up exactly the same amount of space. Some OCR programs require specifying that text to be scanned is monospaced.

Motherboard The main circuitboard of your Macintosh.

Mount To activate a floppy or hard disk for use. Disks must be mounted before you can open them.

Mouse A pointing device used to indicate an area or point on the screen.

Multibit Any scan that uses more than 1 bit to store information about a pixel.

MultiFinder The Apple system software, used prior to System 7, which makes it possible to have several applications open at once. MultiFinder allows you to move quickly between different programs. Some programs, like telecommunications software, can run in the background.

Multisession CD A photoCD that has had images placed on it several times, as opposed to single-session CDs, which are written to only once.

Multitasking The capability of a computer system to handle several different chores simultaneously. Because microcomputers have only one main processor, multitasking is usually done by slicing processor time into individual segments and allowing the programs to share the slices in rotation. DOS is not generally a multitasking operating system, although third-party enhancements can give it these capabilities.

Multiuser The capability of a computer system to handle several different tasks performed by several different users simultaneously. UNIX is the best-known multitasking system among microcomputer users, although it is also available for larger systems.

Negative A representation of an image in which the tones are reversed. That is, black is shown as white, and vice versa.

Neutral color In RGB mode, a color in which red, green, and blue are present in equal amounts, producing a gray.

Noise Random pixels added to an image to increase apparent graininess.

NTSC National Television Standard Code. The standard for video in the United States.

NuBus A system bus that allows you to ad high-speed expansion cards, such as video adapters. It is used in Mac II series computers.

Object graphics Vector-oriented graphics in which mathematical descriptions, rather than bit maps, are used to describe images.

Offset printing See *Lithography*.

Opacity The opposite of transparency: the degree to which a layer obscures the view of the layer beneath. High opacity means low transparency.

Origin The starting horizontal and vertical reference point for a scan.

Overlay A sheet laid on top of another to specify spot colors for printing. In programming, a portion of a program that is called into memory as needed, overlaying the previous redundant section of the program. Overlays allow programmers to write programs that are much bigger than those that could fit into memory all at once.

Page description language A programming language that can be used to tell a printer how to handle a given page. PostScript is the most widely used page description language for printing and publishing.

Palette A set of tones or colors available to produce an image. A row of icons representing tools that can be used.

Pantone Matching System (PMS) A registered trade name for a system of color matching. If you tell your printer the PMS number of the color you want, it can reproduce that color exactly by mixing printing inks to a preset formula.

Parallel To move data several bits at a time, rather than one at a time. Usually, parallel operation involves sending all 8 bits of a byte along eight separate data paths at one time. Parallel movement is faster than serial movement. Most scanners use parallel connections to move image information.

Parameter A qualifier that defines precisely what a program is to do.

Peripheral Any hardware part of a computer system other than the microprocessor itself and its directly accessible memory. We usually think of peripherals as printers, modems, etc.

Photo CD Developed by Eastman Kodak Company, this special type of CD-ROM can store high-quality photographic images in a special space-saving format, along with music and other data. PhotoCDs can be accessed by CD-ROM XA-compatible drives, using Kodak-supplied software or compatible programs such as Photoshop.

Phototypesetting A process used to expose text and images onto materials that will later be used to produce printing plates. Phototypesetters generally have much higher resolutions than laser printers.

Physical A feature that exists in reality.

PICT A graphic image and file format used by the Macintosh and its Clipboard. PICT2 is an enhanced version, which can be used in both 8-bit and 24-bit formats.

Pixel A picture element of a screen image; one dot of the collection that makes up an image.

Plate A thin, light-sensitive sheet, usually of metal or plastic, that is exposed and then processed to develop an image of the page. During printing, the plate transfers ink or dye to a surface, generally paper.

Plugging A defect on the final printed page in which areas between dots become filled due to dot gain, producing an area of solid color. See also *Dot gain*.

Plug-In A module that can be accessed from within a program like Photoshop to provide special functions. Many plug-ins are image-processing filters that offer special effects.

PMMU Paged Memory Management Unit. The optional 68851 chip for Motorola 68020-based Macintosh II computers, which provides special memory management needed by Apple UNIX (AUX) and used with virtual memory modes with System 7. Macs using the 68030, 68040, and PowerPC 601 chips have this memory support built in.

Point Approximately 1/72 inch outside the Macintosh world; exactly 1/72 inch within it. Points are used by printers to measure things like type and other vertically oriented objects.

Port A channel of the computer used for input or output with a peripheral. The serial and parallel ports of the PC are the most widely used.

Portrait The orientation of a page in which the longest dimension is vertical. Also called tall orientation.

Position stat A copy of a halftone that is placed on a mechanical to illustrate positioning and cropping of the image.

Posterization A photographic effect produced by reducing the number of gray tones in an image to a level at which the tones are shown as bands, as on a poster.

PostScript The most widely used page description language for PCs. Developed by Adobe Systems, PostScript provides a way of telling the printer, typesetter, or imagesetter how to generate a given page.

Prepress The stages of the reproduction process that precede printing, particularly those in which halftones, color separations, and printing plates are generated.

Preview scan A preliminary scan that can be used to define the exact area for the final scan. A low-resolution image of the full page or scanning area is shown, and a frame of some type is used to specify the area to be included in the final scan.

Printer command language The instructions used to drive HP LaserJet printers and compatibles, as in Hewlett-Packard Printer Command Language (HPCL).

Process camera A graphic arts camera used to make color separations, to photograph original artwork to produce halftones and page negatives, and to perform other photographic enlarging/reducing/duplicating tasks.

Process colors Cyan, magenta, yellow, and black. The basic ink colors used to produce all the other colors in four-color printing.

Program Code that instructs the computer how to perform a function.

Proof A test copy of a printed sheet, which is used as a final check before a long duplication run begins.

Quadtone An image printed using black ink and three other colored inks.

Quantization Another name for *Posterization.*

QuickDraw/GX Graphics language built into the read-only memory of the Macintosh.

Raster image An image defined as a set of pixels or dots in row and column format.

Raster image processor (RIP) The hardware/software used to process text, graphics, and other page elements into a raster image for output on a printer.

Rasterize The process of turning an outline-oriented image such as a PostScript file or an Adobe Illustrator drawing into a bit-mapped image.

Ray tracing A method for producing realistic highlights, shadows, and reflections on a three-dimensional rendering by projecting the path of an imaginary beam of light from a particular location back to the viewpoint of the observer.

Read-Only Memory (ROM) Memory that can be read by the system but not changed. It often contains system programs that help the computer carry out services.

Reflection copy Original artwork that is viewed and scanned by light reflected from its surface rather than transmitted through it.

Register To align images, usually different versions of the same page or sheet. Color separation negatives must be precisely registered to one another to ensure that colors overlap in the proper places.

Register marks Small marks that are placed on a page to make it possible to align different versions of the page precisely.

Registers The basic memory locations of a microprocessor, through which all information that is processed passes.

Render To produce a realistic 3-D image from a drawing or other data.

Resampling The process of changing the resolution of an image, adding pixels through interpolation, or removing pixels to reduce resolution.

ResEdit The Apple resource editor, which allows you to modify applications, data files, and system files (if you're brave enough to experiment).

Resolution The number of pixels or dots per inch in an image, whether it is displayed on the screen or printed.

Retouch To edit an image, usually to remove flaws or to create a new effect.

RGB color correction A color correction system based on adjusting the levels of red, green, and blue in an image.

RGB color model A way of defining all possible colors as percentages of red, green, and blue.

Right-reading image An image, such as a film used to produce a printing plate, that reads correctly, left to right, when viewed as it will be placed down for exposure.

RIP Raster Image Processor. A device, which is often found in printers, that converts page images to a format that can be printed by the marking engine of the printer.

RISC Reduced Instruction Set Computer. A computer system like the new Power Macintoshes that includes an optimized instruction set designed to complete each instruction in one clock cycle, and that, therefore, operates faster. Such systems depend on the software for functions that formerly were handled by the microprocessor.

Rubber Stamp A tool that copies or clones part of an image to another area.

Saturation Purity of color. An attribute of a color that describes the degree to which a pure color is diluted with white or gray. A color with low color saturation appears washed out. A highly saturated color is pure and vivid.

Scale To change the size of a piece of artwork.

Scanner A device that captures an image of a piece of artwork and converts it to a bit-mapped image that the computer can handle.

Scrapbook The Apple desk accessory that can be used to keep text and graphics available on a semipermanent basis. The Scrapbook is a handy tool for scanner users who want to store or move groups of images, since the Clipboard can hold only one image at a time.

Screen The halftone dots used to convert a continuous tone image to a black-and-white pattern that printers and printing presses can handle. Even expanses of tone can also be reproduced by using tint screens that consist of dots that are all the same size (measured in percentages: a 100% screen is completely black).

Screen angle The alignment of rows of halftone dots, measured from the horizontal (which would be a 0° screen angle).

SCSI Small Computer Systems Interface. An intelligent interface that is used for most scanners in the Macintosh world and for other devices, including hard disk drives.

SCSI ID The number from 0 to 7 assigned to each device on the SCSI bus. You make this assignment by adjusting a jumper or DIP switch on your equipment or, sometimes, through software. No two devices can have the same ID number. The Mac itself always has SCSI ID 7, and the boot disk is typically ID 0.

Secondary color A color produced by mixing two primary colors. For example, mixing red and green primary colors of light produces the secondary color magenta. Mixing the yellow and cyan primary colors of pigment produces blue as a secondary color.

Sector The smallest section of a track, containing 512 bytes of data.

Selection To mark various portions of an image or document so that you can work on them apart from the rest of the image or document.

Selection The area that has been marked, usually surrounded by a marquee or an outline that is sometimes colorfully called "marching ants."

Separation See *Color separation.*

Separations Film transparencies, each representing one of the primary colors (cyan, magenta, and yellow) plus black, used to produce individual printing plates.

Serial Passing information 1 bit at a time in sequential order. Some scanners use serial connections.

Serif Short strokes at the ends of letters. It is thought that serifs help lead the eye and make text easier to read. Sans serif type lacks these strokes. Serifs can sometimes touch in tightly spaced text, causing problems for OCR software.

Shade A color with black added.

Shadows The darkest part of an image, generally with values ranging from 75 to 100%.

Shareware Software that can be copied and distributed freely for evaluation purposes but that must be registered, usually for a small fee, if you decide to keep using it.

Sharpen To increase the apparent sharpness of an image by boosting the contrast between adjacent tones or colors.

SIMM Single in-line memory module. The small circuitboards used to add memory to Macs and other devices such as the LaserWriter. Today, SIMMs usually contain 1 MB to 16 MB of memory, but there are other sizes, including the 256K SIMMs used for VRAM.

Smooth To blur the boundaries between tones of an image, often to reduce a rough or jagged appearance.

Smudge A tool that smears part of an image, mixing surrounding tones together.

Snap A feature that causes lines or objects to be attracted to a visible or invisible grid or special guidelines in an image or drawing.

Solarization In photography, an effect produced by exposing film to light partially through the developing process. Some of the tones are reversed, generating an interesting effect. In digital photography, the same effect is produced by combining some positive areas of the image with some negative areas.

Source code The program code generated by a programmer. If the code is not directly executable by the computer, it is translated by an interpreter, assembler, or compiler into machine language object code.

Spot The dots that produce images on an imagesetter or other device.

Spot color Individual colors used on a page. Usually limited to one or two extra colors besides black to accent some part of a publication.

Spot color overlay A sheet that shows one of the colors to be used in a publication for a given page. A separate overlay is prepared for each color, and all are combined to create the finished page.

Static RAM (SRAM) Memory that does not need to be refreshed and that, therefore, does not lose its contents when power to the computer is turned off. SRAM is more expensive and typically faster than DRAM.

Strip To assemble a finished page by taping or otherwise fastening pieces of film containing halftones, line art, and text together in a complete page negative or positive. The most common format is as a negative, because dirt and other artifacts show up as pinholes that can be easily spotted or opaqued out before the printing plates are made.

Subdirectory A directory created within another directory, which stores its own separate files.

Substrate A base substance that is coated with another. In printing, the substrate is generally paper or acetate, and the second substance is usually ink or dye.

Subtractive colors The primary colors of pigments. When two subtractive colors are added, the result is a darker color, which further subtracts from the light reflected by the substrate surface.

Surface properties The transparency, texture, and reflective qualities of a 3-D surface.

System file The file used to start up your Macintosh and regulate the transfer of information among all the other components of the system software.

System level interface An interface over which information is passed in logical form.

System software Your Mac's operating system, which includes the System file and Finder, as well as other components.

Template A publication that is used as a framework to provide the basic structure and layout for a publication.

Terminator A device that absorbs signals at the end of a bus, preventing electronic "bounce-back." Your SCSI bus must have two terminators, one at the first and last devices. Some devices are internally terminated; others require an add-on device.

Text file Usually an ASCII file, often created by selecting Save Text Only from within an application.

Thermal wax transfer A printing technology in which dots of wax from a ribbon are applied to paper when heated by thousands of tiny elements in a printhead.

Threshold A predefined level used by the scanner to determine whether a pixel will be represented as black or white.

Thumbnail A miniature copy of a page or image, which gives you some idea of what the original looks like without opening the original file or viewing the full-size image.

TIFF Tagged Image File Format. A standard graphics file format that can be used to store gray scale and color images.

Tint A color with white added to it. In graphic arts, tint often refers to the percentage of one color added to another.

Tolerance The range of color or tonal values that will be selected, with a tool like the Magic Wand, or filled with paint, when using a tool like the Paint Bucket.

Toner A pigmented substance used in page printers (and office copiers) to produce an image on a page.

Trapping The capability of an ink to transfer as well onto another layer of ink as to the bare paper itself. In halftoning, poor trapping results in tonal changes in the final image. In desktop publishing, trapping has an additional meaning: printing some images of one color slightly larger so that they overlap another color, avoiding unsightly white space if the two colors are printed slightly out of register. Printers call this technique *spreading* and *choking*.

Triad Three colors located approximately equidistant from one another on the color wheel. Red, green, and blue make up a triad; cyan, magenta, and yellow make up another. However, any three colors arranged similarly around the wheel can make up a triad.

Trim size Final size of a printed publication.

Tritone An image printed with black ink plus two colored inks.

True Color A system in which any pixel in the image can be any of the 16.8 million colors available in a 24-bit color mode. This is in contrast to systems that also access the full 16.8 million color gamut but limit a given image to a smaller palette of colors chosen from the larger range. For example, you may be able to use only 256 colors even though any of the millions available can be selected for that palette.

Type code A four-letter code that tells the Macintosh what kind of document a file is. It is used with the creator code, which represents the particular application that created the file. Some applications can create several different types of documents.

Undercolor removal A technique that reduces the amount of cyan, magenta, and yellow in black and neutral shadows by replacing them with an equivalent amount of black. It can compensate for trapping problems in dark areas. See also *Gray component removal*.

Unfragmented A hard disk that has most of its files stored in consecutive sectors rather than spread out over the disk. Such an arrangement allows more efficient reading of data, requiring less time to move the read/write head to gather the information.

Utility A program that performs some useful system or maintenance function, as opposed to an applications program.

Vector image An image defined as a series of straight line vectors. The beginning and ending points of each line are stored and later adjusted as the image is sized.

Vignette In prepress terminology, an image with a continuous gradation of tones.

Virtual disk An electronic, or RAM, disk created in memory to mimic a real disk drive—only much faster.

Virtual memory Hard disk space used when there is not enough RAM to carry out an operation. Photoshop and your Mac each have their own virtual memory systems. If you use Photoshop a great deal, you'll want to turn off the Mac's version and let Photoshop work exclusively with its optimized version.

Wire frame A rendering technique that presents only the edges of a 3-D object, as if it were modeled from pieces of wire. Using a wireframe is much faster than modeling the entire object, including all surfaces.

WORM Write Once Read Many (or Mostly). Optical disk technology that allows writing to the disk by the user, although a given section cannot be erased and reused.

Wrong-reading image An image that is backward relative to the original subject—that is, a mirror image.

X-height The height of a lowercase letter, excluding ascenders and descenders.

Zoom To enlarge part of an image so that it fills the screen, making it easier to work with that portion.

INDEX

'ou Will Find
e CD-ROM

ntents break down into the ies:

'orking copies of filters from the Adobe Gallery Effects 3lack Box, HSC's Kai's Power Tools, Intellihance, and

of exclusive filters prepared just for this book which you 's Custom filter.

Shareware. Great programs like Plug-In Manager, and the best of the shareware filters from Chris Cox, Paul Badger, and others.

Chapter Files. These are full-color versions of all the figures in the book, along with many intermediate TIFF files used in the examples. Each folder is given the chapter number it corresponds with.

TIFF Images. Separate folders containing TIFF images you can work with, in Spain, Miscellaneous, Portrait, and Glamour categories. You can use these royalty-free images in your own work. Some have flaws that you can correct with filters, others are ready to manipulate.

Filter Examples. You'll find hundreds of examples of images with filters applied on this CD-ROM. The Spain, Miscellaneous, and Glamour folders each have a SpecialFX folder with examples of other images transformed with filters. In the Chapter 12:Working.12 folder, you'll find 50 Photoshop-format files, each with three to four (or more layers) showing a different effect. The layer names tell you what setting was used to achieve the effect.

Macintosh F/X Sampler. Some sample images from the companion MIS:Press book, Macintosh F/X. Different images in the same categories as above.

Seamless Textures. Dozens of seamless textures in PICT format you can use with your image editor and filters that accept PICT or texture files.

Antique Artwork Sampler. From the American Antique Graphics Society, some 50 MB of antique images.

In all cases, I don't recommend using any of the files directly from the CD-ROM. Image files, in particular, load very slowly from a CD-ROM drive, and with images on this disc up to 7 MB in size, you can wait quite awhile for one of those to feed into RAM. Instead, I recommend the following:

Tryout Software. Drag the folder containing the application or its installer to your hard drive. Many won't run properly from the CD-ROM either because they must be installed to use, or because they need to write files to the disk they're launched from. System 7 treats the nonwritable CD-ROM as a "locked" disk.

Shareware Filters. Drag these to the Plugins folder used by your image editing application.

Custom Filters. Drag to your hard drive, then access Photoshop's Custom Filter and load these when the dialog box asks for a file.

TIFF files, Textures, Samplers. Leave these on the CD-ROM until you need them. If you have an image browser application, you can create thumbnail images to use as a reference for finding the picture you want. All but the glamour/figure photographs have reference thumbnail images as their icons, anyway, although these are a little small for serious study.